FOLLOW THE LEADER
CHARLES MILLES MANSON

He spent more of his life in prison than he did on the outside, yet he nurtured his family on visions of love. Then came the Beatles' *White Album*, with the song "Helter Skelter." His message suddenly changed to bloody holocaust.

Susan (Sadie) Denise Atkins, Leslie (Lulu) Van Houten, Patricia (Katie) Krenwinkle, Charles (Tex) Watson, Lynette (Squeaky) Fromme—Manson's personal girl friend—and others followed his command blindly, without question.

Paul Watkins, Southern California golden boy turned high-school drop-out and Family man, was groomed as Manson's successor. He begged, borrowed and stole for Manson. He endured Manson's ravings and rages. But he refused to be an architect of the ultimate Helter Skelter vision —even if refusal virtually guaranteed that he would be its first victim.

THIS IS THEIR STORY . . .

My Life with Charles Manson

Paul Watkins

with
Guillermo Soledad

BANTAM BOOKS
TORONTO · NEW YORK · LONDON

MY LIFE WITH CHARLES MANSON
A Bantam Book | June 1979

*Grateful acknowledgment is made to G. W. Yuscarán for per-
mission to quote passages from his book,* Desert Winds, *published in Tegucigalpa, Honduras, by Guaro Press in 1973.*

ISBN 0–553–12788–8

Published simultaneously in the United States and Canada

*Bantam Books are published by Bantam Books, Inc. Its trade-
mark, consisting of the words "Bantam Books" and the por-
trayal of a bantam, is Registered in U.S. Patent and Trademark
Office and in other countries. Marca Registrada. Bantam
Books, Inc., 666 Fifth Avenue, New York, New York 10019.*

Author's Note

It's been ten years since I lived with Charles Manson and the Family. Yet, people still ask me: "Weren't you shocked by the Tate–La Bianca murders?" Sure, I was shocked, revolted. But in many ways (certainly in retrospect), not surprised. I went through Charlie Manson's whole trip. I knew Charlie, Tex (Charles Watson), Katie (Patricia Krenwinkle), Sadie (Susan Atkins), Leslie (Leslie Van Houten), Clem (Steve Grogan), and the others before they became murderers. As brothers, sisters, and friends we shared the daily experience and dramas that became Helter-Skelter. What happened to them might well have happened to a lot of people at that time. It is a bizarre, frightening, yet enlightening story: a full-circle story. Nothing that has been written thus far has come close to explaining it. But it can be explained. I can explain it. It's taken a long time, I've paid my dues, and I want to tell it now, as it really was. I ask only that the reader recall the ambience of the late sixties—perhaps the most turbulent and chaotic time in America in the last thirty years. I ask too that he or she attempt what may well be impossible: to see Charlie Manson afresh, as I did, before the murders and violence.

These are the facts as I remember them.

only when I have flowered will the hillsides come to color ...

—W. G. Yuscarán

Part
One

I Am You
and
You Are Me

1

On the day I met Charlie Manson—March 16, 1968 —there was enough wind to drive the clouds and the smog out of the L.A. basin. I remember standing on a ridge above Topanga Canyon looking out over the valley. The mountains beyond San Fernando were clearly delineated and I could make out the confluence of highways which compose the L.A. freeway system and beyond it the congestion of greater Los Angeles. It felt good to be miles away from all that, shirtless in the afternoon sun. I took a leak, then hiked back through the oak grove to my campsite to smoke a number.

Several months before, I had left my home in Thousand Oaks and had dropped out of high school, giving up my senior year and the office of student-body president. By that time I'd lost all interest in my studies. I preferred smoking grass and playing music to sitting in a classroom. The world seemed utterly insane to me and I began experimenting with other drugs, until I was busted for marijuana and put on probation in December 1967. That same week, two friends of mine came back from Vietnam, dead. Others my age were enlisting; there was racial violence throughout the country—riots daily; plus, the overriding awareness that a nuclear holocaust could wipe out everything. But the roots went deeper. I remember my parents on the day John Kennedy was shot and how that event devastated them and so many others. It seemed, in a way, that many never got over it, that afterward they just stuck their heads in the sand and decided to live without feelings, without seeing. They didn't recognize in the midst of all the violence, assassinations, profiteering, and suffering of the late sixties that there was a new spirit being born, something hopeful in the

3

air. I saw that hope in what later became known as the "psychedelic revolution," the movement of America's youth. While police described me then as a hippie and a "runaway," I considered myself a fugitive flower child in search of enlightenment and truth. I took a hit off my joint and lay back in the waving mustard weed to let the hot sun bathe my face.

From the hillside where my tent was pitched (near the top of a ridge in the middle of a mustard-weed patch), I looked directly down through a stand of eucalyptus and oak to Topanga Canyon Boulevard, which stretched from the valley to the Pacific Coast Highway. Hidden from the road, I could observe at my leisure the endless procession of cars weaving back and forth through the canyon. I had chosen this vantage point for strategic reasons: probation authorities were still searching for me following the December marijuana bust at Half Moon Bay.

That bust was a real revelation. Certainly it made me more sympathetic later to the plight of Charlie and the Family. It happened while I was living in the mountains around Big Sur with a friend called Black Beard Charlie (Charlie Melton). Black Beard was another "runaway" from L.A. who had shined-on suburbia to take to the hills. He was nineteen, a full-on Kerouac "dharma bum" who could assume the full lotus at the drop of a hat and fall immediately into trancelike meditation. He was tall and slender with a gaunt, El Grecolike face which seemed compatible with his vagrant life-style. Brown, wide-set eyes highlighted his dark complexion. His hair hung to well below his shoulders and was tied at the base of his skull with a strip of rawhide. Black Beard was a student of Eastern religions and he taught me a lot about survival in the wilderness with a pack on my back. We had made camp at Hot Springs Canyon, near Esalen, and were committed to the gypsy life, wandering through the forests and along the California coastline.

Two weeks after we arrived at Hot Springs, however, the weather turned unbearably cold and rainy, and we agreed to pack up and go looking for a warmer, drier scene. That fateful morning we rolled out early to watch the sunrise through a gray drizzle beside our tepee. We shared a breakfast of apricots, raisins, and camomile tea before loading our packs and setting out for the highway.

We were both wearing Levi's and moccasins, and I was carrying a pound of grass in a bag strapped to my waist, a stash I had earlier escaped with during the bust of a hippie commune in the valley. We cut holes in our blankets to make ponchos which covered our bodies and helped keep us dry on our trek out of the canyon to the highway.

We didn't care much which direction we went, so once we reached the road, Black Beard stood on one side and I went to the other. It didn't take long. Within five minutes we had our first ride—a freezing-ass ordeal in the back of a Chevy pickup which took us to Daly City. From there we flagged down an old-timer driving a fifty Plymouth who must have been blind as a bat—he was a trip —kept asking if we were in the military, said he used to be; said he didn't know what the world was coming to, couldn't trust anyone, not even your own mother, but that his mother was dead and that having arthritis didn't help "a damn." He told us his name was R.D. and that it stood for "Real Dirty," "but you boys kin call me Red." We drank a shot of brandy with him before he let us out on Polk Street in San Francisco, then we stood on the curb and waved as he disappeared into the morning fog.

The city seemed cold and inhospitable that day. We spent the morning wandering the streets, lugging our packs around, resting on corners, watching people. Sometime around noon, we took a bus ride to get warm but the driver gave us the evil eye for ten blocks so we got off. All the Christmas shit was up: window displays, Styrofoam Santas, colored lights, phony greenery, most of it dripping wet and pathetic-looking. We hiked over to Hippie Hill and found it nearly deserted. The mood had changed completely since the summer of '66 when I first visited the Haight. Instead of hippies and flower children we saw only derelicts and hard-core junkies trying to score booze and smack. Everything seemed depressed and stony and by late afternoon we wound up in Golden Gate Park drinking hot tea and feeding the gulls. When it started to rain again I was ready to split.

"Hey, man, let's boogie outta here."

"What's up, Paul?"

"The rain, man . . . I'm catching cold. I feel like getting dry."

"Where to?"

"Anywhere, let's just go."

We packed up our gear, took a hit of acid, and left the park, trudging all the way to the highway. By the time we got there it was bitter cold but the rain had stopped and through a mist reminiscent of that morning, we watched the sun disappear into the sea. One ride with a jocular young sailor and his beer-swilling girlfriend took us to the outskirts of Half Moon Bay. From there we set out walking toward town in silence, still coming onto the acid. The road was wet and the wheels of passing traffic made a hissing sound against the pavement. I thought of the highway as a snake, hissing as we moved along its back. We hadn't walked a hundred yards when a highway patrolman pulled over, wanting to see our I.D.'s.

The cop was a big, swaggering dude with a wide, sanguine face and freckles; the more I looked at his face the more the freckles looked like islands on some vast sea of skin. He said I'd been walking like a drunk and he stood over me with his flashlight while I fished through my wallet for the I.D. I had two, one a driver's license that was legal, the other a draft card that wasn't. I found the cards and he seized them both. But I was feeling confident, even friendly.

"Which one of these is you?" His voice was hard.

"The license is for real. But hey, man, I'm old enough to be on the road; it's cool. Hey, I'd like you to meet my friend Black Beard Charlie."

The cop ignored my introduction and told us to walk on down the highway to the drive-in restaurant where there was more light. We did and he followed us, radioing in the meantime to another squad car, which careened into the parking lot just after we got there. By then Black Beard was all Buddhaed-out in the full lotus, under a neon light. In front of him he had laid out his driver's license, his draft card, and a Bible. The big cop was still examining my I.D. "What's with Moses?" he asked, gesturing toward Charlie.

I shrugged. The other two cops were looking at his I.D., but he didn't bat an eyelash and they didn't disturb him; they just looked at the I.D., then set it down again.

"What do you have on your back, Mr. Watkins?" the big guy wanted to know.

"Camping gear."

"Let's have a look."

"You can't search me without a warrant!"

The cop sniggered, reaching for the poncho. "Take it off, Mr. Watkins."

"Hey, man, you're supposed to be the law." I pushed his hand away. "This is my house . . . you can't enter my house! I didn't do anything!" The acid had slowed things down, had removed the filters from my vision. The cop seemed enormous to me now, like Goliath or King Kong, and I felt as though I were acting out a role in some ancient, preordained myth, and that somehow the outcome was already a matter of destiny.

The cop was furious now. *"I said take it off!"*

"Fuck no! I'm a sovereign being . . . you're violating my universe, man!"

He grabbed at the pack and the other two cops lurched over to help. I was more exhilarated than scared, driven by an impulse I could only obey as I listened to the cops grunting while trying to pinion my arms; my blood was surging, my adrenaline pumping, and for a time I held them off. But then the big one slammed a leg in behind my knee and threw me to the ground; he had one foot on my neck and the other on my hand, which he crunched into the pavement. I felt the toe of his boot grinding against my fingers at the same time the gravel was cutting into my face. My flesh peeled away onto his boots, onto the gravel. I was aware of warm blood trickling across my skin. I could smell it. Panicked again, I began kicking and flailing like some beached mammal; that's when Black Beard came to life and tried to help me—but one of the cops collared him.

"Hey, Paul," Charlie shouted. "Give it up man! Shit, it ain't worth it!"

"No! No! They can't do this," I gasped. "This isn't the law!"

"This is the law, sonny," the big guy snarled, ripping my pack from my back. "This boot on your neck is the law . . . and don't forget it!" His words fell on my ears like some sort of substance pounded out of cold air. I heard the words being repeated over and over again, then I felt them like a liquid being poured into my head; but it was my own blood I felt, dripping. And I knew he was right, that one man overpowering another, inflicting his will, is the bottom line of the law. Ironically, this revelation elated me.

I was in a spaced-out daze when the big guy jerked me to my feet and held me while one of the other cops rummaged through my pack, scattering food, clothing, and utensils on the ground. Patrons from the drive-in had gathered in an excited gaggle outside the door to watch. I was bloody and exhausted, yet filled with a sense of buoyance, as though I had played my part well and was being cosmically rewarded. Black Beard, meanwhile, had resumed the lotus beneath the light, his eyes closed, his face mirroring an inscrutable calm.

"I found the marijuana!" came the proclamation as the cop jerked the bag from the debris, as if to prove to everyone, including the spectators, that it had all been worth it. His proclamation struck me as uproariously comical and I burst out laughing and cheering at the same time. It seemed to me then that we were all members of some comic acting troupe, a band of gypsy thespians performing on the roadside. And as the proclamation continued: ". . . in the name of San Mateo County, district . . . you are hereby . . ." I continued to cheer and to clap my hands. That's when I noticed the other cop gaping at my hands in unmasked horror; then they were all looking at them. I looked down. Both hands were crumpled, my shirt torn to shreds, my arms cut and bleeding; my face was a gouged conglomerate of gravel, dirt, and blood. For several moments I stared down at my hands; they looked mangled beyond repair. The big cop had taken off his handcuffs and he stood over me, hesitating. Then I calmly reached down with one hand and straightened the fingers of the other, feeling the bones crunch and crackle back into place, resetting both hands while the cops gawked at me. At last I opened and closed both hands several times to make sure they worked, before holding them out like raw hamburger to the big cop they called Ben. He slapped the cuffs on me, then heaved me bodily into the back of his car.

"Get your ass up and outta here, Moses!" he barked as I maneuvered into a sitting position in time to watch Black Beard collecting the gear from the parking lot and stuffing it into my pack. Then Big Ben got in his car, and the other two cops got in theirs, while the crowd around the restaurant began to disperse.

That's when Charlie ran up to the car and shouted, "Hey, Paul, hang tough, amigo . . . see you soon!"

We Brodied out onto the highway amid a swirl of gravel and mud, and all kinds of things flashed through my head: like maybe I'd go to jail for twenty years; marijuana was a big offense in those days. But I wasn't really scared; in fact, I felt a strange sort of satisfaction: the acid brought me to the realization that I had created the episode myself, had generated my own personal catharsis at the cops' expense. I didn't blame them; if anything, I felt slightly guilty for deceiving them. Sitting Indian-style in the cage in the back of the squad car, I watched the clouds clear. I could see hundreds of stars glittering crisply in the heavens. Everything seemed clean and promising, and gradually a flood of emotion swelled up inside me; tears streamed down my face. It seemed as though I had just returned from the bottom of the world, that I had been stomped on and stamped with the mark of civilization, but that I had survived and was still free. I flashed on Black Beard sitting in the full lotus and smiled through my tears. I saw the strength in his face and the light in his eyes when he shouted at me through the window, and I felt like a warrior. The moon broke through the clouds and Big Ben and I watched it out the window. He saw the tears and asked if my hand was okay.

"Yeah, it's okay."

I was booked in San Mateo and released the following morning to the custody of my parents in Los Angeles. I ran away again, and a week later I met Black Beard in Malibu; we palled around together for several weeks before he split for New Mexico. That's when I moved into my tent in Topanga Canyon, which is where this story started—on the day I met Charlie Manson.

After watching a wedding caravan scream up the canyon—I remember horns blaring and the flowing streamers and tin cans tied to the cars—I pulled my pack out of the tent and ate some dried peaches and a handful of raisins, which I washed down with water from a canteen. Then I kicked off my moccasins and took out my French horn. The instant I started to play, two blue jays who hung out in a nearby scrub oak came out and started squawking; they'd been there ever since I set up camp, and they squawked each time I played music. But no one else did. There was no one else around.

It was my custom to sit on that hillside for hours, playing the music to trees and wildflowers, watching the leaves blowing and twisting as if they were dancing to the tune I played—the sensitivity of massive, gnarled limbs betrayed in their nimble leaves. And when it was hot, there were always the white butterflies fluttering in pairs across the canyon, and a myriad of droning bees in the mustard weed. From my hideout I could see the elegant homes of the wealthy perched on surrounding hillsides, and a few shacks back up the canyon. But around me was only a feral expanse of nature, now abloom in early spring; perfect; living in a pup tent on my own private mountain in the middle of L.A. But those crazy birds made me think of my friend Jay, who lived up the canyon on Summit Drive, and I decided to hike down there to visit him.

It was around four o'clock when I put the horn away, grabbed a sweater, and started my hike down the hill toward the riverbed which leads up the canyon to Summit Drive. Descending the slope through the oaks reminded me of similar terrain just north of Taos, New Mexico, where, the previous summer (1967), I had spent two weeks in a hippie commune. That entire summer, in fact, I'd devoted to hitchhiking around the country, from Haight Ashbury to Taos, looking for people to live with and make music with—people who sensed then, as I did, that there was a new awakening of consciousness; a generation utterly alienated from their parents by the seemingly unbreachable gap of time and acid.

I had become acutely aware of this phenomenon on my first trip to the Haight that same summer: playing music in the city—in parks, crash pads, parking lots; smoking grass; feeling good. It was the beginning of the psychedelic revolution and it captured the awareness of youth like nothing else in my lifetime. I met people from everywhere, hiked with them through the city and up into the mountains behind Berkeley, where we sang songs and picked flowers; we were like gypsies spreading love, giving love and flowers to people in the street; people of all ages—children, old men, women, bus drivers, cops, newspapermen, grocery clerks, ex-convicts. It was real love and it was contagious. People have forgotten how deeply it was felt because in time it turned into a heavy rip-off drug scene and lost its potency. In fact, by September 1967 (two months after Jimi Hendrix brought "a new soul sound of love" to the Monterey Pop Festival), Haight Ashbury had degenerated from a scene of smiles and flowers into a cesspool of violence and hostility: it had become a terror-stricken ghetto where those "hippies" who remained became victims of phony slop-bucket liberal do-gooders, vicious con men, or worse. But in the beginning the love was real; it had integrity; and it turned my head around. So much so that by the time I went back to Thousand Oaks the following September to finish my senior year, I couldn't handle school any longer. I became one of two or three out of 2,500 students who started using psychedelics: "outrageous behavior" for a student-body president. School officials said I should be "setting an example." I thought I was. Two months later, I was removed from office. The only president in the school's history to be so honored.

I hiked along the creek bed which parallels Topanga Canyon Boulevard, taking my time, hopping from rock to rock over the silver trickle of water that glistened in the light. After an hour I stopped on a protruding hunk of gray granite, big enough to stretch out on, and there I smoked a joint while contemplating the shadows on the rocks and the changing textures of the hillside. When it grew cold and started to get dark, I moved on.

Jay's house was located at the end of the creek where the road slopes up and dead-ends against the face of the hillside. All but hidden in a grove of oak, it gave the illusion of total isolation from the world. Beyond it, the rugged hillside swept up into an overgrown mane of mustard weed and wildflowers which looked from the floor of the canyon to be the jumping-off place to the sky. Though there were other houses around, within a stone's throw of Jay's, they were hidden by dense foliage and the rolling contours of the landscape. Being at Jay's, you had the feeling of living in a mountain retreat. Jay was a musician who played drums for a local rock group on the

Sunset Strip. I'd met him only recently and had visited
him a number of times since moving to my hideaway in
Topanga. But I hadn't seen him in over a week.

It took twenty minutes to hike the half-mile up to the
dead end where Jay's car was usually parked on a slope
above the house. But his car was gone. In its place was
an old black school bus with a large storage rack on top,
secured with rope and covered with an embroidered
psychedelic canvas tarp. From a distance, and because
of the angle as I approached the slope, the bus looked
like the head of a minstrel wearing a top hat. When I
turned off onto the dirt driveway and started down the
gully which plunges into the oak grove, I spotted a dim
light in the living-room window. By then it was downright cold, so I jogged down the hill, hopped up on the
porch, and knocked on the door. A can of paint sat in one
corner of the porch with a brush lying on top of it; Jay
had intended to paint the trim around the windows of the
house, but apparently had not gotten around to it. The
house was small, made of weathered pine, and painted
white. It was old and run-down, but it had a woodsy
charm. The fireplace was spewing smoke and I was eager
to get warm. I was ready to knock again when the door
opened.

Two naked, wispy-legged teenage girls with waist-
length hair stood in the doorway, greeting me with
quizzical, appraising smiles. I felt the heat from the fireplace waft across the porch and I smelled the fragrance
of marijuana.

"Is Jay around?" I stammered.

"Jay doesn't live here anymore," the taller girl said;
she pulled a strand of hair away from her eyes and
smiled. "I'm Snake and this is Brenda. . . . Would you
like to come in?"

They asked my name and I told them as they stood
aside to let me enter the house.

Brenda (Nancy Pitman) led the way. She was about
five-three, and had wavy blondish hair that hung to her
butt. Her body was slender and suntanned; she looked
like the classic little surfer girl from Malibu, which, as it
turned out, is what she was. Snake (Diane Lake) was
about five-five and had a more rounded, voluptuous body;
beautiful, upturned boobs and an incredible jungle of
fire-red hair, so thick it seemed to coil out of her head as

though charged with electricity, all but obscuring her pixie face and large fulgurous green eyes.

The living room we entered was spacious, with windows fronting on the thickest part of the oak grove. A luminous glow emanated from the fireplace and the smell of pot was intoxicating. Ten or twelve people, all but three of whom were girls, sat on the floor around a knee-high wooden table, the top of which was covered with a red embroidered cloth. There were three or four candles on the table and two bowls filled with candy bars. About half the girls were naked; none of the guys were, though the one at the head of the table who held the guitar was shirtless. At my feet, lying across the entrance to the room like some exotic Playboy Bunny in repose, was a pretty dark-haired girl who was subsequently introduced to me as Sadie (Susan Atkins).

"This is Paul," Brenda announced in a husky voice, a childlike voice which seemed compatible with her rosy, cherub face; she addressed the guy at the head of the table, the shirtless one who held the guitar and who smiled warmly, raising his hand in a gesture of welcome.

"I'm Charlie," he said. "Won't you stay and make music with us?"

2

My full name is Paul Alan Watkins and I was born on the twenty-fifth of January 1950. I was one when my family moved to Sidon, Lebanon, where my father worked on the pipeline and where we lived in a sprawling, rather barren apartment complex for Americans near the outskirts of the city, within walking distance of the Mediterranean and a boat-filled harbor.

I don't remember a lot about the four years I spent there but I do recall playing in dusty garbage-strewn streets with Lebanese kids and walking with my mother through a marketplace teeming with people. I can still visualize mazelike networks of narrow aisles littered with peelings, fish heads, and debris; flanks of hanging blood-red meat, roving fishmongers laden with squirming mackerel; women mending nets; smells of incense, spices, urine, oil, and sweat; dark faces of young and old chattering in Arabic—a vast sea of color, motion, and humanity; and seagulls scavenging for food.

I remember Arula and Rudi, the two seventeen-year-old girls who took care of us while our mother was gone. From them I learned to speak Arabic and to play the street games of children my own age. Once a week they took us with them to the *masjid* (mosque) to light candles. I knew nothing about the Islamic religion and have only vague recollections of worshipers gathered to pray. My most vivid and precise recollection is of Arula lighting incense in my bedroom each night after dinner, a memory that to this day triggers a deep and pervasive feeling of sensuality that I will always associate with Lebanon and the Middle East.

We left Sidon when I was five and moved to Beaumont, Texas; we remained there a couple of years, then traveled to Thousand Oaks, California, where I attended school from first through eleventh grades and became active in a variety of church groups.

Unlike most kids, I always liked church. There was something about being inside one that filled me with a sense of humility: maybe it was the stained-glass windows or the singing of the choir, but somewhere in that ambience I felt a deep reverence for life, a sense of spirituality that sustained me while growing up in Thousand Oaks. I experienced the same kind of feelings in nature, in the fertile rolling hills beyond home—the sloping oak groves of the Conejo Valley—where as a boy I often hiked alone or with my brothers.

At the tender age of eight I became a student of the Bible and I was active in youth organizations and church camps until the time I entered high school. My family were Methodists and I attended weekend youth groups regularly. But religion didn't get funky until my thirteenth year, when I went to hear an outdoor evangelical meeting with a friend named Toby: it was a breezy autumn evening and we had just eaten dinner before hiking across the ravine to the outskirts of town where the meeting was assembled in a clearing under the oaks. We sat in the front row, Indian-style. I remember hearing the traffic

in the distance and I could see the lights from Thousand
Oaks casting a glow along the rim of the foothills. There
must have been a hundred and fifty people there that
night, most of them from out of town. About a third of the
congregation were black, and you rarely saw blacks in
Thousand Oaks. There was a lady playing a piano and
singing. She was short and pudgy and wore a battered
straw hat laced with artificial flowers. Since she sat directly in front of us, we could look up her dress and ogle
her enormous thighs, which slid together like two juicy
hams. After singing a medley of rousing spirituals, she
introduced herself as Lydia, then asked everyone to welcome Preacher Bob.

I'll never forget Preacher Bob. He was tall, bald, and
limber. Blue veins bristled in his wiry white arms, as he
stood up and raised his hands over his head, then smiled
like a Cheshire cat. A gold hexagon-shaped ring flashed
from his little finger. He stood directly in front of us,
wearing pressed white slacks and a white shirt with the
sleeves rolled above the elbow.

He began at once to rave about Jesus. Through Jesus
he had found salvation and a new life. After five minutes
under the floodlights (which were strung up around the
stage on pieces of cord tied to the oak trees), he was
spewing sweat in prodigious salty drops. *"There's still
time, friends! There's always time to take Jesus into your
lives!"* His voice reeled higher and higher. People started
shouting: *"Hallelujah . . . Glory to God!"* Preacher Bob
just grinned, wiped his brow, and raised his hands in
praise. Then Lydia banged the keyboard and we all sang.
Pretty soon I was clapping, clomping, and singing up a
storm. I didn't care much about being saved. What revved
me up was the emotion and intensity—the almost primal
sensuality of being out there under the stars with all
those people, singing my guts out.

For months afterward I attended services, got saved,
felt fine. But I grew tired of weekly salvation. By the
time I reached high school, my fervor for evangelism had
waned, while my interest in music and singing had become a passion. During those days I played the trumpet,
and on weekends performed as a member of the Conejo
Valley Youth Band. Often, I'd play solos and dig on the
crowd's reaction. I'm certain that it was during those per-

formances, while I stood before all those eyes like some latter-day Elmer Gantry, that I first sensed my potential as a performer.

For the most part (with the exception of my religious orientation and the four years I spent in Lebanon), I enjoyed a pretty standard middle-class American upbringing. If, as some were later to assert, I became an "alienated young man," I was no more alienated than thousands of other youths of my own generation. I did not come from a miserable home life where I was beaten, abused, or grossly mistreated. My affinity for rebellion and the psychedelic revolution went deeper than family. I loved my parents and they loved me, and while I was one of six children (three boys and three girls, I being the second son), I did not feel rejected or neglected by my folks, nor was I ever a social outcast among my peers. If anything, up until the time I took to the road, I was considered an unusually well-adjusted kid. I made decent grades and was always popular in school; in fact, I was elected president of every class I attended from first through eleventh grades. I was regarded by my teachers as bright, gregarious, even "gifted," which seems to blow the minds of those who learned of my later involvement with the Manson Family.

What disturbs these people—the public at large—is that they usually expect me to be some sort of spaced-out weirdo. When they learn otherwise, it scares them, and they become defensive. The reasons for this are clear to me now: the public has always known Charles Manson as a murderer. They did not meet him, as I did, on that evening in March 1968 in Topanga Canyon. When I met him, there was no violence in the Family, no talk of Helter-Skelter; in fact, it was the complete opposite. Charlie's love then was real. It had some integrity. But the public met Charlie through the media only *after* the murders; by then, the whole story was tainted with blood. To understand Charles Manson and the Family you have to see *how* they evolved, you have to make that journey as I did, from one end of the spectrum to the other.

Brenda lit two sticks of incense while Charlie and the others introduced themselves. Then I squatted beside Brenda and Snake at the far end of the table facing Charlie. Snake offered me a candy bar and Charlie began to tune his guitar. I allowed my eyes to feast on the bevy of beautiful, unclad women. If an orgy was in the offing, I was more than ready for it. Snake wore a garland of tiny red roses as a headband, though I hadn't noticed them at first, so thick and red was her hair. But when I sat down beside her, she removed the band and placed it on my head. Then Brenda handed me a joint.

The exact number present that night, excluding myself, was twelve: Charlie, Sandra Good, Lynette (Squeaky) Fromme, Bruce Davis, Snake (Diane Lake), Brenda (Nancy Pitman), Katie (Patricia Krenwinkle), Sadie (Susan Atkins), Mary Brunner, Stephanie Rowe, Ella Jo Bailey, and a guy called Motorcycle Mark. All but Mark were part of the original Family Charlie had began in San Francisco the year before. Had anyone told me that four of these people would later be convicted of the most sensational murder of the century and that the little guy named Charlie would be compared to men like Hitler and Jack the Ripper, I would have laughed outloud. The vibes pervading the scene that night were only mellow. Violence was the farthest thing from my mind as I glanced around the room.

The floor, except where the table was positioned, was covered with mattresses, which in turn were overlaid with blankets. Several Indian tapestries were tacked to the walls, and three potted ferns hung from the beams of the ceiling directly over the table. In the corner, leaning against the wall, was Mark's Harley Davidson Sportster, covered partially with a beach towel. Charlie raised his eyes and nodded at a tall slender, red-headed girl—Lynn (Squeaky) Fromme—who got up at once and left the room, returning moments later with a glass. Charlie took a drink, then smiled: "Sody water," he said aloud. He set the glass down, got to his feet, and stretched.

I noted immediately how short he was: about five-three (two inches shorter than I). He wore motorcycle boots and faded Levi's, the pockets of which were embroidered with flowers. Tied around his neck was a leather thong. With his arms over his head, his ribs protruded, but his body was sinewy and he looked strong. A Zapata-style mustache and shoulder-length brown hair highlighted the even, boyish features of his face and his dark, darting brown eyes. He seemed like a jovial little dude, which I could well imagine, what with all those delectable

ladies surrounding him. He was obviously older than the
others and the focal member of the group, though at the
time I was much more aware of Brenda and Snake, who
sat beside me smiling warmly.

"Did you guys know Jay?" I asked Brenda, trying not
to stare at her boobs, "the guy who used to live here?"

She shook her head. "The house was empty when we
moved in last week."

"You're all together?"

She nodded. "We're a Family," she said simply, "an
extension of Charlie's love."

I didn't know what that meant, but I was beginning
to get an impression.

Charlie sat down and one of the girls placed a joint
in his mouth. I wondered to myself: how does this guy do
it; he's like a friggin' sultan. Then Charlie smiled at me,
before saying something to Bruce about the Harley;
moments later, Snake asked me where I was from and
everyone talked quietly and I gradually felt the purely
sexual vibes being dissipated and absorbed into a general
feeling of closeness, a rapport which was like nothing I
had experienced in such a large group. I sensed that
these people were really "together," and it intrigued me.
I didn't understand it then, but I felt it strongly. This, I
thought, is what I'd been looking for.

Charlie took another hit from the joint, then began to
sing. He bent forward, hugging the guitar, his hair hanging over his face; he really leaned into the music with
body and voice. And he was good, damn good, timing the
notes and modulations with a loose-jointed, natural
rhythm. Manson had soul and there was genuine merri-
ment in his manner, a contagious style that got everyone
off. As a musician I admired his talent for improvisation; it
gave the music vitality. Plus, it was right up my alley,
'cause that's the kind of music I do best and that's why
Charlie and I connected so well that night.

Those who have written about Manson have always
implied that drugs and sex were his primary means of
programming the Family. But music was perhaps even
more influential. No other art form better expresses and
transmits the nuances of the soul. While Charlie was
never a great instrumentalist, his voice was strong and he
had a good range. He could wail, croon, and get funky.
That night he was lighthearted and full of love.

He got it moving by making up songs, singing nonsense verses with uncanny timing. I felt completely relaxed and into it. When he suddenly began a new verse, then hesitated halfway through it, I obeyed an impulse and sang the rest of it.

"Right on, Paul! . . . Let's do it!" Delighted, he bounced up and came around to my side of the table and started to play again. Pretty soon we were taking turns, first Charlie, then me, one verse following another, a full-on duet—all of it spontaneous, all of it coming together; everybody digging it. Afterward he sang a song and the whole group joined in: it was a song I was to hear hundreds of times as a member of the Manson Family.

> *Your home is where you're happy*
> > *It's not where you're not free*
> *Your home is where you can be what you are;*
> > *'Cause you were just born to be.*
>
> *They'll show you their castles,*
> > *And diamonds for all to see*
> *But they'll never show you their peace of mind*
> > *'Cause they don't know how to be free.*
>
> *So burn all your bridges,*
> > *Leave your old life far behind you*
> *You can be what you wanna be*
> > *Just don't let your mama find you.*
>
> *Anywhere you might wander,*
> > *You can make that your home*
> *Just as long as you've got love in your heart*
> > *You'll never be alone.*

Later, Charlie sat beside me strumming the guitar. Bruce Davis had moved over and sat facing us from across the table. Bruce, whom I would come to know well and who was subsequently convicted for his part in the murder of Shorty Shea, was a thick, heavyset dude with an angular, saturnine face, usually wearing a tight-lipped expression. He had black wavy hair and a very macho demeanor. He was twenty-five. Like Charlie, he had done time. His hands were thick and gnarly, and he gestured with them sporadically while describing a motorcycle ride in Malibu which had resulted in busting up the Harley earlier that week.

"Hey, if that wasn't bad enough, Charlie gets up on the bike and starts riding it around the sidewalk; then he loses control and crashes the son of a bitch through a fucking bakery window!"

Charlie chuckled. A small space was visible between his front teeth. "Yeah, it kinda got away from me," he said.

"Kinda! Dig it, the fucking bike is still running, sitting in the middle of three wedding cakes; the guy who runs the place is screaming like a banshee . . . gonna tell the law—I go in and Charlie's licking his damn fingers and askin' the guy what kind of frosting he uses on the cakes . . . hey!"

I listened while they rapped out their recent adventures in West L.A. Then Charlie asked me where I'd been and what I'd been doing. I told him about traveling to communes around the country and about my hassles with the Man. Then I described what I'd experienced in Haight Ashbury in the summer of 1967. And that got Charlie off.

"Hey, Paul, I can dig it, man . . . 'cause that's when I got out of Terminal Island and went up there." He leaned forward and smoothed his hair back from his eyes with his hands. "It's like as soon as I left prison and went to the city I met this dude who gave me something to eat, you know, and took me up to the Haight. I stayed up there with him and we slept in the park in sleeping bags and we lived on the streets and my hair got a little longer and I started playing my music—and everyone's digging it like tonight, you know; and they're smiling at me and putting their arms around me and hugging me. Hey, I didn't know how to act—like it just grabbed me up, man, that there were people that real. . . ."

Lynette (they called her Lynn) sat down beside Charlie and handed him a joint. He took a hit and handed it to me.

"Then you know, Paul, it's like you were saying, things got bad at the Haight—all the young love split. When that happened, I just got that old bus outside there and said, 'Hey, anybody wants to go can go on this bus . . . the bus isn't mine and it doesn't belong to anyone . . . we'll just put the pink slip in the glove compartment and the bus can belong to itself.' And you know, we just got some people together and turned off our minds and went looking for a place to get away from the Man." Charlie tossed his head to flick the hair from his eyes. "Hey, we went to Seattle, to Texas, to New Mexico, and the Man was everywhere; everywhere we went. And like it was a trip, we were going nowhere and coming from nowhere and just grooving on the road because the road seemed to be the only place where you can be free when you're moving from one spot to another . . . and we're still moving around." He smiled at Lynn and put his arm around her. "It seems like when you're moving like that you have the freedom to take a breath. To take a breath from the city. You know how crazy the city is. . . ."

I nodded, as Snake sat down beside me and offered me a drink from a cold bottle of root beer. Charlie smiled as I handed back the bottle. Then she left the room, returning moments later with two more bottles, which she handed to us. Charlie asked if I felt the love in the room. I said I did.

He smiled, pulling one leg on top of the other into the half-lotus, before flicking his hair from his eyes. "You know, it's like if you love everything, you don't have to think about things. I mean, you just love. Whatever the circumstances hand you, whatever the dealer deals you, you just love the hand you got, dig?" He grinned, squeezing Lynette's hand; then set the bottle of root beer on the table. "I've never had much schooling, no home, in and out of orphanages, foster homes, reform schools, jails . . . and it's good, see, 'cause my head has always remained clear . . . like I have no opinion. But I know the truth, you dig. The truth has no word form. It just is. And everything is the way it is because that's the way love speaks. And when you tune in with love, you tune in with everything . . . that's not really a philosophy, that's a fact, and anybody who's got love in their hearts knows that."

While I drank the rest of the root beer Charlie told me that the love in the room belonged to him and that we should enjoy it because that's all there was to enjoy. With Snake and Brenda sitting beside me again, their sleek bodies delineated by the candlelight, I was ready to enjoy it.

Looking back on that night through the lens of hindsight, it is easy to project interpretations which don't belong—particularly in view of the fact that Charlie, Sadie

(Susan Atkins), Katie (Patricia Krenwinkle), Bruce Davis, all present that night in Topanga, were subsequently convicted of first-degree murder; but what I can say is that I did feel the love Charlie spoke of, not only the anticipation of making love to his girls, but the bond that clearly existed, a bond generated by Charles Manson. What he seemed then is what he was: a hard-core ex-con who had found love in the streets and with it had established an alternative life-style to the rat race he called "the city"—a communal scene that seemed, that night, to be grounded by a feeling of brotherhood. I'd spent two years searching for that kind of ambience in communes throughout California and the Southwest. I found none of them were really "together." Most, in fact, were merely glorified crash pads where people came together to get stoned and fuck. What united them was not this feeling of love but a kind of desperate desperado alternative to the bleak superficiality of the straight world.

That desperation of the late sixties was not an isolated phenomenon. I had seen it on the road everywhere I went. People of all ages—confused, fearful, angry, frustrated, but not defeated. The half-decade between 1965 and 1970 was probably the most violent and chaotic period in America in the last thirty years. Against the backdrop of the Vietnam war were the wars and violence which raged in streets and ghettos throughout the country: the Watts riots, the San Francisco riots, the Black Panther shoot-outs, the Chicago Seven conspiracy, the assassinations of Martin Luther King and Robert F. Kennedy. Yet, through it all, there was a vitality which sustained hope and inspired a search for new direction and leadership. The psychedelic revolution proved a catalyst to the process. The music of the Beatles reinforced it. There was Woodstock. There were books on Eastern thought. I remember reading novels by Frank Waters on the Pueblo Indians; part of the reason for my journey to the Southwest was to find good peyote in the desert. More than anything, I wanted to identify more closely with my inner processes and the cosmic forces which seemed so inaccessible in the wake of a civilization gone mad. What the youth in America were looking for in the late sixties, it seemed to me, was a shared love and a sense of identity.

Charlie took the empty bottle out of my hand, then

rose to his feet: "Would you like to stay tonight and make love with us?"

His question hardly needed an answer and he didn't wait for one. He merely returned to his place at the head of the table. Without recourse to a single word, Bruce and Katie moved the table to one corner of the room, while Mary and Brenda shoved the mattresses together. That's when I noticed Sadie get to her feet and walk to the head of the table near Charlie; she gave me what I interpreted to be an invitational smile while I stood gaping at her well-endowed physique. Sadie was full-bodied and sensual, one of Charlie's original girls. While I didn't speak to her at all that first night, I was aware of her presence; later we would become very close friends.

I was slightly apprehensive as everyone sat in a circle and joined hands. I had never taken part in group sex or orgies of any kind. In fact, where sex was concerned I was a relative novice, not a virgin by any means, but at eighteen, hardly an experienced lover. Had I not been stoned and into the vibes of Charlie and the Family, I might not have made the scene that night; but I was horny, and with Brenda and Snake clinging to me, I was ready to go for it. Also, rapping and playing music with Charlie had created a rapport between us; his presence alone had a calming affect, and I inadvertently focused on the energy he was putting out, as did everyone else. Without being aware of it consciously, I sensed even then that the control was in his hands. In part it was the music and the anticipation of what was coming, but more it was the intuitive certainty that he alone determined all action.

Suddenly Charlie gave out with a gut-wrenching yowl and immediately the others began shouting, moaning and screaming, giving vent to a cacophony of noise; sitting directly to my left, Snake began to jibber while Brenda let go with a high-pitched screech like some berserk jungle feline; though I was initially startled by the raucous outburst, I immediately understood it as a kind of tension release, a collective purging of the soul, and I managed my own halfhearted rendition of what sounded like a dying seal. Gradually the noise subsided into a dull penetrating drone and I felt Snake squeeze my hand. Someone had turned on a stereo with the volume low so that the sounds seemed muted and hazy; the fire was still flickering among the coals and I was aware of how warm the room was becoming. In emulation of Charlie (who sat almost directly across from me), people began closing their eyes; somehow closing mine made it much easier and I began to get into the flow of energy coming into my hands. Months later, when I moved into Spahn's Ranch with the Family, I would come to understand how Charlie programmed sexual energy into the group and how group sex functioned to unify the Family. But that night, my primary concern was to get it on with Brenda and Snake.

For what seemed like hours, we rocked back and forth, hands joined—until at last I realized that people around me were removing their clothes. I opened my eyes and saw Bruce embracing Sandy, and I was aware of Charlie lying alongside Sadie and Squeaky, and of a general tangle of bodies to which I seemed to be remotely attached. I heard the lugubrious sounds of lovemaking and the positioning of bodies. Of immediate and most pressing interest, however, was Snake, who began to unfasten my belt while Brenda helped me pull off my sweater. I was sweating profusely as Brenda lay down, and I lay down beside her, caressing her cheek with my hand. She guided my hand between her legs, while Snake pressed against me from behind so that I was sandwiched between the two girls. The grass had awakened my senses to every nuance of motion; to the slow undulations of our bodies greased with perspiration; to the perfection of everything tactile and audible. Oblivious of everything but the music, we moved together in a kind of harmonious, inventive slither, exploring orifices and contours with an amorphous precision like underwater jellyfish congealed into a single entity. Then I rolled onto my back and felt Snake's tongue press into my mouth while Brenda began giving me head. It was as if my entire body was immersed in sensation, as though together we moved through space like planets on a hot surface of moist and resilient flesh no longer alone in the universe.

During the course of the evening I made love with other girls, but it was dark by then and I was completely spaced-out and never knew who they were. At one point I remember lying beside Charlie and him repeating that the love was his and that we were all brothers and sisters in love. It did not occur to me that night that Charlie was bisexual. I didn't sense those kinds of vibes, and he made no physical moves in my direction, though later that dimension of our relationship would become something of an issue.

Everyone was asleep when I got up before dawn, slipped on my moccasins, and tiptoed out to the porch. The air was crisp; moisture glistened from the blades of wild grass growing around the house. Hundreds of tiny black birds were wide awake and chattering in trees along the ravine. I had awakened with a new plan of action: to return to Big Sur and live alone on the beach. I didn't know why this notion came to me so suddenly, particularly after all the good feelings I'd experienced that night, but it did. It had never really occurred to me to remain with Charlie and the Family after that first night. Even had they asked me to stay, I would probably have declined. I had little inclination, then, to live communally with anyone. Oddly enough, my meeting with Charlie had triggered a desire to be alone: to sort out my life and do my music away from the "madness" he had spoken of, away from L.A. and anything that smacked of civilization. The thought excited me as I pulled on my sweater and started back up the canyon toward my campsite.

3

On April 4, 1968 (the day Martin Luther King was gunned down in Memphis), I headed north on Highway 101. Three rides took me to the outskirts of Carmel, where I camped on the beach. There, I was content to remain alone—meditating, writing music, and hiking along the shore. To me, there is no place more inspiring than this wild stretch of California's coastline. The waters of the sea are vibrant and clear; the surf, spectacular. Wind-ravaged pines cling to the cliffs, convoluted in gyrations of a frozen ballet. What I saw around me turned me inward on myself. I experienced a deep tumultuous confusion, yet sensed it was part of positive inner change. From time to time I did think of Black Beard, wondered what he had found in New Mexico. I wouldn't find out until over a year later, when we met by accident in Topanga Canyon and shared horror stories about Charles Manson.

I spent a week on the beach, alone. Then, early one morning, on the spur of the moment, I decided to hitch-hike into Big Sur. My one and only ride, as it turned out, was a good one; after a one-hour conversation on the beauty of nature and brotherhood, the guy who picked me up asked me to baby-sit his house while he made a trip to Hawaii. I couldn't believe it. Later that morning we arrived at his place. It was perfect: an isolated, rustic, well-cared-for five-room cabin built on a hillside about four miles up Garapata Canyon, just south of Big Sur. The owner, a thirty-year-old hippie farmer named Kevin, had recently purchased the farm and asked only that I take care of his garden and tend to his animals—a big German shepherd named Wiley, a goat called Sheila, a couple of pigs, and a yard full of chickens. "If you need any help, I got a friend named Ray who lives with his wife just a couple miles up the canyon; he's a good man." Kevin showed me around the place; said there was plenty of work—repairing sheds, mending fences, painting the out-house. "Suit yourself," he said. "Don't have to do any-thing if you don't want to, just so long as you keep an eye on the house and feed my stock."

It was a beautiful spread, built on five acres of ground with a year-round stream at one end of the prop-erty and a developed fifty-gallon-a-minute spring (with gravity-flow plumbing) on the other. There were a spa-cious garden area, a weather-tight poultry house, and an abundance of usable building materials; sawn and stacked lumber, pipe fittings, sheet metal, nails, screws, tools of all kinds, a hand plow, and a beat-up engineless Model-T Ford which sat in the middle of the yard.

For the next three months I lived alone on the place, enjoying the natural beauty and solitude. The plump, green hillsides were scattered with oak and pine set against a backdrop of blooming wildflowers. The salt air was invigorating. White gulls soared in daily from the beach, circling and sailing the skies alongside hawks and vultures. I felt like a king living high on the hillside, completely divorced from the vicissitudes and traumas of the outside world—the chaos in Los Angeles. I had no TV set, not even a radio. My life became a ritual of work and relaxation. I got up at daybreak, fed the animals, cleaned the stalls, collected eggs, and milked Sheila. When it got hot I took off my shirt and worked at odd jobs. Using surplus wood and tar paper, I repaired leaks and built a storehouse for the spring harvest. Kevin really knew how to cultivate the soil. By mid-June his garden had produced a rich yield of radishes, beets, tomatoes, lettuce, zucchini, eggplants, artichokes, cucumbers, melons, and beans which Ray and I harvested and took to town to sell. The physical labor was satisfying and my body got hard and lean. Not since I had competed as a high-school wrestler had I felt so strong. When I wasn't working, I baked bread, played music, read, and hiked back and forth through the canyon to the sea with Wiley, who invariably chased lizards and butterflies while trotting ahead of me on the trail. I really felt like I was getting it together, that things were breaking my way. I thought of asking Kevin if I might stay on when he returned.

Then, just two weeks before Kevin was due back, Ray got in a hassle with his wife, Letti, and asked to move in with me; since Ray was Kevin's close friend, I didn't have much choice in the matter. Things worked out for a day or two, until Letti started charging up to the house to cuss and fume and threaten Ray with a lawsuit. She was a big, full-breasted, bawdy gal from the Midwest, with a voice like a foghorn.

Late one night she got drunk and started banging on our front door. Ray and I were in bed. He was snoring and didn't wake up; but I did. I could hear her shouting: "Ray, goddammit . . . Ray, open the door. . . . You prick! You asshole with ears. . . . I heard what you told the lawyer. I heard what you said, you shit-for-brains motherfucker!" I woke Ray and told him to get his ass out there and tend to his wife before she broke down the door. Meanwhile, Wiley was barking and she was calling him names. "Hey," she shouted at us, "I'll make dog-salad air conditioning out of that canine if you sic him on me." That's when I looked out the window and, in the glow of the porch light, saw that Letti was toting a twelve-gauge shotgun.

"What the hell is with you, anyway, dammit!" I heard Ray mutter as he stepped out the door. They yammered at each other for about twenty minutes; then Ray came in and said he was walking her back to the house. "All she needs, Paul, is a good screwin'. . . . I'll be back."

The next morning, just before dawn, I climbed the hill to a vantage point from which I could look down on the highway. Sitting there reminded me of my spot in Topanga Canyon, and I thought about what my next move would be. Across the ravine I spotted Ray trudging toward Kevin's barn carrying a bucket. He was feeding the animals and collecting eggs. He'd already moved back to Kevin's; said his old lady had called her brother, who was coming in from Memphis: "She says he's bad. But don't worry, Paul, it's cool. I can handle that asshole." I didn't want to hang around for that. Suddenly the serenity of Kevin's farm was giving way to a conflict which I sensed was far from over. I wanted to leave but didn't know where to go. Thoughts of camping on the beach no longer appealed to me. I had a trial coming up in L.A. for a second marijuana bust, though it was the last thing I wanted to face. I was in limbo again, about to leave one scene in search of another.

I smoked a joint and watched the gulls glide across the sky, embedded there like flecks of jewelry. I wondered why there were so many cars on the highway that day, then remembered it was the Fourth of July. I watched the sun come up, and went back to the cabin and wrote Kevin a letter. I thanked him and told him I was splitting. Despite his problems with Letti, I knew Ray would take good care of the place. Then I packed my stuff, said good-bye to Ray, and started south.

By noon I was standing on the corner of Topanga Canyon and Ventura Boulevards. It was hot and smoggy and my eyes burned. I'd been there only minutes when two girls driving a battered green Plymouth swerved onto the shoulder of the road to pick me up. I recognized them at once as Snake and Brenda.

"Hey, far-out!" Brenda smiled. "It's you . . . uh . . ."
"Paul."
"Yeah, Paul, right!" She brushed the hair from her

face as Snake leaned forward to let me into the back.
There were several sacks of produce and canned foods on
the seat. I set them on the floor and took off my pack.

"Been shopping, huh?"

"Garbage run."

"Garbage?"

"We just go down and clean out the trash behind
those big supermarkets in the valley . . . those pigs throw
away all kinds of good stuff . . . look at it, all fresh food
. . . help yourself to some apricots." She eased back onto
the highway. Snake smiled at me.

"Where have *you* been, anyway?"

I briefly recounted my adventures in Garapata Canyon, then asked what they'd been up to. They launched
into a duet about Charlie's love; said they hadn't been
doing anything but making love 'cause that's all there was
to do. Their rap sounded a little stilted and corny to me at
the time, though I did have recollections of the closeness
I'd experienced that night in Topanga Canyon. Both girls
wore bemused smiles and exchanged knowing glances as
we purred along the highway amid heavy holiday traffic.
I asked if they wanted to smoke a number, and they declined. Each was dressed in a loose-fitting, full-length
hippie-style dress. Directly in front of me, Snake's hair
hung in a profuse jungled tangle down her back. Looking
at them, I realized just how horny I was after three
months without sex. They said they'd moved out of
Topanga Canyon.

"We're living up at Spahn's Ranch now," Brenda enthused. "It's a trippy place . . . beautiful, away from everything. Ever been there?"

I shook my head at her sparkling green eyes in the
rearview mirror.

"Why don't you come up and say hi to Charlie?"

I didn't think much about seeing Charlie. But I had
nowhere else to go.

"Sure," I said. "Why not?"

We drove up Topanga Canyon Boulevard, past Devonshire to Santa Susana Pass, then up to the Chatsworth
foothills. The girls talked about Charlie and the Family,
how mellow their life was there, how deeply they all felt
Charlie's love. "Charlie," Brenda intoned, "is just a hole in
the infinite through which love is funneled." It all sounded

pretty hokey to me, and I didn't pay much attention, until Snake flashed a beatific smile and said simply, "Charlie is Jesus Christ."

They both giggled. I let it slide, thinking it some sort of inside joke.

It was hot, bright, and smoggy, yet the drive revitalized me as the wind poured through Snake's window. I was still slightly spaced-out after leaving the mountains so abruptly, particularly after the comically bizarre episode the night before with Letti and Ray. I had no clue to what my next move would be as I gazed out at the ocher-colored foothills; I did know that my first priority was to get laid. I'd heard about Spahn's Ranch, remembered friends at various times going there to ride horseback. I knew it was used as a set for Hollywood westerns but I'd never seen the place until that day. I had no idea that I'd soon be calling it my home.

We took a back road off Santa Susana Pass and drove down a dusty dirt driveway onto the ranch complex—a conglomerate of weathered wooden buildings, sheds, and lean-tos, set against a backdrop of rock-studded rolling foothills and rather dense low-mountain vegetation: scrub oak, eucalyptus, mustard weed, and wildflowers. With chickens gaggling, dogs barking, roosters trumpeting their eternal salutation, and people moving through rituals of morning chores, you had the feeling of entering the hub of some funky Mexican barrio. I saw clothing drying on lines and rafters and a young hippie girl carrying a child. A cowboy waved as he came out of a trailer and flipped a cigarette butt. The place looked like a puzzle of tiny, odd-shaped structures put together out of wood, stucco, and strips of sheet metal. There was smoke rising from a trash can, and the smell of breakfast mingled with other smells, the barnyard aromas of horseshit and poultry dust. Because of the holiday, there were large groups of camera-toting tourists moving about the property, ogling the movie sets and renting horses to ride. Intermittently, a firecracker would explode in the distance and reverberate off the walls of the hillside.

As we drove slowly beside the battered boardwalk of the "town," Brenda pointed out the movie sets—Longhorn Saloon, Rock City Café, an undertaking parlor, the jail, the tack room—and out behind these structures, the house of the owner, a half-blind eighty-two-year-old man named George Spahn, whom Snake called "a real cutie." In fact, George was sitting outside his house in the sunlight in a rocking chair as we drove by in a cloud of dust. Farther down the road (about a quarter of a mile off to the left), sequestered behind a stand of eucalyptus trees, was the main ranch house. "George is renting it now to a bunch of hippies," Brenda said. "They're not with Charlie," Snake added. "Just kids George lets hang around." I spotted some of the "kids" sitting outside the house playing music. I was tempted to join them, but the girls insisted on taking me back to what they called "the outlaw shacks," where the Family was then staying: two small dilapidated redwood structures within a stone's throw of the main ranch house.

We were approaching the shacks when down the ravine came a group of riders (a man, a woman, and several seven- or eight-year-old children) trotting at a good clip toward the road. We waved at them and the kids grinned and waved back. One of the boys jerked a toy six-gun from his holster, aiming at us as we passed them. I played like I was hit before firing back in mock retaliation with my index finger. Moments later we skidded to a stop beside a battered green pickup truck.

Before we were out of the car, the door of the shack opened and I looked up to see Charlie, Sandy, and Squeaky standing on the porch. Charlie was dressed in tight-fitting Levi's; he was shirtless and shoeless, and clean-shaven except for a neatly trimmed mustache. He was twirling a set of car keys on one finger. As we approached the shack, his eyes flickered recognition and his grin widened.

"Hey, man, what's happening?" He bounded off the porch. "Long time no see . . . um . . . Paul, right?"

"Paul Watkins." We clasped hands hippie-style. Again it struck me that Charlie and I were close in size.

"You're lookin' good, man. What kind of gig you into these days?"

I repeated the story I'd told Brenda and Snake, while the girls carried the sacks of groceries into the house.

"Hey, dig it." Charlie spun the keys. "We have to split for a while . . . but we'll be right back. Stick around, huh?"

"Sure."

"Far-out. Snake's gonna be here . . . if you need any-

thing. Hey, we can play some music when I get back."
He hopped into the cab of the truck and honked the horn.
Moments later, Brenda, Squeaky, and Sandy dashed out
of the shack and piled in beside him. Charlie grinned,
then fired up the engine. "Later, Paul."

It must have been about two in the afternoon when
Charlie split. I went back into the shack to leave my gear
and get my horn. It all looked pretty familiar, probably
from shoot-outs I'd seen that had been filmed in the same
dwelling. The furniture had been cleared out; the floor
reminded me of Jay's living room that night in March: wall-
to-wall mattresses, blankets, and sleeping bags—one big
communal bed. Snake told me that Katie, Sadie, Mary,
Ella, and Stephanie had gone to Mendocino but would
be back soon. Bruce Davis, she said, had "gone on his
own trip."

I talked to Snake a while, then took my horn and
walked down the road toward the ranch house and the
sound of music—two guitars and a harmonica. It was hot
and dusty, the air pungent with the smell of fresh horseshit along the roadside. There were a dozen or more
hippie kids—guys and girls—still congregated in a circle
under a stand of eucalyptus, smoking dope and jamming,
when I joined them. It was a friendly scene and I got
down with the music, feeling good doing sounds with a
group after three months of solos and solitude.

Later I rolled a joint and hiked up to a rock on the
hillside overlooking the ranch. The air was fresher up
there, and I detected the aroma of coffee being brewed.
Across the ravine on another slope I saw two of the Spahn
Ranch wranglers herding a dozen or more mares toward
the ravine. I waved but they didn't see me. I peeled off my
shirt and began to ponder my options. I really didn't know
what my next move would be: maybe head back to Big
Sur again, after my trial; or set out to find Black Beard; or
go back to school to please my folks. But none of these
ideas appealed to me. I finished off the joint, then stood
up to take a piss. That's when I spotted Snake at the foot
of the hill, strolling aimlessly, it appeared, beneath the
eucalyptus trees. From time to time she glanced up at me
and smiled. She'd changed her clothes. Standing in the
sunlight, her body was silhouetted inside a silky yellow
summer dress. While I didn't know it at the time, I would

later learn that Charlie had left her behind to seduce me. At that point I didn't need too much seduction.

Snake (Diane Lake) was fifteen when I met her, and had joined the Family just weeks before I first saw her in Topanga Canyon. Of all the girls, she was the only one who had come from a hippie background. Both her parents had been members of a hippie commune called the Hog Farm.

Charlie had met her there and had talked her parents into letting her join him. At fourteen she was a veteran of acid trips and orgies. Only later would I learn how strong a hold Charlie had on her. But from the beginning I felt a soul kinship to Snake. I was aware of a deep sensitivity and visceral toughness that would sustain her through experiences which might well have shattered the average person. My bond with her was to remain a strong one.

When she started down the trail toward the creek, I followed her. We spent the rest of the afternoon making love in the sunshine on a grassy knoll just a few feet from the creek bed.

It was dusk by the time we wandered back to the outlaw shacks. Charlie and the other girls were sitting outside on the porch. Charlie was playing the guitar, making up songs. He grinned when he saw us and flicked the hair from his eyes. When Snake went into the house, Charlie followed her. Moments later he returned and asked if I wanted to take a ride with him into Hollywood. When I said yes, he sprang to his feet. "Let's go." We piled into the pickup, fired it up, and took off in a swirl of dust down the road. Charlie was in high spirits; he chuckled to himself as we sped along the rim of the pass toward the main highway.

"Hey, man, dig it . . . Snake made a dandy report on you . . . says you make love real good." He beamed. His face was animated, full of color, his eyes bright and energized.

"Does she tell you everything?"

Charlie hooted. "Hey, she's one of my girls." He pulled some dark glasses from the visor and put them on. "You like her?"

I said I liked her, and Charlie gave me a roguish grin before slapping me paternally on the knee.

We boogied out to the San Diego Freeway and headed south. When I asked, Charlie told me how they had eased into Spahn's gradually by getting to know old George. He explained that so long as they kept George happy—helped around the ranch, shoveled shit, took care of him, and kept their own trip discreet—they could stay at Spahn's indefinitely. "Old George is a trippy dude . . . kind of cranky, but okay, dig. I keep a couple of girls with him most of the time; you know the old fart can still get his rocks off! Yeah, man . . . George has a lot of beauty. He's just like the rest of us . . . just needs a little love."

Charlie eased the truck into the right lane. "You know, man," he said, "you ought to move in with us a while."

"I got some things to do . . . a few other trips."

"What you got to do? Hey . . . I ain't trying to pry . . . a man should never put his business in the street—but the point is, there's nothing *to* do, dig?"

"Got a court hearing coming up . . . then I may go up to Big Sur . . . I had a nice little scene up there . . . I'm not sure yet . . ."

"Look, we have our own little scene at Spahn's. You're welcome to stay if you want to. Everything is there. Mostly what we have is a lot of love. It's my love and I give it to you. . . . Like if you've been on the road and want a place to hang out for a while, rest up, you got people who love you." He spit out the window. "You got some troubles with the Man, hey, I can help you out there. Where cops, lawyers, and jerk-off judges are concerned, I'm an expert. . . . Mainly with the heat, you just mostly play dumb, dig . . . play it by ear . . . just slide right along with their greasy, pig-power games. The pigs aren't really bad, man. Mainly they're just dumb. So you play a little dumber and they suddenly think they're smart. That's pretty much how it is: the dumber they think you are, the better they feel, the more they let you slide."

Listening to Charlie was a trip. Few people I've known could ever compete with Charles Manson when it came to laying down a rap—winding one sentence on top of another from some infinite unfathomable coil of associations. His train of thought had roots in a sea of theory and experiences, and while the logic was never precise—invariably shot through with non sequiturs and bizarre anecdotes—the flow was always spontaneous and compelling, all the more intriguing because the paradox of his personality was built right into the dialogue: a blend of jocular machismo on the one hand, and a kind of soothing spiritual wisdom on the other. It blew my mind.

We were driving down Sunset Boulevard toward Bel Air. Charlie was still talking: "Ya see, I have five girls coming back this week from up north. I'm going to need some help. That's a lot of women to care for, dig? . . . The trip is with women, you have to keep them loved. What I mean is, they gotta be fucked, regular. That's just the way it is. You can say whatever you want, but that's the trip. But if you love them, man, they'll take care of you: feed you, bleed you, clothe you . . . stand by you down the line. They'll make you strong and you'll make them strong, you dig? It's survival, that's all. The more a woman submits, the stronger she is. The stronger she is, the stronger you are. If you got women who'll stand by your trip, Paul . . . well, then you have a good scene . . . it's like money in the bank. Hey, I could use your help, man. . . .

"Look, you want to make a trip to Big Sur, we'll all go with you . . . just pile in the big bus and boogie up there. Our scene is mobile . . . I just leave a couple of girls with George. If it's happening at Big Sur, let's go. . . . You know, man, you're a beautiful little dude . . . you're smart, you make good sounds. Hey, Snake said some nice things about you; you should get into our trip for a while . . . at least spend the summer."

It was not a difficult decision to make. I liked Charlie. And I definitely liked the harem he had going at Spahn's. It intrigued me: how did he do it? Certainly at no time in my life would I ever have so many women available to me. At eighteen, I could handle it. I guess that's what Charlie figured. I was convinced too, in those days, that a person lived best when he flowed with the events and circumstances of the moment. By being on the road at the right time, I had managed to live like a king in the mountains of Big Sur for three months. It seemed more than just coincidence that the day I left Big Sur, I met Brenda and Snake. Also, Charlie's rap about life was in direct harmony with my own feelings: "I am you and you are me," he said. "What we do for ourselves, man, we do for everyone. There's no good in life other

than coming to the realization of the love that governs it
. . . . Coming to 'Now,' dig? People, you know, wear all
kinds of masks to hide their love, to disguise it, to keep
themselves from conquering their own fear. But we have
nothing to hide . . . nothing to be ashamed of. There is
no right and wrong. We're all beautiful expressions of the
same love, and it's this experience that we share."

Some of what he said smacked of sermons I'd heard
as a kid; some of it, at times, sounded pompous. But the
core of it was fundamental to what I believed, and
somehow Charlie's music, his unpretentiousness, his small-
ness, his past, his humility, his general funkiness, made it
all palatable. I had yet to see the other side of the coin.

In retrospect, I realize too that our being about the
same size played a substantial role, not only in the beginning but later on. Being five-foot-five in a macho
world of six-footers was never easy. It's a bit like being a
racial minority, being literally "looked down upon." There
is a definite camaraderie among small men, and there's no
question, where Charlie was concerned, they got the
benefit of the doubt. He had clearly paid his own dues in
that regard; he had, in fact, survived seventeen years in
concrete jungles behind bars and walls, using his brain to
accomplish what his brawn was clearly incapable of. Because of my size—my parents wanted me to become a
jockey (two of my uncles had ridden winners in the
Kentucky Derby)—I did not pose a threat to Charlie
physically. Perhaps because of this, we came to share an
intimacy that was unique within the Family. At the time
I was eighteen, he was thirty-four—old for the hippie
world. I believe he saw in me (standing before him eye-
to-eye) the epitome of the enthusiastic flower child. At an
unconscious level, perhaps, I became his mirror, re-
flecting the emergence of the flower child in him, the
emergence of his own long-stifled love. Though I noted
an urgency in his request that disturbed me slightly, I
dismissed it, not realizing that part of what I sensed was
my own intuitive apprehension—of what, I had no idea.

By the time we turned into Dennis Wilson's sprawling estate and parked the pickup behind Dennis' Rolls-
Royce, I had agreed to spend at least the rest of the
summer with the Family.

4

Dennis Wilson looked about five-eleven and weighed maybe 160 pounds. He appeared agile and athletic, with blue eyes, blond hair, and rather standard California good looks. He seemed to be easygoing, but his jovial exterior betrayed a subtle sense of agitation. Still in his early twenties, he'd been married, divorced, and was the father of a child. When I first met him he came on like a polished playboy bachelor—glib, loose-jointed, and hip. At the same time (unlike the rest of the Beach Boys), he seemed accessible and amenable to suggestion—less satisfied, perhaps, with his own success. Earlier that summer he had met and befriended Charlie. Charlie seemed anxious that I meet him.

Dennis was standing on his porch, barefoot in a pair of Bermuda shorts, when we drove up and got out of the truck. Charlie introduced me to Dennis and we all went inside the house.

I was blown away by the size and beauty of the estate, once the home of Will Rogers. (If "success" was gauged by material extravagance, Dennis sure as hell had made it): the classic Spanish-style Hollywood mansion, complete with magnificent manicured lawns, vibrant recently cultivated rose gardens, and an enormous kidney-shaped swimming pool. The inside was no less lavish: furnished to the hilt with antiques, original French paintings, Persian rugs, and countless mementos and photos of the Beach Boys' international acclaim in the record industry. Charlie's reasons for cultivating Dennis were obvious. In addition to his Rolls-Royce, Dennis had a new candy-apple-red Ferrari, a fine piece of machinery that Steve Grogan (Clem) and I were to total three weeks later on a drive up to Spahn's Ranch.

At the time, I viewed Dennis as an all-American middle-class surfer kid who suddenly made it rich and didn't know quite how to handle it. He was a prime target for the Family. Charlie self-righteously played the role of Robin Hood, taking from the rich, namely Dennis, to give to the poor, namely Charlie. He really went to work on Dennis, made him feel guilty for possessing so much wealth, urged him to renounce it in exchange for a simple communal life based on love: Charlie's love. Because Dennis liked Charlie and saw the potential in Charlie's music, he was willing to help him and arranged for the Family to hold recording sessions in his brother Brian's Beverly Hills studio. Dennis was equally intrigued with Charlie's impoverished childhood, his criminal record, and his eclectic free-lance spiritual rap. As Dennis once remarked to me, "Charlie is the most tuned-in dude I ever met."

For the most part, however, Charlie was merely playing the roles he played best: con man and pimp. He had at his disposal not one but ten attractive girls who were ready and willing to heed his every whim. For a small-time ex-con who had spent seventeen years of his life behind bars, Charlie was doing all right for himself. It obviously impressed Dennis. During the first few weeks I was with the Family, Charlie was always sending over contingents of girls to keep Dennis fucked, sucked, and steeped in Manson doctrine: "Cease to exist . . . just come and say you love me. . . . Give up your world, come on and you can be . . . . I'm your kind, I'm your kind. . . . And I can see. . . ." Dennis all but capitulated. One night he gave Charlie and me not only most of his wardrobe (five-hundred-dollar suits, shirts, shoes, and ties), but all of his gold records, which we later distributed in the streets of Hollywood to passersby, just to blow their minds. It seemed to put things in perspective: what were gold records anyway? What did they mean to the spiritual man? What did they represent other than the epitome of American capitalism? Were it not for the fact that Dennis was deeply committed to the entertainment establishment, committed to people who had their own designs on his dangling purse strings, he might well have renounced everything and joined the Family.

The cast of characters at Spahn's Ranch that summer was awesome. The day I arrived there were four girls living with Charlie: Snake, Brenda, Squeaky, and Sandy. Two days later, Sadie, Katie, Mary, Stephanie, and Ella returned from Mendocino, swelling the female population to nine. The males (in addition to Charlie and myself) included Brooks Posten, a kid named Kim, Steve Grogan (Clem), and a good-natured Texan named Charles (Tex) Watson, who had been living with Dennis Wilson before joining the Family shortly after my arrival. Tex was twenty that July, one of the most affable, good-natured people I'd ever met. An excellent carpenter and mechanic, he stayed busy by keeping the Family vehicles in running order. He also served as a buffer between the ranch hands and the Family. Being from the Lone Star State (McKinney), he spoke in a languorous drawl—"I jes come here t'see what was goin' on"—and was able to relate to the cowboys on their own terms. During the months that followed, I saw Charlie get inside his head. Within a year Manson turned Tex into a death-wielding robot who thought of himself as an avenging angel.

There were other males who drifted in and out of the Family that summer: one was Juan Flynn, a flamboyant, strapping Irish Panamanian who worked for George Spahn as a wrangler; another was Bobby Beausoleil, a super-hippie Hollywood kid and a fine musician who later introduced two new girls to the Family—Catherine Share (Gypsy) and Leslie Van Houten. The average age within the Family was twenty. The oldest girl was Gypsy, twenty-six; the youngest, Snake, fifteen. The oldest guy other than Charlie was Juan Flynn, twenty-six; the youngest guy, Kim, seventeen. While there would be fluctuations in size from time to time, new faces coming and going, this nucleus remained fairly consistent. The only child born to the Family at that time was Pooh Bear (Michael Valentine Manson), Mary Brunner's four-month-old son, sired by Charlie. Sadie, meanwhile, was five months pregnant, and Charlie had spread the word: he wanted all his girls to bear new life and for the Family to grow.

The day after my arrival at Spahn's we moved out of the outlaw shacks into the jail, which adjoined the saloon. We still had designs on the back ranch house but would have to wait until the hippies gave it up. In the meantime, we converted our new quarters to accommodate the entire Family. The saloon was authentic old-West, complete with hand-tooled mahogany bar, mirrors, and low-hanging overhead fans. The girls cleaned the place thoroughly and we knocked out a wall to connect the jail with the saloon. We covered the floor with mattresses and bedizened the walls with tapestries purchased at the Topanga Plaza. All our food was stored in George's house, and the girls cooked on his stove, an arrangement which pleased the old-timer, since his own meals were prepared by the Family. Charlie always assigned one or two girls to minister to George's needs. Lynn (Fromme) became his favorite and spent hours sitting beside him while he rocked in his chair in the front room while country music blasted from an old portable radio. One of George's greatest pleasures was to fondle Lynn's knees as she sat beside him. When, on occasion, he slid his hand up her leg and pinched the inside of her thigh, Lynn would invariably flinch and make a little "eeak" sound while George chuckled to himself demonically. That's how Lynn came to be dubbed "Squeaky." And the name stuck.

Living so close to George and the main hub of ranch activity forced us to keep our scene discreet. We didn't want to offend the tourists nor to piss-off the ranch hands, some of whom lived in trailers and shacks on the property. Charlie was always urging us to cultivate the wranglers. So we did: saddling and currying the horses, shoveling shit, and cleaning up for George. They never had much to complain about. Only one among them really ever bad-mouthed the Family—a part-time stunt man and movie actor named Donald Jerome (Shorty) Shea.

Shorty was in his mid-thirties, a rugged, seemingly easygoing cowboy who aspired to become a big-time movie star; he had worked as a horse wrangler for over fifteen years and was a good friend to George. He was always taking off to try out for a movie role that "would land him in stardom." But it never happened; and he kept coming back to Spahn's to work for George. I always liked Shorty. Juan considered him his friend. I'll never forget the horror I experienced (a year later) when Clem described what they'd done to him.

In addition to Shorty there were three wranglers who lived at the ranch full-time: I knew them by their first names—Randy, Benny, and Larry.

Randy Starr was ranch foreman—tall, wiry, about forty-five. He wore his black hair long under a felt stetson. His face was gritty and pockmarked, and he ate "bennies" by the roll and swilled gallons of vodka. Shorty used to say his eyes looked like "two piss holes in the snow." Randy'd been a stunt man most of his life and had sustained an injury to his spine which rendered his left hand all but useless; it hung at his side like a hunk of rubber. Still, he considered himself something of a ladies' man and was forever trying to sweet-talk the "gals" into his trailer to show them his "stunts." But Charlie, wishing to keep our scene separate and secret, forbade girls in the Family to socialize with any of the wranglers—except for Juan Flynn. Since Juan was such a big, powerful dude—hip to the drug scene and well-liked by all the ranch hands—Charlie figured it best to have him on our side. And, Randy liked Juan.

Benny was the number-two man—jovial, easy-going, about five-nine and 160 pounds, somewhere in his mid-thirties. He'd been married more than once and reportedly had a whole passel of kids. But he lived in the bunkhouse on the boardwalk and only saw his family on the weekends. Benny claimed he was the best stunt man in the business. "Do any damn thing, if ya pay me for it." More than once I saw him fall off the barn for twenty-five dollars. About a month after we got there, someone gave him a tab of acid, and on a dare he walked all the way to Corriganville without his boots.

Then there was Larry, retarded by a horse fall in childhood, a hardworking twenty-eight-year-old. He had long blond hair and carried a bowie knife, which he knew how to handle. But he was always even-tempered and well-liked, constantly living out some cowboy-kid fantasy. He loved to do the "Blackfoot shuffle" and was forever galloping up to a group of us to announce: "Looks like I'll be headin' for Abilene today."

But George and the wranglers weren't the only people we had to deal with at Spahn's. There was also Ruby Pearl, a sixty-three-year-old red-headed latter-day Annie Oakley who had been a friend of George's for years. She'd also been a stunt rider in the circus and knew as much about horses as anyone at the ranch. She ran the finances, handled the wranglers, and pretty much managed the ranch. Since Spahn's supported some seventy head of horseflesh, Pearl was continually buying and selling them, as well as renting out stagecoaches, wagons, and sometimes the wranglers themselves to local movie companies. Pearl didn't live on the ranch, but she came every morning at dawn and worked energetically until late in the evening. Where the Family was concerned she was friendly and unobtrusive. So long as we did our share of the work and took care of George, she had no complaints. I liked her a lot. So did Charlie.

But the most bizarre personality among George's close friends was a wizened, beady-eyed dyspeptic little lady in her seventies who lived in a dilapidated lean-to (once a tool trailer) behind 'the saloon. Her name was Dody and she shared her low-slung hovel with a handful of yapping brindle-marked dogs. Her clothes were filthy, her teeth yellow. The only time we'd see her was when someone took her some food. Then she'd crawl out the entrance to her shack on her hands and knees. She spoke very little, and what she said was usually unintelligible. She seemed frightened and suspicious around people, childlike, yet wary. There was talk of committing her to a mental institution, but no one wanted that to happen. George let her live there because he liked her.

The general atmosphere at Spahn's was like that at most horse ranches. There was dust, leather, and the ubiquitous smell of horseshit. There was a well-stocked tack room filled with saddles, bridles, harnesses, whips, blankets, and sometimes bails of hay. And there was dust. Everything at Spahn's was seen through a veil of dust. In addition to the horses, there were scores of chickens who had the run of the place—laid their eggs everywhere—plus a scroungy one-horned goat who roamed the property bleating continually while scavenging for food. And there was always the full crew of cowboys—dressed daily in tight-fitting Levi's, work shirts, and soiled stetsons: walking around, rolling cigarettes, talking in a drawl, spitting into the dust. Sometimes they hunkered on a boardwalk outside the saloon, bullshitting with Charlie and the Family. They liked Charlie's stories and told their own. Texas talk. Merle Haggard and the good ole boys. They told jokes, cussed, farted, and when they spotted Pearl, sauntered jauntily back to work. On weekends they went to "shit-kickin' " bars in the valley and got drunk, then told stories about it during the week. Randy sang in a small country-western combo in one of the bars and asked some of the musicians in the Family to come down and play with them. We did a couple of times. It was okay. The ranch was comfortable, really. Except for the flies. There were flies everywhere, millions of them. Charlie used to sit on the boardwalk in the sun and laugh, letting the flies crawl all over him: "Man, you gotta submit to the flies. . . . Let's face it, they own this place."

Charlie (Charles Milles Manson) was born on November 12, 1934, under the sign of Scorpio. His mother, Kathleen Madox, was sixteen at the time of his birth, and was living with a man named William Manson, who may or may not have been Charlie's father, but who, nonetheless, provided him with the surname he was to use the rest of his life. While Charlie would later claim that his mother was a teenage prostitute, other relatives described her simply as submissive and "loose." In any case, it is clear that she lived with a succession of men during Charlie's childhood and was frequently absent from him. Charlie spent much of his time with obliging friends or with his aunt and maternal grandmother, moving back and forth between Ohio, West Virginia, and Kentucky.

In 1939 Kathleen and her brother, Luther, robbed a gas station and assaulted the owner with Coke bottles, knocking him unconscious. The next day they were arrested and incarcerated. While his mother served her sentence, Charlie lived with his aunt and uncle in McMechen, West Virginia, remaining with them until 1942, when Kathleen was paroled and again took custody of her son.

From 1942 to 1947 Charlie lived with his mother and a succession of "uncles," moving from one run-down neighborhood to another, until at last Kathleen tried placing her son in a foster home. When none were available, she sent him to the Gibault School for Boys, a care-taking center in Terre Haute, Indiana. Charlie was twelve. Ten months later, he escaped and returned to his mother. When she rejected him, he took off on his own, and began burglarizing private residences to survive. He was finally caught and sent to Juvenile Center in Indianapolis. But due to an error in filling out his papers, he was listed as "Catholic" and sent to Father Flanagan's Boys' Town in Omaha, Nebraska. Less than a week later (together with another boy named Blackie Nielson), he stole a car and drove to Peoria, Illinois, committing two armed robberies while en route. His life as a hard-core criminal had begun. He'd just turned thirteen.

For the next twenty years Charlie was in and out of federal and state prisons for car theft, forgery, burglary, and pimping. During that period, he was married twice, once to a seventeen-year-old girl from McMechen named Rosalie Jean Willis, who bore him one son, Charles Manson, Jr., and later (1959) to a California girl named Leona, who also bore him a son, Charles Luther Manson. Seventeen of those twenty years (from the time he was fourteen to the time of his release from Terminal Island at the age of thirty-four), Charlie was behind bars. "Gettin' educated," Charlie used to say, "in them institutions of higher learning." In the joint he studied music and learned to play the guitar. He wrote hundreds of songs. He also became interested in Eastern philosophy, Buddhism and Scientology.

Scientology was just becoming popular when he went to prison for the tenth time at the age of twenty-six. While in confinement at McNeil Island, Washington, he began studying Scientology under the guidance of a convict named Lanier Rayner, who had been a student of L. Ron Hubbard, the discipline's founder. Charlie would later claim that within a matter of months he had achieved Scientology's highest level, "Theta Clear." From these studies he extracted certain phrases such as "cease to exist," and "come to Now." Utilizing these, together with other precepts gained through reading, music, friendships, and his own observations of human nature, Charlie evolved an eclectic "theology" of his own which seemed to harmonize beautifully with the budding spiritual notions of the new generation of flower children. At the time Charlie left prison on March 21, 1967, and went to San Francisco, flower power at Haight Ashbury was in full bloom. For a seasoned ex-con and onetime pimp who had associated with some of the toughest criminals in the country, the dewy-eyed kids standing on street corners in San Francisco must have appeared like something out of a dream. Charlie had spent seven consecutive years behind bars before that summer. It was like returning from a time warp. Charlie had never known love; he had never really had a family. In the summer of 1967, nine months before I met him, he started one.

Shortly after my arrival at Spahn's, I had to appear in court on my marijuana bust. Charlie read my citation and advised me how to handle the situation. He said I didn't need my parents there. Two days before the court date we had one of Dennis Wilson's white sequin-studded five-hundred-dollar suits altered to fit me. Squeaky and Sandy cut my hair while Charlie briefed me on what to tell the judge. That morning in court, while Charlie stood at the rear of the room, I stood before the judge, indignantly demanding a speedy jury trial. "I was busted, your Honor, for being in a place where marijuana was being smoked. . . . Where I was, was the side of the road. Now, I don't know if marijuana is smoked on the side of the road or not. I don't even know what this proceeding is about . . . but I do want a jury to decide my fate and—"

The judge sighed and said two words: "Case dismissed."

It was the first time I'd been in a courtroom with Charles Manson, but it would not be the last. We walked out together arm in arm, grinning like loons, and returned to the ranch.

After living alone in Big Sur for three months, the adjustment to life at Spahn's was by no means easy. It was like living in another world—Charlie's world. And like Charlie, it was always intense, paradoxical, comical, unpredictable, often beautiful, and in time, frightening.

On the surface, the Family routine was simple and fairly consistent: most of us, unless we had wrangler duty, generally got up at our leisure and, if we wanted to, made our own breakfast. Rarely did we eat as a group in the morning. While the girls cleaned up the place, took care of George and Dody, made garbage runs, or helped Pearl, the guys worked on the ranch, played music, or hung around with Charlie, who was usually scamming in town or tuning the scene at the ranch. At noon the girls would prepare lunch for those who wanted it. The evening ritual was always the same: we'd eat dinner, listen to Charlie rap for an hour or two, play music together, then make love—either in small groups or as a Family. Once or twice a week we'd set aside an evening to take acid. Use of drugs in the Family was never indiscriminate or casual. Rarely did we smoke grass during the day, and Charlie forbade anyone taking acid on his own. Drugs were used for a specific purpose: to bring us into a higher state of consciousness as a Family; to unify us.

Economically, we managed well. Much of our food came from garbage runs in the valley, or from money derived panhandling. Mary had a contact at a local bakery in Santa Monica who supplied us with bread, cakes, cookies, and other assorted pastries. Several of the girls had credit cards we used for gasoline. Charlie's scams in the city always netted us old cars and donations. People were always giving Charlie things, people like Dennis Wilson and Bobby Beausoleil, who contributed not only money, but automobiles, clothing, and food. Meanwhile, all bank accounts became communal property, so that we generally had a reserve of cash when we needed it.

On one level, this life seemed easygoing and mellow. Since, as Charlie had said, "There is nothing to do but make love," there were, at least in theory, no pressures. But it's hard to do "nothing" without getting bored, and harder still to make love in a group without freaking out or getting hung-up. Thus, pressures were created and people became "discontent." Charlie insisted that only those who were "discontent" had to work with the wranglers. If you couldn't cut the sex scenes, you were obviously discontent. I was generally able to handle the sex trip consistently without going off into some heavy psychological number, which meant the other guys— Clem, Brooks, Kim, Tex, and T.J.—had most of the discontent duty. That left me and Charlie together much of the time, and I wound up palling around with him nearly every day. That's how I got close to Charlie and came into a position of power and freedom within the Family. I picked up on the scene right away—got it together with the music, and really hit it off with the rest of the Family. I don't know why it happened so fast. I guess I was ready to learn about myself. I'm sure it surprised Charlie. I hadn't been there more than a week when he said: "You know, Paul, one of these days I'm going to pass the power on to you, dig?" At that point, I wasn't sure just what the power was.

If there was a goal in the Manson Family during that first summer (1968), it was to have no goal other than arriving at a plateau of inner harmony as a group, a plateau of love that might be an example to the desperate and alienated world. Without saying so directly, Charlie espoused the doctrines of Buddhist teachers and Zen masters: "turn off the internal dialogue and come to Now." What it meant was an inner cleansing of the psyche and the soul—a confrontation with self on the deepest levels of experience—not privately or secretly, but in front of the Family, in front of Charlie. What it meant was the heaviest psychosexual therapy imaginable. I learned more about myself and human nature through that group experience than from any other in my life. If I hadn't felt a real love from the Family in the beginning in support of the changes I was going though, I would never have remained.

From the beginning, Charlie believed the Beatles' music carried an important message—to us. He said their album *The Magical Mystery Tour* expressed the essence of his own philosophy. Basically, Charlie's trip was to program us all to submit: to give up our egos, which, in a spiritual sense, is a lofty aspiration. As rebels within a materialistic, decadent culture, we could dig it. We were ripe for it. I know I was. It was particularly attractive to me because I'd always been spiritually oriented, into the Bible and Eastern thought. But generally, the girls were easier to program than the guys. It was easier for them to submit; they were more ingenuous and didn't have as far to fall, as much ego to drop off. They'd already been programmed into a form of submission by society. Yet, in a way, by submitting, they became superior to the guys. Like when it came to accepting their bodies—being naked—they were generally more comfortable than the men. Particularly Charlie's original girls; they were not only physically "liberated," but sexually confident.

Certainly Charlie's conception of love was a sexual one: "Hey man, like Jesus, when he rapped about love, wasn't talking about some mealymouthed muttering and stuttering . . . he was talking about love with a real spirit . . . love with a dick and balls! Why do you think all those women hung around Jesus? . . . Hey, he showed those Romans how to ride their chariots . . . it's just that all these 'latter-day saints' and men in black have tried to fill people's heads with a load of garbage . . . how do they get off talking about love? . . . walkin' around in those black robes up to their eyeballs, choking on those collars, their little peckers shriveled up and ready to fall off . . . what do those motherfuckers know about love? Hell, they never even dip their wicks or know what their bodies look like. . . ."

That was the hardest thing for me, initially—being free and comfortable while naked in front of the others. I overcame this inhibition for the most part by way of an episode that happened just three days after I joined the Family. By then, all the girls had returned and we were living in the saloon. It was around seven P.M. and we'd just eaten a huge welcome-home casserole dinner, with mounds of green salad, followed by our customary dessert of *zuzus*, a name Charlie had given to all junk food and candy. (It was Charlie's contention that candy was traditionally used as a ploy by parents to manipulate children and that we, the Family, should never be subjected to a life without it, the implication being, perhaps, that we were all good children. During the months I spent with the Family, there was never a day when we did not have plenty of zuzus.)

After dessert that evening, everyone sat in a large circle in the center of the saloon on mattresses, waiting for Charlie to initiate things. He had invited a couple of hippie girls from up at the ranch house to join the festivities, partly out of neighborliness, partly because he still had designs on the ranch house and wanted to work on the hippies. Both girls, Bo (Barbara Rosenberg, who would later join the Family) and Shelly, were in their late teens. Shelly was tall and voluptuous; Bo, short, slender, and with full upturned breasts and an engaging, yet nervous smile. They got right into the zuzus and the music, and seemed relaxed.

It was hot and nearly everyone was naked, when Bo, in preparation for the scene that was coming, began to peel off her clothes. She was clearly self-conscious. I sensed her embarrassment immediately and identified with it. Charlie was also aware of her hesitation and he didn't let her off the hook. He confronted her, but did it masterfully, in a direct, yet soothing monotone.

"There's nothing to be embarrassed about, Bo," he said, evenly.

If she hadn't been uptight before, she sure as hell was then. Everyone's eyes were on her, which is what Charlie wanted. He used scenes like that to teach the group, a method I was to see him employ time and again.

"Hey, we're all made of the same ingredients—same stuff: flesh, blood, and bones and like that." He stood up as if to demonstrate, looking down at his own body. "We're all just plain old skin, right?" Bo had already removed her bra and was still holding it in her hand. She dropped it on the floor as Charlie went on with his rap. "So, look, just relax and get down with us. . . . There's nothing to be ashamed of. You were born beautiful. You have a beautiful body. Come over here a minute, Bo."

The girl stood up, still in her panties. When Charlie extended his hand, she walked over to where he stood. Then he led her behind the bar to a full-length mirror. I couldn't see them, but I heard him talking to her, we all did. "Look at yourself, woman. See how beautiful you are. . . . No, no, dammit, look . . . really take a look. Look at your arms, your boobs, your legs. Look at all that pretty hair. That's not a foreign country, that's your own planet, your own beautiful, physical self. Touch it! Go on, touch it! There's nothing but beauty there, nothing but your own beauty to love."

The next day I went into the saloon alone and stood before the same mirror. I took a long look at my own body. I scrutinized everything: my hair, face, legs, arms, hands, feet, fingers, fingernails. I looked at my genitals, examined them carefully. It may sound absurd, but that day I got to know my body by really looking at it. I saw it as beautiful and I accepted it. Without realizing it, I'd spent eighteen years without really accepting my body. Perhaps my religious, sometimes puritanical upbringing had caused me in some way unconsciously to disassociate myself from my body, particularly my genitals. It was a good lesson, one of many I would learn while in the Manson Family.

Charlie was always rapping about letting go of the ego. "Let it die . . . turn off the internal dialogue and come to Now." Pacing back and forth across the saloon, he'd talk for hours, stopping to make a point, gesturing with his hands. "Hey, we don't have to be hung-up on all this past shit. Let it die. It doesn't matter what happened to you when you were three years old, or when you joined the Boy Scouts. Hey, the sound of one hand clapping is the sound of one hand clapping. That's all. There's nothing to figure out. There ain't no background. There's just Now and when we come to Now, we come to love—and get free."

After these spiels, we'd sing Charlie's songs, which reinforced his words: "Cease to Exist," and "Your Home Is Where You're Happy," and "Old Ego Is a Too Much Thing." Then a few of the girls would pass around some grass or a little hash, and Charlie would initiate a game called the Circle, transmitting motion by joining hands and passing the motion around the group. We'd all focus on turning off the internal dialogue, and just get into the rhythm and vibrations of the motion. Gradually Charlie would start programming in sexual energy by touching or feeling the person next to him, and this would be passed along. From that point, we'd progress to positions on the floor, touching each other, trying to get a harmonious sense of energy flowing. Charlie would usually direct things by using sign language (winks and nods), or by physically guiding people. Since there were always fewer guys, the girls would get off by tuning in to each other, trying to get into the rhythm of the whole group. Sometimes small segments, say four or five people, would get a nice thing going. But it was hard to pull off the big transcendental sexual trip of coming all at once, of coming to "Now" in one big orgasm. Charlie believed that if we ever achieved that as a group we would be bound together as one person in a state of love. But invariably, someone would start freaking out or going through some heavy ego death and we'd have to help that person through it.

One night, during my first week at Spahn's, Sandy freaked out on acid—started screaming about death—said death was crawling across her skin.

Sandra Good was one of Charlie's original girls, and among his most devoted followers. She had a pretty, cherub face with rosy cheeks and a well-proportioned Rubenesque body. She had come from a wealthy family and had been a debutante; her only blemish was a small scar on her throat, where years before she had undergone a tracheotomy. Sandy was always sensitive and high-strung, given to hysterical outbursts and tantrums. She was true to form that night.

"Charlie! Charlie! . . . It's Death. . . ."

Charlie was seated at the head of the table beside Squeaky, but he quickly went to Sandy and knelt beside her.

"Look at it!" he shouted. "Feel your skin . . . what does it look like? Look at Death!"

"Volcanoes . . . volcanoes! Volcanoes and worms! Worms on my skin! Eating my skin. It's green with worms!" She broke away from Charlie and started crawling across the saloon floor; then suddenly she stopped beside Clem and Stephanie and rolled over onto her back, gasping for air.

Charlie was right there. He grabbed her by the hair, jerking her head back. "Look at it. Don't avoid it!" Then he was talking more softly, soothing her while she screamed while the rest of us sat there spaced-out and stunned, tripping out.

Sandy's voice sounded like the screeching of some jungle bird. "I can't . . . I can't!" she stammered.

"Look at it all, dammit!" Charlie urged. "Look at the love! Take off the masks and see the love! Volcanoes are beautiful. Fire is your love . . . yours and mine!"

Sandy rubbed her arm with her hand. Gradually her breathing slowed down.

"Charlie," she said softly, pronouncing the word as though it were a mantra.

He let go of her hair. "You're warm," he said, touching her neck. "You're like silk."

"Charlie."

"Yeah?"

Sandy started to laugh lightly and put her arms around Charlie.

"Let it go," he said. "Let everything go where it wants . . . give it up. Let it die. . . . Feel the love."

"It's like . . ."

"Don't let anyone into your head but me."

"I hear the wind," she said.

"So do I," Clem intoned.

"Me too," Snake whispered.

Later, during that same trip, Ella erupted, shouting angrily at the fire: "Stop it! Stop it! Don't put it there . . . I can't stand it!"

She sat facing the flames. Her hair hung in loose pliant curls down her back. I could see the side of her face, flushed, aglitter with perspiration. Ella too was one of Charlie's original girls—tall, slender, and one of the most adept lovemakers in the Family. She would later leave the Family in the company of an ex-con named Bill Vance who arrived at Spahn's a few months prior to the murders. Ella's most striking feature was her smile, a smile that seemed to radiate from deep within her. But she wasn't smiling that night.

"Don't!" she cried. "I can't stand it!"

"What is it?" Charlie broke in, seizing her arm. "Who is it?" Ella pushed him away and he grabbed her hands with his. They struggled, and he muscled her to the floor, still clinging to her hands. "Let go," he said. "Submit to the motion . . . submit to my motion . . . quit fighting me."

Gradually Ella stopped flailing; she relaxed and her hands and arms became one with Charlie's. He rotated his arms, holding on to her hands; soon their arms were moving in a smooth rhythmic pattern.

"Who is it?" Charlie asked again.

"It's Candy. . . . It's my friend Candy." Ella spoke without turning her head. "I can't stand it . . . I can't . . ."

"Talk to her!" Charlie urged. "Tell her what you're feeling. Listen, Candy, listen to Ella." Then Charlie motioned to Snake, and it was understood that she was Candy. She crawled up to Ella.

"Candy!" Charlie shouted at Snake. "Listen to Ella."

Throughout my experience with the Family, we often acted out roles, becoming parents, brothers, sisters, and friends for one another. Some of the scenes were devastating. But we always got through them. Invariably Charlie took control with a blend of physical force and a soothing monologue, asking that we submit to what we encountered and submit to his motion. We all took part in these scenes, and a strong kinship resulted. We did become brothers and sisters. Acid only intensified it, made it more indelible. Charlie directed it, but he could not control it. It was something no one could control. As much as anyone, he too was submitting to the forces of the unconscious.

But not all the scenes were heavy: some, in fact, were crudely comical. One night during that same first week, we were into a sex scene, split up into small groups of five or six. I was making it with Sadie and Stephanie, really getting into it, when Charlie sprang to his feet. "Wait a minute," he shouted. "Hold everything!" He was standing over Clem, who, apparently, without much success, was trying to give head to Katie. Katie had signaled to Charlie that Clem wasn't cutting the mustard.

"Look, man." Charlie knelt beside Clem. "Don't you know how to give head yet?"

Clem grinned sheepishly.

Charlie walked to the bar to get a cigarette; everyone sat up. "Look," he said, lighting the cigarette. "You heard of Freud? Well, the dude was always talking about sucking on something . . . right? Oral fixations. We all got 'em. See, I mean the cat was right . . . you need to suck on something: that's why you got a mouth . . . that's why women got tits." He took a deep drag and the smoke billowed out around his head.

"I mean, dig it . . . you see kids sucking their thumbs or their fingers, or chewing on suckers or jawbreakers or long wiggly pieces of licorice; licking off frosting. People are always sticking pickles and smokes and zuzus into their face to suck on, dig. So, if you're gonna suck on something, you should know *how* to do it." He set the cigarette down. "Hey, Katie, come up here a minute. Get up on the bar, will ya. Please . . . Yeah, right, just lie down there. Good."

Katie (Patricia Krenwinkle) was twenty-one. She had been with Charlie for nearly a year prior to my arrival in the Family. She was a strong, large-boned, tough-minded girl. Though not as loquacious when it came to spouting Charlie's rap as the others, she exuded confidence and had respect within the Family. She was not beautiful but had a plain, appealing face and a good body. Nothing seemed to daunt or fluster Katie, and it was this attitude, together with her unflappable devotion to Charlie, that made her such a dominant figure in the Family. Where sex was concerned, her own self-confidence seemed to consistently intimidate the younger men.

"Okay," Charlie barked. "Everyone gather round a second and watch this. I mean, shit, if ya can't give head, we might as well stop everything! Spread your legs, Katie . . . okay . . . good." Charlie bent over and gently parted the lips of Katie's vagina with his fingers, exposing the clitoris. "See this? . . . Do you see this, Clem? Look, dammit, see it! . . . Good. Everyone take a gander at it. Okay, this"—he pointed— "is the little bugger that needs attention." With that he went down on Katie to demonstrate.

A few days later, during my second acid trip with the Family, Charlie pulled off another of his instructional demonstrations. The rule when taking acid was that no one leave the room during the trip, not even to use the bathroom. A trip usually lasted about twelve hours. In case it was needed, we installed a portable shitter in one corner of the room. By that time, Charlie had made me the "dope monitor," which meant that I passed out whatever dope the Family used. I'd just handed it out and everyone had taken a tab. We were gathered in a circle: Brooks was strumming on the sitar. Charlie was seated, shirtless, at the head of the group, already into his rap:

"To lose the ego is to die," he said. "And when you die or a part of you dies, you release that part to love. So what it means is overcoming your fear of death. Fear is the beginning of growth. Yet, it's what holds us back. Fear is a higher form of consciousness, 'cause it gives us a glimpse of the love. So it's like you have to submit to your fear . . . your fear is your pathway to love."

We were starting to come on a little to the acid when one of the girls—another visitor to our scene—had to use the little pot. She got up during a pause in Charlie's rap and started for the shitter. But when she got there, she stopped, turned around, and started back, embarrassed to use the toilet in front of us. Charlie was on his feet at once. He took the girl's hand and smiled. "You gotta use the pot?"

"I can wait."

Suddenly Charlie became the clown. "Hey . . . hey," he said. "We all got assholes, right? Anyone here without an asshole?" The little brunette hurriedly sat down, her face flushed. "Hey, like everyone look at my asshole." Charlie bent over and spread the cheeks of his anus. "That," he declared, "is an asshole. . . . We all got 'em, we all use 'em—without 'em we'd be in real trouble, right? Anyone else got an asshole they'd like to show us? Hey, Paul . . . come here . . . show us your asshole. Right on! There's another one, folks, pretty much the same, aren't they? Sadie, can we take a look at yours?" Sadie smiled, stood up, and spread her cheeks. "Amazing." Charlie beamed. "That's the one thing that don't change—the asshole. Men got no tits to speak of; women got no pricks. But we all got them assholes." He grinned at the girl. "So go on over, use the son of a bitch, and let's get on with it."

While the girl proceeded to the toilet, Charlie, without breaking stride, went right on with his rap.

"The human soul," he said, "doesn't hear 'Don't' and 'No.' 'Don't' and 'No' are contrary to nature . . . dig? Life is 'Yes' and 'Do.' Even when people say 'No' they mean 'Yes.' What it means is don't get hung up on the negative vibes. Hey, if you got to shit . . . you shit. You stay positive. You confront your fears. You always move toward 'Yes' and 'Do.' That's the way to overcome fear and get to love, get to Now. You say 'Yes' to your fears, you look at them and submit to them. And then it's like they dissolve into the love that you are, into the love that we all are. You do what your love says."

5

From the day I arrived until the day I left the Manson Family there were always girls working on Charlie's ceremonial vest—a vest embroidered by hand in every imaginable color, a vest begun the day the Family was started by Charlie's first female follower, Mary Brunner. During the Summer of Love it was embroidered with flowers, which flowed across the shoulders on vines; then little scenes were added depicting the Family's odyssey across the country, and finally, their arrival at Spahn's. There were scenes of making love, riding horses, smoking dope, dancing, making music, going to the desert. In time the vest became a vibrant, living chronicle of events within the Family, all the way through the period of Helter-Skelter, the murders and the trials. Over a two-year span more than fifteen girls worked on the vest continually—sometimes twenty-four hours at a stretch. It looked like a medieval tapestry depicting a legend or a myth. During the trials, after the girls cut their hair, great locks of it were sewn into the fabric. From time to time Charlie (and only Charlie) would wear the vest during music or therapy sessions, only to remove it afterward so that more work could be done on it. Or he would let *me* as if he were granting knighthood. It was never finished, and to this day I don't know what became of it.

One morning during my second week at Spahn's, I got up around ten and headed down toward the stables. After several days of relative indolence, I felt the need for physical exercise. I missed the strenuous workouts I'd enjoyed at Big Sur. It was already hot and I removed my shirt as I walked, draping it across my shoulder. I spotted Benny and Larry herding four Appaloosa mares out of the corral. Larry waved, and I waved back. My shoulders were sore from where Snake had scratched me during the lovemaking the night before. From the onset, I'd found myself gravitating toward Snake, but I had to keep it cool. Charlie didn't go much for people teaming up. He was always breaking up little alliances that formed within the Family, since, as he put it, "this only weakens the Family and causes dissension. The Family is one. I am you and you are me. Love has no individuality; it belongs to all of us and it belongs to no one."

Still, after nearly ten days at the ranch, I was getting on top of the scene. I'd made love to nearly all the girls and felt I was pretty much accepted by everyone. I knew as much when Charlie reiterated how glad he was I'd decided to stick around. I still had some weighty hang-ups to deal with, but at that point, at least compared to the other guys in the Family, I was clearly ahead of the game.

I picked up a rock and fired it at the corral fence. It ricocheted off, and Tommy Thomas, Randy's black-and-white bulldog, came yipping out to greet me. I gave him a pat, then trotted up the hill toward George's house, deciding to get the keys to his pickup so I could take a load of horseshit from the stables and dump it. The screen door was ajar when I banged on it, and a little bell affixed to the inside doorknob clinked. I could smell sausage and hot coffee. I knew Squeaky was inside making George's breakfast.

"Come on in," I heard George call out. "I'm blind as a bat, ya know, can't see a thing."

We exchanged amenities and Squeaky asked me if I wanted a cup of coffee, so I sat beside George at the table while Squeaky brought another cup.

Squeaky (Lynn Fromme) was attractive in a bird-like, ethereal way. She had light red hair, an abundance of freckles, a lithe agile body, and was perhaps more devoted to Charlie than any other woman in the Family. Like most of the girls, she had grown up in the Los Angeles area, where her father had worked as an aeronautical engineer. Though she was consistently mellow on the surface, Squeaky's abrupt movements and nervous laughter belied a frenetic uneasiness that showed itself as full-blown paranoia during subsequent acid trips. I never understood the mechanism of Charlie's hold on Squeaky until many months later when I made love to her for the first time. But she was in good spirits that morning, as she poured the steaming coffee into my cup and pushed the sugar within reach.

I stirred my coffee and glanced around the room. George's house was always a trip: chock-full of saddles, bridles, and tack-room gear. It looked more like a bunk-house than a ranch owner's living quarters. The house was old and weathered, the paint peeling off the walls in places, the floors strewn with faded throw rugs. The living room was good-sized, fronting directly onto the kitchen. There were also a bathroom, two bedrooms, and a storeroom off the back porch. Furniture was sparse: a couple of wooden rocking chairs, two straight-back antique chairs pulled up to the dining-room table, and a dusty old couch.

There were a lot of stories about George Spahn: one was that he had more than ten children and that each of them was named after a favorite horse. He could always remember the horses' names, but never the names of his kids; it was also said that George could tell the quality of a horse just by feeling its muscle tone. I remember days when new horses would be brought to the ranch and George would be led out to the corral by Pearl to pass his hands over the animal before giving the approval to buy. We always wondered just how blind George was. One afternoon more than a month after I arrived, we took Snake into George's house and had her strip naked in front of him. George didn't say anything, but everyone agreed he turned a vibrant shade of red.

George rocked back and forth in his chair, swilling his coffee, a reflexive grin playing across his lips. He was clean-shaven and wore baggy, old-timer-style pants with suspenders, a white shirt, and vest. His eyes were hidden behind dark glasses. At his side, resting against the rocker, was his cane.

I told him I wanted to borrow his pickup to dump a load of horseshit down the canyon. Without hesitating, he reached into his vest pocket and pulled out the keys.

"Jes' drive it careful, ya hear?"

Squeaky took the keys and handed them to me,

winking. She'd spent hours with George. Whenever anyone would ask her how George was in bed, she'd just
grin her benign, space-cookie grin and spout back some
of Charlie's rap: "George is a beautiful person . . . I
love George."

I finished the coffee and took off at a trot toward the
corral. The mustard weed on the hillside was a bright yellow in the matinal light. I felt refreshed. My surroundings
already seemed comfortable and familiar; I liked the
ranch, its isolation, all its characters. I liked the open air
and the sloping mountains. I was beginning to feel more
and more that I'd made a good decision. As I entered the
stables, I heard the guttural sounds of grunt labor; someone was shoveling shit out of the stalls. I saw it come flying out in great heaps at the end of the corridor. It was
Brooks Posten. No member of the Family had more discontent duty than Brooks. No one shoveled more shit.
"Tons of it," he used to say. "Fucking tons of it."

I peeked into the stall. "What's happening, Brooks?"

He looked up, lifting a shovelful, and grinned.
"Horseshit's happening." I stood aside while he tossed it
into the pile at my feet.

"I got George's pickup, if you want to take a load up
the canyon and dump it."

Brooks nodded.

"I'll grab a shovel and back the truck in."

Brooks was from Borger, Texas—tall, blond, blue-
eyed, with sharp irregular features. He was nineteen that
summer. He'd left Texas the year before, dropped out of
high school to begin his own psychedelic, experimental
odyssey, which took him throughout northern California
before coming to L.A. He'd met Charlie just one week
before I came to Spahn's and was trying like hell to make
the scene. He was a good guitarist and had a strong singing voice. In time, we became close friends, and from our
combined vantage points—Brooks at the bottom shoveling
shit, me at the top as Charlie's number-one man—we were
eventually to glean a comprehensive overview of what the
Manson Family was all about. But that morning was the
first time I'd really talked to Brooks.

I drove the truck in and we began shoveling out the
stalls. While we worked I asked Brooks what he'd done

before coming to Spahn's. He told me about living in Mendocino County in the town of Ukiah, where he met a Methodist minister named Dean Morehouse.

"Yeah, Dean was pretty far-out. He's the one who first turned me on to LSD and told me about Charlie. Said Charlie was the most tuned-in dude he'd met. Old Dean was right on . . . I couldn't believe it either, man, 'cause Charlie had made it with Dean's virgin daughter, Ruth Ann, down on the beach in Mendocino. Dean was pissed plenty at first, said he'd kill Charlie . . . but shit, after Charlie turned his love on Dean, Dean just said, 'Far-out!'"

I leaned my shovel up against the truck and sat down, wiping the sweat from my face with my sleeve. Flies swarmed around us like hornets; their incessant drone permeated the air. Brooks sat beside me, hawking a glob of spittle against the side of the stall as he did so.

"Yeah, you should have seen it, Paul, when I went with Dean over to Dennis' a couple of weeks ago. Dean hadn't seen Charlie for a while . . . I didn't even know Charlie then, really. But he walks into Dennis' house and sees Dean . . . goes right over, kneels down, and kisses Dean's feet. Blew my mind! A few days later, I was stoned on acid and Charlie was sitting in Dennis' living room tuning his guitar. The next thing I know Dean crawls up to Charlie on his hands and knees like a puppy dog and just looks up at him. Charlie says, 'Are you ready to die this instant?' Dean says, 'Yes, I am.' Then Charlie says, 'You can live forever, brother.' Blew me away, man."

Listening to Brooks, I realized how deeply dependent he was on Charlie. But at the time, it seemed right, that the power Charlie had was good.

Later, Brooks told me that his father had died while he was in high school and that he had felt somehow responsible—guilty for not having shown his father more love. "In a way, I think I helped kill him." After he had told me this, I began to understand why Charlie's death rap got so heavy for Brooks. Unconsciously, he took the death command almost literally. There was a part of him that thought he should die, that he deserved to die. That summer Brooks got totally spaced-out; not only could he not function in the sex scenes; at times, he was rendered completely catatonic. One day, a month or more after I'd been at Spahn's, I found Brooks lying outside on an old couch, motionless, with his head hanging over the edge, his limbs rigid. There were flies buzzing all around his head, and I could smell where he'd shit in his pants. At first I thought he was dead. Then I felt his pulse and began shaking him. Finally I got him to his feet and took him into the house to clean him up. It scared me to see a guy that strung-out. But I never attributed any of it to Charlie. To me, it was just Brooks going through his changes. If anyone could help Brooks, I figured it was Charlie.

Brooks and I worked until sundown, then went back to the saloon to eat dinner. Charlie seemed agitated during the meal, and afterward kept pacing around the saloon.

"I don't like the part I'm playing," he declared. Without looking at anyone he strode to the mirror behind the bar and jerked off his cowboy hat. "Hey, Mary, get me another hat." While Mary went into the room behind the bar to get a hat, Charlie untied the red bandanna from his neck and tied it around his head, then studied himself in the mirror. "Hey," he said to himself, "if you don't like the part you're playing, change it . . . it's a magical mystery tour . . . we can change the mask whenever we want."

Mary handed him a weathered, misshapen stetson. He tried it on. "What's wrong with the part I'm playing?" he asked himself. "It's a drag, man," he answered. "George is always bitchin', the cowboys got their redneck heads up their ass, that motherfucker Shorty is badmouthing us . . . . no one can make the scene here. . . . I think I'll just die and start over." With that Charlie clutched at his chest and dropped to the floor as though struck dead. Then he got up grinning, hopped up on the bar, and began to play his guitar and make up verses, one leading into the next:

> Hey, Snake and Brenda pushin' all the time,
> trying to be like Sadie, gettin' out of line . . .
> and Gypsy too. . . .
>
> Paul and Snake got a cozy thing going . . .
> looks real good but its belly-button's showin'. . . .

Leave your thoughts . . . don't control your mind
Leave yourself and just be
Leave yourself far behind you. . . .
Now, is where you should be. . . .

The trouble with you all is ya can't get free
Got a wireless phone to mama . . . won't let you be
Ya seem to be fine, but you're always on the line
. . . the party line. . . .
'Cause you really don't wanna know how . . . to
make love . . . and
Come to "Now"

Oh I had a little monkey and I took him to the
country
And I fed him on gingerbread
Along came a choo-choo and knocked my monkey
cuckoo
Now my little monkey is dead. . . .

Charlie was always rapping about "making love" and "death." Those words went together, flowed effusively through all his songs and raps. In time, "death" and "making love" became almost synonymous. "It's through death [ego death] that we come to love." Only later would I realize the extent to which those notions applied when I learned that Sadie had had an orgasm while committing murder. Yet, at that time, what I saw in Charlie's program was positive. I understood that if I were to become tuned in to myself, a good bit of my ego would have to die. Like everyone else, I was going through my changes, trying to become one with my love. And since Charlie was love, I was in some sense, like everyone else, becoming Charlie. Not infrequently during some heavy acid trip someone would shout, "But who am I? . . . I don't know who to be." Charlie would just tell them not to worry about it: "Be whoever or whatever you want to be. If you want to be someone, why not be me?"

One evening during that same period, Charlie and I took a hike up to the outlaw shacks before dinner and sat on the porch. He told me how he envisioned the Family once people got the shit and the ego mucked out of them, once they got "clear."

"It's like when people are really tuned in to each other, they don't have to think or speak. They just know.

One thought becomes all thought . . . they move together, they feel together, they breathe together like one organism. In a way, they become more like animals—more instinctive. They don't worry about the shit in their heads . . . they're clear . . . they just react and feel. Then, whatever they do is right on: making love, making music, just getting into the flow of the natural scene. That's what I see happening, man . . . dig? That's the direction we're moving in . . . that's the direction we have to move in in this life, 'cause sooner or later the shit is going to come down."

Later that night we drove into West L.A. to pick up a car. Some guy was turning over a '62 Chevy to Charlie and the Family. It was uncanny; people were always giving Charlie things: cars, tools, time, women, money. It was something in his personality—a kind of mystic, hypnotic humility that prompted them to submit to his incessant catechizing.

Another gift came to Charlie just two days later: a seductively packaged gift by the name of Ruth Ann Morehouse—none other than Dean Morehouse's "virgin" daughter Brooks had told me about earlier. Ruth Ann (who became known in the Family as Ouisch) was sixteen, small, elegant, and sensual, with black hair and a lustrous, curvy body. She was a delicious-looking girl and Charlie kept her close to him during the first few weeks of her stay at Spahn's. That was generally the procedure when a new girl arrived: Charlie would indoctrinate her with his concentrated presence on all levels, then turn her loose to the fold.

The day she arrived was the same day Bobby Beausoleil brought another new girl to the Family, Catherine Share, better known as Gypsy—dark-skinned, seductive, and built like a brood mare. Charlie's trip was particularly heavy after dinner that night. We had all smoked good grass and were playing music. He was singing a song he had written that particularly appealed to the women in the Family. Since there were two new members of the fair sex present, he really got into it:

There's a time just for livin'; time keeps on flyin'
You think you're lovin' baby; all you're doin' is
    cryin'.

Can you feel? Ask yourself: are your feelin's real?
Look at your game, girl: go on. Look at your
game, girl.

Just to say you love is not enough, if'n you can't
be true.
You can tell all those lies, baby, but you're only
foolin' you.
Can you feel? Ask yourself: are those feelin's real?
Look at your game, girl: go on. Look at your
game, girl.

If'n ya can't feel, and the feelin's ain't real
Then ya better stop tryin' or you're gonna play
cryin'.
That's the game. Oh, that's the game.
The sad, sad game: the mad, mad game.

While Charlie sang, the girls sat around him, the looks on their faces almost reverent. Ouisch sat on his left, her eyes wide, her mouth slightly ajar. She reminded me of a teenager watching Elvis Presley in his prime. All eyes, in fact, were riveted to Charlie; every motion in the room was prompted by the movement of his body as he sang, leaning forward, then backward, his hair loose about his shoulders.

As a singer, Charlie was always magnetic. All his vibrance and vitality were expressed through his music. Without question, the Manson Family was programmed most effectively through music. Had the general public been exposed to Charlie's music, they might well have understood, at least to some extent, the intensity of his presence. Music transcends the spoken word—explodes it into color and feeling; makes it live; gives it soul. All one need do is witness a good rock concert: people going berserk; ripping off clothing; dancing; moving; gyrating; submitting like participants in some voodoo hex. Even the most sedate and dignified have been known to flip out, leap onto the stage in a frothing frenzy because of music. Music—cutting through all the barriers and blocks; liberating passion.

Only later would I become aware of just how powerful a force it was; how easily ideas are programmed into the subconscious by way of music—the very core of commercial advertising; little musical jingles that lead you to a box of corn flakes without even realizing it; musical jingles repeated over and over again nightly: "Submission is a gift . . . cease to exist."

Later that night Charlie sang another song he had written: "Old Ego Is a Too Much Thing." He sang it several times in a raspy Okie style. Soon everyone was singing along, belting out the refrain with real fervor: "Old ego is a too much thaang . . . old ego is a too much thaang. . . ." I guess the response inspired Charlie, because after the song he began to rap in earnest about egos being programmed into us by society. I was turned on that night by Ouisch and watched her as she sat beside Charlie gawking up at him as he spoke:

"The idea is to kill off the programs society has stuck us with . . . to deprogram ourselves . . . to get rid of the past shit . . . to submit to the love and come to Now. That's why we sing and make love together and see our fears for what they are . . . steps to a higher consciousness. It's like the man on the cross, dig. He just loved. He just submitted to his love and all his body carried was love; there were no programs inside him. He was clear, just a hole in the infinite that love poured out of."

Charlie would often refer to himself as a "hole in the infinite"; the implications were obvious, and I remembered Snake's comment the first day I came to Spahn's: "Charlie is Jesus Christ." It was all the more intriguing and compelling because Charlie was never Christlike in any traditional classical sense—turn the other cheek, stuff like that. Maybe that made it easier to buy; it seemed more real, more plausible. And we never considered ourselves hippies in that regard either. Charlie pointed out that while the ideas of the hippies were okay, they didn't have the balls or the soul to do anything for society; they hadn't been through their changes; they hadn't seen the truth. Brown rice, flowers, and beatific smiles weren't enough. He said the hippie had his chance at Haight Ashbury and blew it. I remember at one point he suggested we call ourselves "slippies"—like slippery; just slipping beneath the awareness of people. He told how in prison he just played beneath the awareness of the guards and prison officials.

"Like I just played it dumb, man . . . like an idiot boy, you know? And they just left me alone to do my trip, to play my music. It's like inside we have all we need; inside ourselves we have the love, and if we listen to the love and don't fall for the hype, we can get by and see the beauty. It's not that hard, really, if you just open your eyes to it." He took Ouisch's hand and squeezed it. "I see it," he said, looking at Ouisch. "I see the young love coming and getting free of all the programs."

He stood up and stretched, then rubbed his throat. Moments later, Squeaky got up and fetched him a glass of soda water. He took a sip and handed back the glass. Then he walked across the saloon in front of us. He was wearing buckskin pants and sandals; a piece of leather was tied around his neck, and a bowie knife was strapped to his waist in a leather sheath. He'd recently cut his beard. His eyes were clear. Everyone was really into his rap:

"It's like the Man, dig . . . always programming us all the time . . . like society . . . programming us with all the garbage on TV: to wear certain clothes and eat certain foods, dig . . . to buy and produce all the rot that pollutes the earth. . . . Like when I was in the Southwest, you know, I see man destroying things as fast as he can. I see man shooting the animals. I see these big fat dudes coming around with guns, shooting lizards and birds and anything they can. Just killing and killing. Hey, they're all programmed to kill. . . . It's like the cop in Malibu who pulled me over last week, man. And I look on his helmet . . . right there on his forehead, and I see this beast . . . this bear. Hey, why can't people see the mark of the beast . . . it's right there . . . it's not a hard thing to see.

"You see it all the time . . . in the war. You see eighteen-year-old kids . . . all the young love . . . programmed to be marines . . . to hate gooks or Japs and to kill them with a bayonet in the name of democracy or the flag or whatever . . . but they make it out to be heroic, like an all-American dude, a hero, dig . . . just killing.

"What I see in the animals . . . sometimes here on the ranch . . . you know . . . what I see is the animals are smarter than the people. In jail I hardly ever saw animals around. But then I get out and see the coyotes and dogs and snakes, rabbits and cats and mules and the horses. And I see the animals and watch them. And that's where the love is. Most of the love is in the animals and in the people, man. And that's where my love is. I don't really have a philosophy. My philosophy is: don't think. You know, just don't think. If you think, you are divided in your mind. You know, one and one is one in two parts. Like I don't have any thought in my mind hardly at all—it's all love."

"Intense" is the word that best described Charlie during these raps. He seemed totally energized and focused. He exuded an electric, almost seething passion. His words were infused with feeling, as though they had been issued from a bubbling caldron of soul. When he spoke of love you felt the warmth to your core. When he sang, his words were even more compelling. Being so small physically and so large psychically made it even more dramatic. There was a beauty in his face, a bold, confident directness. There was also subtlety and cunning—a lupine glint in the eyes—the look of the wolf, the jackal; the soul of the scorpion. I would later meet an old desert rat in the Panamint Valley who said these characteristics are common to most Scorpio personalities to different degrees. Scorpio, he believed, was the most powerful sign of the zodiac, particularly when it came to sex. Certainly Charlie's sexual appetites, though erratic, were voracious. His desire to bring off the cosmic orgasm was genuine. He said often that if we shared that experience we'd make it through "the last door." His passion and vitality inspired us.

Charlie smoothed his hair back from his face, looked around the room, then sat down beside Ouisch, taking her hand. Squeaky handed him the soda water and he took a drink. I was sitting beside Stephanie and Snake. There were at least twenty people in the circle, including Tex, Juan, Clem, Bobby, and Bo. We'd all smoked a little hash and I could sense a real mellowness in the wake of Charlie's rap. We went through the preliminaries of joining hands and making sounds, but most of it was unnecessary. Everyone seemed tuned in. Generally, just one person's uptightness was enough to throw discord into a scene, but not that night. The vibes were right. It was all the more unusual, since we had two new girls in the Family, Ouisch and Gypsy.

Before long I was lying on my back with Snake on my left. I had my hand on her thigh while Stephanie lay on my right with one of her legs draped over mine. Stephanie Rowe was another girl I grew very fond of. She was quick-witted and capable, and at times would engage in friendly verbal fencing matches with Charlie. She had dark strong features and thick brown hair. A slight tendency to corpulence inhibited her on occasion, but for the most part she was very much on top of the scene. She'd been with Charlie since the San Francisco days, and was a passionate lover. She smelled clean and fragrant that night as she rolled over and put her arm around my waist, while Ella moved over from the left and began giving head to Snake.

Since there were always fewer men, the women prepared each other by initiating foreplay—readying themselves for the men, who would subsequently move from girl to girl while trying to maintain the rhythm of the group. I was aware of the breathing in the room. It sounded like one organism, as if I were connected respiratorially to everyone. The fire was still crackling, spewing up smoke through the flue. The back windows were open so that fresh air circulated like some invisible external aphrodisiac moving in a rhythm with the breathing and the languorous sounds of the lovemakers.

I don't know if the whole Family was in tune with the little scene that five or six of us had going, but I do know that at no previous time had I experienced such a free, natural flow of movement. I had complete control as I rolled from one girl to the next. It seemed as if I were penetrating all of them simultaneously and that we were all in tune—an alchemy of human juices mingling and swirling in orifices belonging to us all. There was no hesitation, no holding back. It was as if the "Love" of the Family on a sexual-spiritual level had stood up to orchestrate its own rhythm. Everyone disappeared into the vortex of sound and sensation. What Charlie had said was true: there was no thinking, no leaders, no rules, no individuality. Where was Charlie? We were all Charlie. And there was no Charlie. Perhaps Charlie *was*, that night, a hole in the infinite.

For me, the climax was not shattering or wildly passionate—more, it was like a quiet, gradual release, a single wave which had broken far out at sea to flow shoreward. The sounds of people coming were like the sounds of waves being dissipated on the shore, spectacularly unspectacular, the infinite, whispered sounds of fulfillment.

No one spoke afterward. I remember people clinging

to each other without moving—bodies relaxed and interlocked; the sounds of quiet breathing. I remember Charlie muttering something aloud, but what he said was muffled and remote, as though it had been uttered from a great distance. Snake laid her head on my chest. I had my arm around Stephanie and was aware of other bodies which had gravitated to me and were now draped across mine; aware of hands resting on my flesh like warm hearts, beating.

Much later that night, Charlie came over with a new girl named Darcy. I was aware of them lying beside me. Almost everyone else was sleeping—a sea of bodies sprawling across the saloon floor. It was dark except for a candle burning on the windowsill that fronted the boardwalk. Charlie asked her if she felt the cosmic vibes that night. She said yes. Then he said sex was just an expression of love: "If you love, you just love . . . physical and spiritual love are one love." Then he told her to give him some head. When she went down on him, he stopped her. "Hey, no, no, not like that . . . Paul can do better than that. Hey, Paul . . . show this girl how to give head, will ya." Charlie was testing me, and I knew it. The thought repulsed me as I looked at him and then at the girl. But I was starting to believe in Charlie. I wanted to please him so I showed her.

"Freedom," Charlie said later, "is a turn-on to cosmic law, and in cosmic law there is no gender, it's just love."

6

But it wasn't all love those first days at Spahn's. Though rare, there were occasions when Charlie vented an explosive violence, particularly if someone challenged his authority. Only in retrospect would I understand the portent of those outbursts.

One night we were gathered around the low dining table waiting while the girls served dinner. It was dark outside but the saloon was illuminated by a series of candles set along the top of the bar and several that flickered from the windowsills fronting on the boardwalk. Gypsy had lit some incense and its ambrosial fragrance wafted through the room, reminding me momentarily of Lebanon, of Rudi and Arula, the housemaids. Several girls walked back and forth across the floor carrying utensils, glasses, and plates of chop suey and salad from George's house. Charlie was tuning his guitar. I was sitting beside Juan Flynn, who had just come in from work and was still wearing his dusty trail clothes and boots. As usual, he was ebullient and animated.

"I been riding thee focking horse for five hours weeth Benny behind me telling me to go faster . . . son-tine I theenk he's crazy, Benny."

Juan stood about six-five and weighed 220 pounds, most of it muscle. He was always garrulous and lusty, a powerhouse personality, one of the few guys Charlie could really never get a handle on. Half Panamanian and half Irish, he had light brown Afro-style hair and steel-blue eyes. He reminded me of a hybrid Zorba the Greek. He'd grown up in Panama and had fought in the Vietnam war. At twenty-six, he was a seasoned young man, intelligent and strong-willed. Still, he was intrigued by Charlie's scene, and I could tell that Charlie's rap confused him. But never for too long. For it wasn't so much Charlie that kept Juan's attention; it was Brenda. At five-three and less than one hundred pounds, she had become in a short period of time one of the heaviest little gals in the Family; a real cosmic sex-cookie, fully capable of handling the big Latino cowboy.

That night she sat on the other side of Juan. He was joking about the Family living inside a jail (the mock jail at Spahn's); then he began describing the time he was jailed in Panama for riding his horse into a bank. Squeaky knelt behind Charlie and began giving him a back rub. Tex sat next to Katie strumming Charlie's guitar.

"I don' know," Juan concluded, "but eet seem to me dat een jail I talk to some very interesting and intelligent men . . . I hate thee jail but I see there is son-thing to learn . . ."

In the other room Pooh Bear was crying. Charlie signaled to Stephanie and she went into the room (behind the bar) to check on the baby. Charlie grinned at Juan, then flicked the hair from his eyes.

"Dig it, Juan . . ." he said. "It's like all my life I felt like all the bad people were in jail and all the good people were on the outside. Then, I would get out of jail and find out just the opposite—that the people outside smiled and pretended they were groovy but shit, they never kept their word, you know. And then I'd go back in the jail. . . . Hey, I think my longest time out of jail in the past twenty years had been about eight months at a stretch . . . up until the last time I got out.

"Then, Juan—dig this—just before they let me out the last time I told the man, I sez, 'Hey, I can't cut society . . . I'm just digging being in here with people I know, being in here playing my music, doing my trip.' So what happens, they kick me out and I go up to Berkeley, you know. . . . And I meet this kid . . . about fifteen. I ask him, 'Hey, where do you live?' And he sez, 'Well, I live out of my sleeping bag.' I sez, 'Well, don't you work?' He sez, 'Hell, nobody works.' So I sez, 'How do you eat?' The kid sez, 'Well, I eat at the Diggers.' Then he put his arm around me like I was his brother and said, 'Come on,' and showed me the love . . . the first time I really found love in the world."

After all the food was on the table and everyone was seated, Charlie took a bite of salad; then we all started to eat. Moments later, he looked up from his plate, screwed his face into a scowl. "Hey, who made this salad dressing?"

Sadie said she did.

"Smells a little bit like piss," Charlie grinned.

"Hold your nose," Sadie quipped.

"I might have to."

Sadie got up and started to walk toward the doorway with a plate. More than five months pregnant, her belly was beginning to ripen and protrude beneath the Mexican blouse she wore. Moving past Charlie, she made some comment which to me was unintelligible. But Charlie leaped to his feet.

"Don't give me that shit, woman!" He grabbed her by the arm and started slapping her. "I don't listen to that kind of talk. You can just take that shit on down the road. Dig what I'm saying!"

Sadie cried out and I felt Juan's body tense. But he didn't get up, nor did anyone else. Sadie kicked and grappled with Charlie until he pinned her arms against the side of the bar. "I'll break your goddamned fingers off! Let go, dammit!"

"Stop it! Charlie . . . stop it!" Her breathing came in short gasps.

Finally he forced her to the floor, bending her fingers back against her hand. She groaned, but he wouldn't let go. "Just relax . . . dammit . . . quit fighting!!" He crouched over her, forcing her arms to move with his until gradually she submitted to the motion and was following his movements. It lasted only an instant; then he was talking soothingly to her, almost like a passionate lover might—stroking her hair. "Just let go, Sadie . . . let go . . ." It was starting to turn Sadie on and she began caressing Charlie. Then he jerked her to her feet and told her to go on in the kitchen and take care of her business.

Later, I was to see many such outbursts from Charlie; short, violent ragings—sometimes verbal, sometimes physical, but always resolved by a form of submission, either physical or mental, or both (motion hooked to emotion), and always balanced by a soothing aftermath. Another of his releases was to smash a guitar to smithereens. He must have destroyed a dozen while I was with the Family. Later, the split in his personality became increasingly more apparent, but always his violence was more than balanced by his softer, more loving side; his patience. Again, it was a paradox, since Charlie was generally much more patient than anyone else in the Family. "After spending two thirds of your life behind bars, you learn a little patience." There were times, for example, when there would be a delay or we'd have to wait someplace in line. Charlie would never get uptight; he'd just find a stick or a rock on the ground and turn it into some kind of toy or game; or he'd start talking to a kid and entice him into the game. It was beautiful the way he'd get so absorbed in it. And it impressed the Family, giving more credence to what he preached about coming to "Now" and being alive in the moment.

When he did vent rage or displeasure, most of us felt responsible, believing that we were to blame by being too hung-up on our own egos. What made us resist, or question, he said, was ego. He taught submission; a submission to "the love." And since Charlie *was* "the love," submission to him. He said too that there was no such thing as right and wrong so long as we followed "our love." The implications were clear, and in time these notions became a reality for most of us. When, on several occasions, he was challenged for being too rough on one of the girls, his rap would always be the same:

"No one was hurt, man . . . I didn't hurt anyone. You don't see blood . . . you don't see any marks. Dig it, pain is a sensation; there is no pain, really. It's like any change, and change you pass through produces sensation. Pain is like fear . . . it expands your consciousness. It's essential. It brings you to Now. Only through pain and fear do you come to love."

What inhibited my reacting to Charlie on these occasions was partially due to the passivity of the girls. Most of them had been with him for months. They were used to it, and even seemed to thrive on the attention. They were committed to Charlie on very deep levels, just how deeply committed I wouldn't learn until much later. It seemed too, in retrospect, that they all felt guilty for certain unnamable sins, so that unconsciously they deserved punishment. I see it as common in this culture. In part, it's the whole guilt trip religion has laid on people. It would appear that unconsciously the Family was as much attracted to Charlie's negative, violent side as they were to his warm, loving side. Generally people repress negative feelings and are afraid to release anger. You don't have to be in prison to store up anger. People are attracted to real violence because they see it vented so rarely. It's like a magnet. But what they're really responding to is their own repressed anger. That helps explain the paradox of Charlie's appeal and also why the murderers got so charged up while committing their crimes—particularly Sadie.

Susan Atkins was only twenty when I first saw her in Topanga Canyon sprawled across the floor of Jay's house, naked. She had long brown hair, pepper-brown eyes, high cheekbones, and a full sensuous mouth. Her body was sleek, supple, and curvaceous. She thrived on sex. Her nickname was Sexie Sadie.

Sadie was born in San Gabriel and raised in San Jose. Her mother died of cancer when she was still in high school. Not long afterward she ran away from home, traveling to San Francisco, where she used her abundant pulchritude to best advantage—working as a topless dancer, hooker, and gun moll. By the time she met Charlie in the summer of 1967, she was prime for his scene. When, during the course of my stay with the Family, some hard-core macho type would show up at the ranch, Charlie would sic Sadie on him. She unfailingly neutralized even the "baddest" of dudes.

Sadie had a seductive, unctuous voice, tinged with a fine patina of bitterness—the voice of a girl who had become a woman too fast. Both precocious and promiscuous, she had come to know men at a tender age; yet she knew them primarily as animals; in their eyes she had always been a sex object. What she did not know how to deal with was real love. To her way of thinking, only Charlie had showed her what that was all about. "Getting hit by the man you love is no different than making love to him . . . Charlie gives me what I need."

Like all the girls, Sadie soaked up Charlie's rap—we all did. That was the game in the Manson Family. When Charlie left the ranch, the rap we spoke was his rap. In time, it got so that we rarely spoke at all of personal experiences or our pasts. We spoke only of love, of coming to "Now," of tuning our scene.

Being at Spahn's made it easier. We were isolated from society. We had no TV sets, no newspapers, and we rarely left the ranch except to drive into town on garbage runs or into the valley to pick up a truckload of corn for the horses. We were nearly always together: sleeping, eating, making love, playing music, working on the ranch. There was nothing more important to any of us than putting Charlie's scene together. If anyone raised a question, Charlie would just dismiss it. "There are no questions," he'd say. "Every question contains its own answer. Therefore when you pose a question, you pose it to the void. A question is just a statement."

Living with the Family became primarily a game of awareness, being aware primarily of what Charlie wanted, anticipating Charlie. My success in the Family was based on my ability to play the games. I learned to pick up on Charlie's signals, knew when he moved a certain way or assumed a certain expression just what he wanted. Sometimes we picked up girls together and brought them back to the ranch. Occasionally they were afraid of Charlie because he was so much older. I bridged the gap. Because we were the same size and spoke the same rap, they were able to make the transition. Charlie benefited from my presence. More and more he put me in charge of details he would generally have handled himself. It was clear too that the veteran girls found it easy to deal with me on all levels. In the process, I got closer to everyone in the Family. During the heavier therapy sessions when someone would freak out, I was able to help them through their changes and I got good at it, thereby gaining rank in the Family. Charlie allowed this; it took the pressures off him, gave him a chance to rest and observe. When Sadie's belly swelled even larger, I took a paternal interest in her; helped her with heavy loads, watched out for her well-being. It was an unconscious process on my part. But I was beginning to feel a strong tie to the greater Family—a real kinship with this band of people who had gathered in the Chatsworth mountains at Spahn's movie ranch.

At the same time, deep within myself I began to experience a vague uneasiness. Initially I thought it stemmed from the trauma of my sexual number with Charlie. But that passed as he had said it would: by confronting whatever latent homosexual fears I may have harbored, I had discovered that I could perform bisexual acts without freaking out. Sex to Charlie's way of thinking was merely a vehicle to assist in "getting free." There were times, for example, when we'd take a little orgy contingent to Dennis Wilson's house just to blow the minds of his "hip" guests, who thought they were so sexually liberated. They'd never seen real uninhibited lovemaking and many of them couldn't handle it. Charlie took a perverse delight in exposing their hang-ups so blatantly; then we'd leave like a well-trained band of commandos and return to Spahn's to do it for real. Both Charlie and I were heterosexuals. But being locked up with men for seventeen years of his life had pretty much dictated a certain amount of homosexuality on his part. "In the joint, you ain't got much choice . . . pretty soon it happens whether you like it or not . . . and after a while, you're just flat on it." When, on occasion, a gay dude would show up on the scene, we'd run him down the road in a hurry. With all those horny women, the last thing we needed was what Juan called a *maricón*.

No, the uneasiness I began to experience went deeper than that. Something scared me, and I didn't know what or why.

One evening, less than a month after my arrival at Spahn's, I left the ranch and hiked up past the outlaw shacks to the hillside where I could look down upon the ravine. I heard the screen door slam and knew that Squeaky was taking George his dinner. There were crickets whirring in the grass and the lights from passing cars on the highway were visible beyond the ridge. Moments later I heard approaching footsteps and saw Charlie coming up the trail carrying his guitar. He was wearing Levi's and a full-sleeved scarlet shirt. He had a smile on his face and reminded me of a campesino on his way to a fiesta.

"Nice sky tonight, huh?" was his comment as he hunkered beside me, looking off down the ravine.

We sat without speaking for a time while he strummed the guitar. Then he began talking about how glad he was I had joined the Family and said again that someday he'd be passing on the power to me: "In time, you'll have your own Family, your own tribe. We'll spread the love around, dig . . . share it with the world." The sky was a brilliant red-orange at the base of the hillside which loomed beyond the ravine like a miniature volcano. My eyes were riveted to the horizon.

"Anything wrong, Paul?" Charlie spoke without looking at me.

"I don't know . . . I just feel sort of . . . frustrated . . . and afraid."

"What are you afraid of? . . . Are you afraid of me?"

"Maybe a little . . . I don't know . . . but I'm afraid of something."

"You know what I think, man? I think you're afraid of yourself . . . and that's okay, 'cause fear is what helps you see yourself. Once you get past the fear, you can see the love. You're starting to look inside yourself, and it scares you."

For some reason, Charlie's words opened up a well of emotion and I began to cry. He put his arm around my shoulder. "You know, brother, the way I look at it, fear is a state you should not resist; it's a state you grow in. Through fear you come to Now, to the very moment of living, and that's where the love is. That's where you're going and where we're all going.

"Hey, you know, up here we got it made. Everything is right here. . . . Dig it: we're not hungry; we got nature all around us; and mostly, we got all the love anyone could want. So don't be afraid of yourself and afraid of the love. Down there, you know, they got madness—they got six million freeways and smog and cars and ugly women and all the poison of TV sets and insurance policies. Hey, the only place they're going is nuts. We got no ulcers here. We got music, a ranch, good hash; we got horses and nothing to do but make love and music. Dig it, Paul, people aren't bad . . . not even the pigs are bad—it's just they don't know where the road starts. They think the road is made of concrete; they don't see the blood veins in their own arms and legs. They don't see the rivers of their own blood; they don't see that the heart is what makes the roads and that roads are invisible until you quit running after them and start listening to your heart." He flicked the hair from his eyes with a jerk of his head.

"You know, man, you might like to take a little ride up north to Mendocino . . . take the girls up there for their dope trial—take the bus and go for a nice ride up the coast and have a good time; see some scenery and greenery . . . get on the road a little bit . . . can you dig that, Paul?"

Ten days later, we moved from the saloon into the back ranch house. Charlie had convinced the hippies to seek another residence, explaining that if they traveled together to another spot their unit would be more cohesive. He had also convinced George that since we were taking care of the ranch, we should be allowed to live in more comfortable quarters. Now we had the seclusion we needed and could feel free to relax. Also, with Pooh Bear, and Sadie's baby due, we needed more room. Since the ranch house was at least a quarter of a mile up the road from George's and the movie sets, no one would be bothered by us.

Like the rest of the buildings at Spahn's, the ranch house was in a general state of disrepair. But it was warm, rustic, and smelled of wood, generating the feelings of a mountain cabin. It had a huge living room with a fireplace and plenty of windows facing the road. Two good-sized bedrooms in the back fronted on the creek, and beyond it, a sloping forest of scrub oak, eucalyptus, and poison oak. The girls went to work at once, scouring floors, cleaning cabinets, and washing windows. We moved the mattresses, furniture, and food supplies in from the saloon, and afterward decorated the walls and the ceiling of the living room with Moroccan tapestries. It felt good to be out of the dusty confines of the saloon into a more bucolic, picturesque setting away from all the tourists.

The very first night we built a roaring fire and ate a lavish meal: cheese-and-noodle casserole, fruit salad, and chocolate cream pies. In celebration, we played music, then dropped acid. I was in good spirits. The fears I had experienced earlier in the week had dissipated for the time being. I felt happy in our new surroundings. Everyone did.

We were all naked. Charlie sat across from me with Squeaky on one side, Mary on the other. Between Mary and Charlie I could see the fire expanding and contracting—rolling like some kaleidoscopic organism as the flames popped and crackled and smoke spun in tight circles around the logs. Snake sat on my left, Ouisch on my right. While holding their hands, I watched the heat spreading out from the inferno's gaping maw in pulsating, luminescent waves, as though drawn to the feeling waves given off by the Family. Charlie moved his hand across his forehead and I saw the aura of his fingers wafting an arc of light—a soft blue stream in front of his face. Then suddenly he rose to his feet and crouched like some predatory beast. Without warning, he lunged directly at me. Before I could react, his weight sent me reeling back against a huge bean-bag pillow and I felt his hands fasten around my neck.

When I looked up into his face, expecting to see that playful twinkle in his eyes, I saw only a leering, demonic expression—a face I'd never known before that day. His eyes were wide and bright—almost blinding—a fifty-thousand-watt stare that told me he wasn't kidding. Jesus! I thought. What the hell is happening? There was even a register of delight in his irises as his fingers tightened around my throat. He was loving it; he was loving choking me and I was stoned enough to see it all as though in slow motion, as though the infinity of my own death might be a spectacle like the sunset—like the ebbing flames of the fire. During those first few moments all paradoxes seemed to coalesce and to burn like the flames.

My fear seemed somehow separate from my thinking—enough so to enable me to have a clear vision of what was happening.

Charlie's face was contorted with madness; it was a face in transformation, fast becoming rigid, losing its fluidity. He can't see! I kept thinking. He can't see me. The madness has blinded him! His weight and the feel of his fingers around my neck brought recall of the cop at Half Moon Bay whose foot on my neck was the same madness, the madness of the law. Gradually everything slowed down even more until I was conscious of each one of Charlie's fingers tightening around my windpipe and of the gurgling sounds coming from my throat.

Then it occurred to me, as I sank deeper into the pillow, that he *couldn't* strangle me. My neck muscles were too strong to penetrate. I tightened the muscles and locked my hands around his forearms. I tried to grin. But there was no sign of give in his expression or in his hands. If anything, he got stronger. His breathing came hard and tight in my face, until suddenly I gave way to my fear; my air was being closed off. I began sputtering.

"What the hell is going on?" were the words I attempted to utter, but the sounds were garbled, completely unintelligible. I tried to push his arms away. Then the thought came to me as it had at Half Moon Bay: I am a sovereign being; there is sovereignty of the spirit; no one can take my life without my allowing it. This thought seemed to bring my awareness into sharper focus, until I felt the saliva dripping from my mouth onto Charlie's hands, then down my neck. I could feel the saliva foaming.

What was happening, I knew, at the deepest levels of consciousness, was not possible; he could not destroy me. Yet the paradox was all too clear: he was doing it! What perplexed me even more was that no one seemed at all concerned over what was happening—Charlie is strangling the shit out of Paul—so that part of me thought: this must be a routine game; no big deal. And it was then that I looked up at Charlie and realized *where* his strength was coming from. I saw the waves and pulsations of my own fear being absorbed into his hands. I saw streaks of sweat running along his forearms like tiny rivers toward my eyes. I saw that he was strangling me with *my own fear!* And I realized too, during the eternity of that episode, that what was prompting me to endure it all—to violate my own survival mechanism (which is fear and the adrenaline it pumps)—was a deeper, cosmic consciousness which had seized my curiosity.

"Okay, Paul," he said, "I'm going to finish it off now . . . I'm going to kill you."

At precisely that moment, the fear began to leave me. I relaxed and looked up at Charlie. And it happened: as I withdrew my fear, I felt his power ebbing; he was losing strength. His hands began to shake. Then his whole body was shaking. Moments later, his hands popped off, and he was literally ejected from me. I sat up, and he faced me on his knees, his body dripping with sweat. He seemed as shocked as I did, yet there was a twinkle in his eye.

"You saw it, huh?" he said, almost reverently.

I nodded, rubbing my neck with one hand. "Yeah, Charlie . . . yeah . . . I saw it."

And what I had seen (though it would take time to sort it out in my mind) was the game Charles Manson was playing; the game of fear manipulation which was his way of controlling the Family. He had set me up for the episode during our little talk on the hillside. Had I submitted to the fear and thrown Charlie off, or had I passed out and come to later, I would always have lived in fear and would have either left the Family then, or, had I stayed, remained completely dominated by Charlie.

Ironically, from that point on I operated on a plane of vision which in some sense put me on a par with Charlie. Later, I realized that Charlie had staged the incident to test me. It was the classic confrontation of the master and his prize pupil. Yet, it was a dilemma for him: on the one hand he loved me like a brother and needed my help; on the other hand, I posed a threat to his absolute rule. My own reaction was also a paradox. While I had been terrified, I had also made a great step forward within the Family. Perhaps Charlie *was* passing the power to me, without meaning to.

Few if any of the others really saw what transpired. In retrospect, I see that they were governed not only by their love for Charlie but by fear of the demons inside him which were every bit as powerful as the love, and which, in time, would destroy that love. During the months that followed, I would see this fear mechanism

operating on many levels. By resorting to physical violence and domination with the girls—twisting their arms,
smacking them, but never hurting them seriously—he was
able to maintain and instill fear, which was balanced by
his love and his seeming infallibility. The words Charlie
uttered were invariably rich with truths. Not only his
words but the motion games, which were based on principles of yang and yin—force versus resistance, mascu-
line versus feminine—the polarity of the world of matter;
Charlie had discovered that the harmony of opposites is
at the core of cosmic law and that submission (in the
way Sadie had submitted to him that night) was fundamental to an achievement of that harmony. There was
beauty in these principles which Charlie clearly understood and knew how to implement.

Yet, on a deeper, more insidious level, he was programming us through fear. He did so by locating deep-
seated hang-ups in a person's psyche. Later, when we
went to the desert, I would see dramatic and harrowing
instances of this under acid. On acid these personal
blocks, inhibitions, fears, nightmares, and frustrations became all too apparent to Charlie. At the same time, he
would ask that we submit to him and to our fears. Instead
of reprogramming or dismantling the fear or hang-up, he
would leave it operational on a subconscious level, telling
the person (who is open and vulnerable on acid), "Don't
let anyone into your head but me." In a very real sense,
Charlie took up residence in people's heads. "I am
you and you are me" was something we were programmed for. With a handle on people's fears (a handle
they were unaware of), Charlie could trigger and dissolve
those fears practically at will. For most people, then, he
became both Satan and savior. Simultaneously, he had
programmed people to give up their past lives ("Give up
your world . . . come and you can be") so that eventually
they had no point of reference, nothing to relate back to,
no right, no wrong—no roots. Their only reference point
became Charlie and his program. Thus a new reality was
created. While this reality would soon become frightening, at the time (and in view of the insanity of the "civ-
ilized world," which to many of us was more frightening),
it seemed worthy to endure.

Until that night, however, I had never fully absorbed Charlie's central message, a message repeated

nightly in the music: "Cease to exist, just come and say you love me . . . give up your world . . . come and you can be . . ." When, during that confrontation, I literally "submitted" (and perhaps could well have "ceased to exist"), it blew Charlie's mind. In a very real sense I may even have transcended his own wildest expectations. Because of this, I became at once more valuable and more threatening. Charlie and I had shared an experience which gave us a glimpse of the core—a taste of the same revelation. In this case his counsel had proven correct—fear had been an obstacle to growth. Fear had been the incipient stages of a higher consciousness; fear had placed me at the jumping-off point where destiny revealed itself in a game of chance. I saw that there are no losers, save for those who dare not play the game. Maybe like most good gamblers, I was just lucky. But from then on, while Charlie and I would remain brothers, we were brothers in a different sense—like wolves in the same wolf pack, always wary of each other and continually on guard.

7

If acid does anything, it dissolves filters and buffers through which perceptions are ordinarily channeled. Three-dimensional physical reality is suddenly expanded. It puts you in direct contact with the energies all around you; nothing is dead or inanimate. It magnifies and expands your awareness in all directions at once—a grain of sand becomes a planet, a single voice becomes a symphony. If you resist it, the slightest fear can become a nightmare. These energies fuse and you see yourself, not as separate, but as part of the great kaleidoscopic whole of life, melt-twisted and free of pretension in timeless spirals of movement. You see that what was and what will always be, is. With these filters removed, you are no longer divorced from what you perceive. Knowing this makes it easier to understand how Charlie was able to get inside people's heads; there were no barriers to obstruct him; his energies moved in and out like the tide; he was everywhere at once. When he said, "No sense makes sense," and, "I am you and you are me," he was, in terms of acid consciousness, absolutely correct. When he came to you in love, there was beauty. But when the demon took control, it was frightening.

I would not forget the look on Charlie's face the night he choked me. The episode confused me, made me more fearful and at the same time more committed to Charlie, or if not to Charlie specifically, to what was happening to me in the relationship. Years later, I read *The Autobiography of a Yoga* and was struck by the story of a young man who went into the Himalayas searching for a guru. When he found the guru he asked to become a disciple, saying that his life had lost all meaning. He said, too, that he had ultimate faith in the guru's knowledge and powers. As a test of that faith the guru said simply, "Then jump off the mountaintop." The young man did so, and his apprenticeship began.

Charlie had taught me something. I had faced my fears and had gained knowledge. Yet, there was always the enigma of contradiction—love and hate, elation and rage. Somehow the resolution of those opposites seemed at the core of my own spiritual growth, and while I little understood the dynamics of it, I was instinctively drawn to it. I had seen the split in Charlie, had observed him as both saint and Satan; perhaps it was those elements of my own psyche which responded. While there was never talk of revolution or murder during that first summer (Helter-Skelter didn't materialize until three months later), I had certainly tasted Charlie's rage as well as the intimations of my own mortality. I had seen the monster. But because my own ego was under such assault via the programming session within the Family, I wasn't sure just who I was looking at: was it Charlie? Was it me? Was it the rest of the Family? Or was it something more awesome than any one of us?

The morning after the acid trip, I took the pickup into town for George. I was still uneasy and spaced-out, driving down the Ventura freeway. I started to change lanes and glanced into the rearview mirror. Suddenly, all the headlights behind me became glassy, glaring eyes and the cars took on their proper proportions. I saw them for what they were: living, breathing robots. Their grilles twisted into leering smiles—the gleaming chrome teeth of civilization. And there I was sitting inside one of them myself doing sixty-five mph. I pulled off the freeway onto Ventura Boulevard. I felt sick. Yet, even after I had parked, I was aware of cars everywhere—stationed in lots, along curbs, hoisted atop hydraulic jacks, lurking in closed garages where I couldn't see them—thousands, millions of them in every color. The world had been transformed into concrete to accommodate them. The air was polluted by them. I got out of the truck and puked in the gutter outside a market in Canoga Park, then I drove back to Spahn's on the back roads. When I told Charlie later that morning, he took me down to Malibu and we sat on the beach and watched the sea.

Months later, it occurred to me that nearly everyone in the Manson Family came from the L.A. area or someplace like it: cemented in by freeways, tract homes, shopping centers, and parking lots—living in an atmosphere polluted perhaps beyond redemption by machines and the corporate monster. No wonder the youth of the sixties had flipped out to go searching for their souls. They had lost contact with their parents, their blood, their roots, with nature and the very air they sought to breathe. Humanity had become an echo chamber in the middle of an L.A. freeway.

One of the most beautiful experiences of that summer happened in early August, just two weeks after the acid trip. I was sitting outside the ranch house with Clem under a eucalyptus tree, playing the guitar while watching a handful of blue jays squawking among the branches. I was feeling better about myself at that point, feeling as though I'd become stronger, yet more vulnerable to my own destiny. It was not a feeling of independence from Charlie, since I attributed much of my own growth to my relationship with him. Neither was it subservience to him. More, it was like a precarious balance that I had paid dearly to achieve.

It became clear that I enjoyed a level of awareness that few shared. Clem, for example, was at the other end of the spectrum; in some sense, he was the "dodo" of the Family. He acted most of the time like some bumbling, vapid-eyed hippie who didn't care what happened. It wasn't that Clem was dumb, it was just that he adopted Charlie's program of playing the idiot (playing beneath the awareness of people) so completely that he became an idiot.

Still, he was always a likable character—unkempt, lanky, and awkward. He had long blond hair, freckles, and was fair-complexioned. Before joining the Family (shortly before I arrived at Spahn's), he'd lived with the hippies in the back ranch house. He played the guitar and sang pretty well, and unlike Brooks and Tex, was able to survive the sex scenes without undue trauma. He didn't tune in much to the nuances of the group sex, but when it came to a one-on-one situation, he could ball his brains loose.

We were both in good spirits that morning, feeling lucky to be alive: the day before, we'd borrowed Dennis Wilson's Ferrari, to make a garbage run and then to drive around the mountains near Spahn's. Clem was at the wheel, hauling ass up the mountain on Santa Susana Pass, speed-shifting and burning rubber on the curves. We came blazing up the hill into the steepest curve on the grade, doing about eighty. Clem was beside himself: "Yeeya-hoo!" he bleated. I knew instinctively that we'd have to accelerate to make the turn. "Go for it, Clem . . . *tromp the son of a bitch!*" We boogied into the turn and my heart leaped into my throat. "Yeeoow!" Clem bellowed. The tires squealed and Clem lost it, hitting the brakes. We skidded onto the shoulder, then spun out into the middle of the road before smacking into the guardrail. I thought it was all over. But we bounced off again and came shuddering to a halt in the middle of the road. The car looked like a crushed tin can, nothing left but a twisted mass of glistening metal and broken glass. Miraculously, we were both unhurt. We climbed out through the windows, then hiked back to the ranch. Dennis and Charlie were sitting under a tree in front of the ranch house along with Brenda, Snake, and Sandy, when Clem and I ambled down the road.

"Hey, man," Clem said to Dennis. "Like we kinda had an accident in your car. . . ."

Dennis lay supine on the ground beside Charlie. He raised himself to his elbows. "What happened?"

"Totaled it, man," I said. "Completely."

Charlie drove us back up there in the pickup. But when we got to the curve, the wreckage was gone—not a trace of it except for the long set of serpentine skid marks. "Looks like some motherfucker come along and grabbed up your wheels, man," Charlie mused. "Too bad, that engine's probably worth some bucks."

Later we called the highway patrol. They knew nothing about it. Dennis filed a report, but to no avail—that was the last he ever saw of his car. I figured we survived the crash simply because Clem was too do-doed out to get snuffed.

We were discussing the accident that evening under the tree when we spotted Sadie riding by on one of George's old geldings. I yelled at her but she didn't seem to hear. Minutes later she came trotting up the road on foot. She was wearing faded Levi's about three sizes too big and an old sweater pulled over her plump belly. After nearly six months of pregnancy, her breasts were huge, bouncing gingerly beneath her sweater as she hurried past us toward the house.

"Where's Charlie?"

"Up at the outlaw shacks. Why . . . what's up?"

"I think I'm going to have my baby."

Clem and I exchanged glances as Sadie disappeared into the ranch house.

"Go get Charlie!"

Clem sprinted up the hill toward the outlaw shacks. I raced to the house.

The girls had gathered around Sadie in the middle of the room.

"Get the towels and boil some water in the big pot . . . . Let's pull these mattresses together so she can lie down." Mary Brunner took charge immediately. Just four months earlier, she'd given birth to Pooh Bear under similar circumstances.

"Give her some room, dammit," Katie said, tugging on the mattress.

Sadie lay down in the middle of the floor. The girls helped her off with her clothes and Brenda brought a pillow. Snake sat perched on a chair like a little bird, her eyes wide with anticipation, her face all but hidden behind her hair. The other girls gathered around like Mexican women in an open marketplace. I looked over the tops of their heads.

"You okay, Sadie?"

"Yeah, Paul . . . but the baby is coming . . . I know he's coming. Where's Charlie?"

"I'm right here!" the front door slammed behind Clem and Charlie. They'd both been running.

"Back off a little and give her some room," Charlie ordered, kneeling down beside her. "How you makin' it, honey?"

Charlie was shirtless, his body filmed in a light perspiration. He wore Levi's, cowboy boots, and a red bandanna tied around his head.

Sadie grimaced. "Uh . . . ahhh . . . okay, Charlie . . . okay . . ."

"Paul, why don't you play some music, dig . . . we want this little motherfucker to come out dancin' . . . right?"

Charlie went to the bathroom to wash his hands. Sandy and Squeaky came in with two buckets of hot water and a tray full of steaming towels, setting them on the small table. I picked on the sitar. It didn't take long: soon the contractions were less than ten minutes apart.

Mary, Ella, Squeaky, Sandy, Stephanie, Katie, and Ouisch lifted Sadie up to support her body—just raised her up into a half-sitting, half-reclining position, two girls on each leg, two holding her upper body. Gypsy held her head.

"Ahhh . . . ahhh . . . oh, Jesus, Charlie! Charlie!" Sadie groaned.

"Nice and easy, Sadie . . . just go with it . . . go with the motion." Charlie squatted between her legs, laying his hands momentarily on the inside of her thighs.

"Somebody sterilize a razor blade and bring it in here."

Snake bolted off the chair, got a razor blade from the bathroom, then took it to the kitchen to sterilize it. She was still in there when Sadie's water broke in a gurgle, spraying Charlie and the girls holding her legs. "Shit, the little dude is taking a swim," Charlie quipped. Sadie grinned. Sweat poured off her face; the veins in her arms stood out like tendons as she squeezed Brenda's hands.

The next contraction was a doozie.

"Ahhh . . . ahhhh. Oh, God . . . aghhhh. Charlie!" Strands of wet hair hung across Sadie's forehead. Gypsy brushed them back and wiped the skin with a towel.

"Push, honey," Charlie urged. "Give it all you got . . . push . . . he's starting to come now . . . Damn!"

I stood directly behind Charlie, watching over his shoulder.

Snake handed him the razor blade.

"Easy," Mary soothed. "It's coming fine. It's coming real good. You're about to be a mama!"

"Hang on, honey." Charlie leaned over, his face flushed. He made a small incision at the apex of Sadie's vagina. Instantly blood spurted from the tiny cut, drenching his hand.

"*Aghhh . . . ahhhhh . . . Charlie!*" Sadie wailed. Katie reached in to soak up the blood with a towel.

Moments later, I could see the top of the baby's head pulsating in the opening, enveloped in a quivering glutinous film.

"*Push! Come on! Push . . .* Sadie, have your baby . . . he wants out!"

Then we could see his shoulders, and his little arms.

"Jesus!"

"Here he comes, Sadie!"

"Come on outta there, brother!"

Suddenly the top part of his body tore free in a spurt of crimson.

"Wow!"

"*Push . . . more!*"

Then, as though he understood the command, the baby pushed off with his arms and more or less delivered himself into Charlie's outstretched hands. Sandy wiped off Sadie's face with a towel; her eyes were glazed. Dried white mucus clung to the corners of her mouth. But she was smiling.

I couldn't believe how small he was! He just sat there for a second in Charlie's hands, then blinked with those big, foggy, steel-blue eyes, as if to say: where the hell am I? Then he closed his eyes. Snake reached over with a pair of scissors and snipped the umbilical cord. Charlie tied it off with a piece of guitar string, then handed the baby to Brenda, who began to suck the mucus out of his nose. Finally Charlie gave him a pat on the ass and he started to sputter and cry. Charlie grinned: "Dig this little dude, will ya, mama!" He held the baby out to Sadie.

"He's beautiful, honey," Sandy cooed. "Isn't he just perfect!"

Moments later, the afterbirth plopped out like some amorphous jellyfish. The girls cleaned Sadie up, then made the bed for her in the back room. Charlie began dancing around the room with the guitar, composing

capriccios and rhymes in honor of the "new leader."
Manson always claimed that the children were the real
leaders. Unencumbered by well-developed egos, their
responses were more instinctive and pure; they were always "at Now," which is where we wanted to be. Later
he took me aside and suggested we go someplace and
figure out a name for the boy. So we piled into the
pickup and drove around Chatsworth concocting names
and sobriquets of all kinds. By about three A.M. we'd considered hundreds of names. We were both exhausted.

"Hey, why don't we just call him Caesar," I finally
suggested halfheartedly.

"Uh . . . uh . . . hey, that's good, you know . . . I like
that . . . yeah, maybe just Zezo."

"How about Zezos ZeZe?"

"Right on." Charlie laughed. "Yeah, Zezos ZeZe . . .
Zadfrak. How's that, Zezos ZeZe Zadfrak."

"Zezos ZeZe Zadfrak . . . sounds good to me."

"Dig it, that way he'll always be at the end of the
line . . . and the lines will be so long, he just won't wait in
them . . . you know?"

Years later, I would reflect back on the joy of that
night: the unity of the Family; the birth of Sadie's child
—only to be jolted and repulsed by the chilling realization that just one year later (almost to the day), Sadie
would butcher Sharon Tate and her unborn son.

Even though we were pretty firmly ensconced at
Spahn's, during the first three months, Charlie always had
his eyes open for alternative headquarters. The Family
had moved frequently in the past and we never knew
when we might have to do so again. Bad vibes between
Charlie and some of the cowboys had become increasingly apparent. It was for that reason that we cultivated a
religious order just over the hill from Spahn's called the
Fountain of the World.

The Fountain was a nonprofit spiritual order of men
and women (primarily women) just north of Spahn's in
Box Canyon. It was an impressive complex, built at a
bend in the gorge by a stream (almost hidden) by oak
trees and a sprawling well-irrigated garden. The buildings, all constructed of hand-worked stone, included a
chapel, two dormitories, and a small auditorium where
daily meetings were held. To the right of the auditorium

on a knoll above the garden, a wooden cross was cemented into the ground. From a distance the Fountain
looked like an ancient fortress hewn into the base of the
canyon wall.

One morning not long after the birth of Zezos,
Charlie woke me up and told me to come with him. I
pulled on a pair of Levi's, a T-shirt, and my boots and
followed him out of the ranch house. We hiked up to
the saloon where the pickup was parked and climbed
in.

"Where we headed?"

Charlie fired up the truck and backed it out onto the
highway. "The Fountain of the World."

"What?"

Charlie told me what he knew about it as we wound
our way up Santa Susana Pass to Box Canyon and turned
left. "It might be a good place to hang out . . . you know,
hide under the cross when the shit comes down at
Spahn's. And the way Shorty's been running at the mouth,
it might be anytime."

We got there around ten A.M. and parked the truck
on a hill, then trudged down the path to the auditorium.
The place was about half full, and one of the brothers
was already into his rap. He acknowledged us with a
smile as we sat down. After a long uninspired spiel pro-
claiming the virtues of moderation and human compassion, the speaker—tall, stoop-shouldered, and clad in a
flowing full-length robe—told the history of the Fountain
and how Krishna Venta, its founder, had undergone a
rigorous purification process, part of which included hanging on the cross for three days.

Charlie sat beside me fingering the beads around his
neck, his hair long and uncombed down his back. He
sniggered to himself as the speaker raised his arms to
symbolize the crucifixion.

"For three days the honorable Krishna Venta remained pinioned to the cross you see there on the hillside." He gestured toward a window which fronted on the
ravine.

"For three long days . . ."

Charlie couldn't contain himself. "Hey, brother, that
ain't nothin'," he blurted out, smiling.

"Sir?"

"That's nothin' . . . three days ain't nothin'. Paul here

could hang on the cross for a week. No problem . . . right, Paul?"

The audience, most of them brothers and sisters of the order, gawked at us. I was a little startled by Charlie's boast at first, but I knew his games pretty well by then and I went along with it.

"Sure," I grunted. "Sure, I could do that."

"Come on!" Charlie urged, getting to his feet. "Let's go on out there, Paul, so you can hang. Come on!"

I got up and started up the aisle with Charlie right behind me. But as we stepped out the door, one of the brothers stopped us. "I'm sorry, but I don't think that's such a good idea. It might elicit some unfavorable publicity . . . you understand." He gave Charlie an imploring yet conciliatory smile.

Charlie chuckled. "Sure, brother," he said. "Maybe some other time."

After that little episode, Charlie began sending contingents of girls to the Fountain to work with the sisters—soliciting donations, passing out literature and spreading the precepts of Krishna Venta. Sometimes they remained for days at a time, posing as devout and pious ladies of the cloth. But the Family, as a whole, was never warmly received and things didn't work out as Charlie had planned. We finally gave up on the Fountain. We didn't learn until later that Shorty had paid them a visit.

The irony of that whole scene (I later learned) was that Krishna Venta's Family bore a striking resemblance to Charlie's: according to the records, the order was started when the honorable leader (sometime in the 1950's) recruited a nucleus of women and a few men to enlighten the world with his spiritual teachings. But Krishna Venta's teachings were never, it appears, divorced from the pleasures of the flesh. Under his leadership, group sex, or what he likened to tantric, transcendental self-realization, was a common practice. Most of his critics, however, including an irate husband of one of the sisters, didn't consider this form of "self-realization" quite kosher. One night, during a small service held in the chapel, that same husband arrived with a case of dynamite and blew Krishna Venta, himself, and thirteen others to kingdom come. The ruins of that explosion were left intact as a monument to the order's founder.

Charlie always thought that a hilarious story.

Part Two

Charlie?
Who the Hell
Is Charlie?

8

I found myself anticipating the trip to Mendocino—a chance to get out on the open road, away from L.A., away from Charlie and the ranch. But we needed a vehicle. On the first of September 1968 we bought one—a fifty-six passenger International school bus. The girls had to appear in court for their drug bust on the tenth, so it gave us several days to ready the bus. We parked it between the saloon and George's house, and after sanding it down, painted it a brilliant kelly green with a white stripe around it. While Tex and T.J. tuned the engine, the girls spliced together chunks of thick red carpet to cover the floors. They also made velvet curtains and a black satin headliner, embroidered with sequins. We took out all the seats and converted the interior into two rooms partitioned by a piece of blue velvet. In the back we constructed a plywood platform and beneath it a storage cabinet for food, tools, and spare parts. On top of the platform we laid out mattresses, satin sheets, and mounds of fluffy black- and red-flowered pillows. In the front of the bus, behind the driver's seat, we set up a narrow table surrounded by pillows, and next to the door, a stove.

By the end of the week the bus was ready. So was I.

We set out about four P.M. from Spahn's on a Sunday; eleven of us: Stephanie, Brenda, Mary, Clem, Kim, Sadie, Katie, Gypsy, Ella, and T.J. (Thomas Walleman), who, along with Clem, had lived with the original hippies in the back ranch house before joining the Family. I was driving. We took Topanga all the way to the coast highway and headed north; we were all in good spirits. Kim and Clem lounged in the back with the girls while T.J. and I sat up front bullshitting and munching zuzus.

"Damn thing's got some power," T.J. mused as we

93

barreled out of Malibu, heading toward Oxnard. "Runs better than the last bus Charlie had."

T.J. was about five-ten, a chubby 170 pounds—an unlikely member of the Manson Family in some respects, since he was older than Charlie and going bald. He looked like the heavy in some B-grade western. He wore upper false teeth and was forever popping them in and out of his mouth, a habit that seemed to delight him. Though the girls were never particularly impressed by T.J., he had managed to cultivate their affectionate tolerance. He was useful to the Family (to Charlie), and they knew it. He was earthy and stubborn, and walked with an air of *hubris* which belied his insecurities. He never pulled much weight in the Family and was used primarily to score dope and vehicles. Later, when we got heavily into the revolutionary programming (Helter-Skelter), T.J. used his connections to score motorcycles and dune buggies. He could be obsequious at times, but for the most part I got along well with him.

We spent the night in Oxnard, then drove straight through the following day to Garapata Canyon. The next morning, near Big Sur, we stopped along the road and hiked down to the beach. I sat on a rock beside Brenda and took off my shoes. She pointed to the gulls overhead and smiled. The sky was clear, the sea dazzling. It was a rush being on the coast again. We strolled down the beach about a mile, wading in the surf and picking up driftwood and shells; then we walked back toward the car. With Charlie gone there were no pressures; yet, paradoxically, we all felt closer to him, as if our being in the midst of so much natural beauty was somehow his doing. We didn't talk about it; but it was there, his presence. Charlie was right; we *were* free; there were no leaders, no controls. By noon we were headed up 101 toward San Jose.

Just north of Monterey, we stopped for gas. T.J. was at the wheel. I sat beside him. Directly behind us, Mary and Sadie discussed the effects of motherhood on the body. Mary was showing Sadie the marks on her breasts, telling her to use lots of oil on the skin. Pooh Bear and Zezos had been left at Spahn's. Charlie insisted that children born to the Family be the responsibility of all the women so that strong dependency between mother and child be avoided. T.J. shouted to the attendant to check the oil. Sadie was the first to spot Bobby Beausoleil's Dodge camper pull in and stop.

"Hey, it's Bobby!"

"Where the hell has he been?" T.J. muttered, glancing at me.

"Hi, Cupid," Gypsy hailed him out the window.

Bobby got out of the camper and trotted over to the bus. "Hey, Gypsy, what's happening?" He flashed a smile. I rolled down my window. "Hi, Paul." We hadn't seen him since the second week at Spahn's—the day he brought Gypsy to the Family.

Bobby wore bell-bottoms and a long-sleeved white shirt under a buckskin vest; he was always spiffy in the hip Hollywood style and was known as Cupid by many of his Topanga Canyon cronies. At five-eleven he was slender and rather loose-jointed, with large droopy blue eyes and soft, rounded features, handsome in a boyish, almost angelic way. I liked Bobby but always felt he was too superficial and arrogant to make it in the Family on a permanent basis. He had gotten behind Charlie's scene on occasion, but could never stick it out; he was too frenetic, too greedy—always giving orders and trying to usurp power he never really had. Yet he always came back. Before long, a pattern developed; each time he returned he gave Charlie something as a means of buying his way back—a car, a truck, a girl. Then, in the summer of 1969, when he came for the last time, his welcome was worn out. He told Charlie he'd do anything for the Family; that's when Charlie told him: "Then you know what to do with Gary Hinman." Hinman had been an acquaintance of Charlie's, a musician who had apparently owed Charlie money and had refused to pay it back. Two weeks later, Gary Hinman was dead.

The day we met Bobby in Monterey he was on his way to L.A. with his wife, Gail, and a girl he'd met in Berkeley named Leslie. When I suggested we rendezvous at a campsite down the road and smoke a joint, he agreed. We gassed the bus, bought three quarts of oil, then drove south one mile to the campsite overlooking the sea. It was spectacular, lush with cypress trees and wild poppies. Bobby pulled his truck in beside the bus and joined us inside. We smoked some grass and jammed a little, then cooked up a pot of baked beans and made a salad. It was the first time I'd seen Leslie Van Houten.

Leslie was nineteen, soft-spoken and initially shy. When I attempted to engage her in conversation during dinner, she answered my questions with little elaboration. I did learn that several months before she had left her home in Monrovia, California, to travel north and had wound up in Berkeley, where she met Bobby and Gail. When they asked her to join them, she agreed. I sat beside her on the cliff, drinking coffee. Her movements were fluid. An abundance of dark brown shoulder-length hair, hazel eyes, and rosy dimpled cheeks gave her a country-girl air. Yet, there was a softness, a reservation about her that seemed classically feminine and refined, even coquettish. I was attracted to her at once, and after talking to Bobby, it was agreed that he and I exchange sleeping quarters.

That night I made love with both Gail and Leslie in the camper while Bobby got it on with friends in the bus. After Gail went to sleep, I talked to Leslie for hours. She described her youth in southern California, growing up in a middle-class suburban neighborhood. She'd been a good student and a cheerleader; her folks, it seemed, though divorced, were pillars of respectability. Leslie's dissatisfaction, her wanderlust, grew out of a deeper need for love and a sense of purpose—something I thought I'd found in the Family. I told her about Charlie and suggested she come to Spahn's and meet him. She said she would. I later regretted ever having made that suggestion.

The next morning they left for L.A. and we continued north toward Mendocino. The good weather held out—plenty of sun and fresh air and not much traffic. T.J. drove while I sat in back with the others. Clem dozed beside T.J. in the front seat. Stephanie, Katie, and Ella were embroidering designs into the collars and pockets of Charlie's shirts. That's when we heard the clanking of metal and the bus jolted to a stop.

"Son of a bitch," T.J. groaned. "Sounds like a fuckin' rod!"

T.J. got out and opened up the hood. The others piled out behind him, while I searched the back of the bus for tools, only to find that we'd forgotten the toolbox. We held a roadside powwow, deciding to stand beside the bus in a group looking forlorn—the old wait-for-someone-torescue-you routine. And sure enough, within minutes a real live hero (a middle-aged custodian) emerged from the Grange Hall down the road and offered to drive me to a garage in San Jose. There I borrowed tools and purchased a rod cap and bearing. We brought them back to the bus and set to work, only to discover that the crankshaft had been dented. The cap fit, but not the bearing. So we stuffed a hunk of leather into the hole, buttoned it up, and jubilantly proceeded down the road. We got as far as the outskirts of San Jose before hearing a horrendous bang as the rod gave up the ghost once and for all.

From there we sent a contingent of girls into town to hustle some assistance. "Try and find someone who knows something about these friggin' buses," T.J. barked as the girls crossed the road and extended their thumbs at the first passing car. In less than an hour Sadie, Katie, Brenda, and Ella had hitchhiked into San Jose and returned with a young hippie mechanic named Daryl who proceeded to tear down the engine. After he'd dismantled much of it and had it laid out on the highway, he adjourned to the back of the bus with Sadie for a "breather." Sadie must have taken it out of him, because afterward he got in his truck and split.

We sent the girls out again. By late afternoon they returned in a new four-wheel-drive Willys jeep with a dapper-looking Mexican rancher named Díaz. Díaz was a gracious old man, obviously intrigued and charmed by the girls. When he offered to have us towed out to his ranch (some twenty miles east of San Jose) where we could work on the bus at our leisure, we were more than grateful.

By the time we pulled off a narrow, gutted country road onto Díaz's property, it was nearly dark. But the moon provided sufficient light to see the sprawling plum orchards which spread for miles in all directions. We parked behind his ranch house in a clearing in the midst of the orchard. When we invited the old man to eat with us, he politely declined. He told us he'd send a mechanic in the morning to check out the bus. We offered to pay for the towing charge, but he shook his head. He was a genuine caballero—one of the most distinguished-looking men I'd ever seen. With a full, walrus-style mustache and thick steel-gray hair, he looked like an elderly, gentlemanly version of Emiliano Zapata. I found myself wishing that Juan was there to speak Spanish to him. Díaz mentioned that he had twelve men in his employ and that if we needed anything to ask them.

For the next two days we worked on the engine. Díaz's mechanic, a jovial yet fiery Mexican named Gerardo, had trouble finding parts. And when he did, they were invariably the wrong ones. On the third day, I called Charlie and he said to stay with it. "Just get the motherfucker running and get on back . . . make sure the girls get to court."

Two days later, Katie, Ella, Mary, Stephanie, and Sadie returned from Mendocino. The case had been dismissed. By then, the engine had been twice torn down and rebuilt; it had been a marathon of hard work, but to no avail; it wouldn't turn over, much less move. We were all getting antsy, and so were the ranch hands. We deliberately kept the girls close to the bus at night so as to avoid situations that might jeopardize our good graces with Díaz—at least until we had the bus running.

The night the girls returned from town, we ate an early dinner of peanut-butter sandwiches, beans, brown rice, and ice cream. Afterwards we gathered inside the bus around a wood-burning stove. We were tired and on edge. There wasn't one of us who didn't need a bath. Sadie and Katie were describing their scene in court. Clem had just gone outside to take a leak. There was a full moon blazing in the heavens, and I opened a window to look out across the valley. I could hear the muted voices of the ranch hands coming from behind the bunkhouse; they were singing, and the smoke and sparks from their fire were visible beyond the trees.

Clem clomped into the bus. "Those dudes are getting pretty cranked up." He slumped into a pillow beside Brenda, who was wiping her face with a wet Kleenex. "Drinkin' tequila like it's goin out of style," Clem drawled. "Asked me to send a couple of girls down to keep them company. Half of 'em are already shithoused."

"Where's old man Díaz?"

"Didn't see 'im . . . car ain't there . . . no one's in the house, far as I can tell."

T.J. lit a joint and took a hit. "Shit!" He winced, inhaling as he handed me the joint. "I say we leave this pig here and hitch back to Spahn's. We'll get Tex's ass up here with some tools and fix the son of a bitch, or buy a new engine!"

"I'll give Charlie a call."

I left the bus and trotted along the furrowed path between the plum trees, toward the ranch house. It felt good to run, to breathe cold air. The valley was shrouded in a canopy of soft, brilliant moonlight. Díaz had left the porch light on as he said he would.

As I approached the building, the singing of the ranch hands grew louder—funky ranchero songs, slurred, yet spicy with yeehoos and high-pitched ayeees. I opened the screen door and went inside. The phone sat on a table next to a huge meat freezer, by the door. Charlie answered on the second ring.

"It's me, Paul."

"What's happening up there, brother?"

"Still hassling this fucking bus . . . put it together again, but no dice. I think it needs a new block, new pistons . . . the whole nine yards."

"Did the girls make their gig?"

"Got back today . . . no sweat. Judge dismissed it."

"Dig it, just leave the bus and hitchhike back here . . . is it cool to leave it there?"

"If it isn't, we can tow it someplace else."

"Yeah . . . far-out."

"What's happening on your end?"

"Things are a little uptight. George is worked up about paying his taxes. . . claims he's going broke. I think Shorty's been filling his head with bullshit . . . but it's under control. But, hey, ya remember that chick from Topanga named Cappy . . . Cathy? She's here, says her grandma owns a place out in Death Valley, says we can stay up there if we want. Might be a real trip to go out there, you know. Nice and quiet, good vibes . . . get our scene together without all this crap."

"Sounds okay."

"Yeah, we'll see what happens. How is everyone?"

"Copacetic, Charlie."

"Far-out. Look, you just head on back. . . ."

"Right."

"See ya."

By the time I hung up and started back through the orchard, several cowboys were mounted and riding around a small bonfire. I could see them through the trees. I decided to take a closer look and cut back behind the ranch house, coming up beside the bunkhouse. I watched from the corner of the building.

There were eight or nine of them, four on horse-back, the others standing close to the fire, swilling booze out of bottles. Two of the riders wore holstered guns. I watched for a while, then crawled along the side of the bunkhouse, before sprinting across the yard and ducking into the plum grove.

By the time I got back to the bus, T.J. was searching frantically through the back cabinet for a weapon.

"Those dudes are getting pretty wild," I panted.

"We know." Sadie sat down beside me. "They just rode up to invite us to their party."

"They're packing hardware too," Kim intoned, fastening his bowie knife to his waist. Kim was about five-six and built like the proverbial brick shithouse. Born and raised in Malibu, he'd developed his body through years of surfing. He seemed to be enjoying the scene that night.

"Let's not get carried away," I cautioned.

"Bullshit," T.J. growled. "We're out here in the middle of no-fucking-where . . . anything could happen . . . no one around to hear a damn thing . . . I thought we had a twelve-gauge stashed back here . . . I found the shells . . . but . . ."

"Charlie took it out."

"Shit!"

"Here they come!" Clem pulled the door shut.

Five riders galloped through the trees, yipping and shouting in Spanish. We jacked up the windows and gathered in front of the bus to watch them. T.J. had a tire iron in one hand. Clem was toting a ball-peen hammer.

The riders raced around the bus a couple of times, then reined up outside the door. "You want to come and make a fiesta with us?"

I opened the door slightly and leaned out. "Hey, man, not tonight . . . really. We just got back from town . . . maybe tomorrow we can have a party." The guy I addressed looked like one of Pancho Villa's mestizo guerrillas—stocky with a round, ruddy face and a luxuriant black mustache. I'd met him before while watching them crate plums, but he was too drunk to recognize me. He was called Juancho and was pretty much the head ranch hand.

"Maybe you girls want to come to the party," he shouted.

"Not tonight," I repeated.

"Tomorrow night," Brenda shouted from inside.

"Shut up!" Mary Brunner's voice rang out.

"Really, man," I said, "let's just call it a night."

Juancho gave me a long appraising look without speaking, his eyes steady, his left hand holding down the tossing head of a big chestnut mare; the other four riders, meanwhile, trotted around the bus trying to look in the windows.

"Sure," he said at last. "Tomorrow, maybe . . . okay." Then he whirled his mount around, shouted to the others, and they galloped into the trees again, firing off a volley of shots into the air.

None of us slept. We barricaded the front of the bus and took turns on watch. But nothing happened. The ranch hands stayed drunk, hooted and hollered and fired their guns, but never really made a move on us. Only once, just before dawn, two of them staggered over on foot to request the company of "*dos chamacas*" to put them to bed. Neither of the men had guns, and both were stinking drunk. Each carried a half-pint bottle of José Cuervo. They were so comical we were tempted to let them in; but we didn't.

The next morning, after leaving Díaz a note to thank him, we had the bus towed to a huge parking lot in San Jose; then we split up into groups to hitchhike back to Spahn's.

I went alone. After weeks of confinement on the bus, I felt the need to be by myself. It was around eleven A.M. when I left the others and walked back through San Jose to the first south-bound off-ramp. I had no luggage and felt energized standing in the sunlight flinging rocks at a telephone pole. I found myself anxious to see Charlie and the others. The ranch was my "home." I felt it. I recalled too what Charlie had said about going to Death Valley. As a kid I'd gone there with my father to camp and collect rocks. I remembered the awesome expanse of sand, mountains, and sky. I remembered hiking across the salt flats and taking a bath in the hot springs. The more I thought about it, the better it sounded. I hadn't been waiting fifteen minutes when a brand-new brown-and-white camper with a girl at the wheel skidded to a stop.

I trotted up to the window. "Where ya headed?"

"Mexico . . . where you headed?"

I opened the door and climbed in. "L.A." She pulled out onto the highway.

"My name's Juanita," she said, still gauging traffic through her outside rearview mirror. She turned and smiled. "Juanita Wildebush."

"You're kidding." I beamed. "I'm Paul . . . Paul Watkins."

Juanita was a big, corpulent, rawboned blonde, with thick hair, thick lips, and generous well-tanned haunches. She wore an embroidered Mexican blouse, a tight pair of white shorts, and sandals. Her teeth looked like chunks of quartz crystal when she grinned, telling me she had just returned from Mexico City but was headed right back. "This culture sucks," she quipped. "After being down there for a year, everything up here seems dead." She said she spoke fluent Spanish and that after stopping in L.A. she'd be driving straight through to Oaxaca.

"We could have used you last night." I described briefly what had transpired with the rancheros. She seemed delighted with the story but felt that we should have gone to the party and had a good time. "It would have been a gas. Latin men are the greatest, let me tell ya." She went on to recount, quite graphically, several romantic episodes that she had enjoyed south of the border. "Those guys don't just ball; they get down!" So imbued was she with anything that smacked of Latin culture, I felt it futile to do anything but nod in agreement.

"Whereabouts you goin' in L.A.?" she said at last.

"I live in the Santa Susana Hills at a place called Spahn's ranch."

"Never heard of it."

We chatted amiably while her tape deck boomed out the Beatles and Three Dog Night. The inside of the van was completely customized, with a full leather tuck-in roll, a canopied bed, a propane stove, refrigerator, and a yellow life raft which sat perched on top of the mattress alongside some scuba-diving gear. I got the distinct impression Juanita wasn't hurting for money. And that she was horny. I told her a little about the Family and

Charlie and that our life-style was pretty much divorced from the rat-race Anglo culture she so abhorred. When she mentioned that she had recently come into a small inheritance, I suggested, circuitously, that she stop by at the ranch and meet Charlie. She said she'd like that.

When we pulled up and parked in front of the ranch house that night, Charlie was sitting outside on the porch whittling on a piece of wood.

"Made good time, Paul," he said. "Only one back so far. Who's your friend?" Charlie stood as we approached the porch.

"This is Juanita, Charlie . . . Juanita Wildebush."

"No shit! That's your name? . . . Jesus! That's real poetic!" He laughed. "Come on in."

We followed Charlie into the house. While I poured a cold glass of water, he proceeded to introduce Juanita to Snake, Squeaky, Sandy, Ouisch, and the new girl, Catherine Gilles, who were seated around the fire. Juan Flynn was lounging on the couch playing with Pooh Bear. Brooks was in the shower, singing. Juanita and Juan exchanged amenities in Spanish and Juanita seemed pleased at this.

Later, Charlie took her aside to smoke a dube while I parked her van down by the corral. I didn't hurry, so as to give him plenty of time to lay out his rap. I'd told him Juanita had money and that she might be willing to part with some of it. At the time, I wasn't averse to hustling money for the Family. It was like a game. I could think of no better cause than our own communal existence. And, like everyone else in the Family in those days, I wanted to please Charlie. By the time I got back, Charlie had the full scoop. Juanita's inheritance was no mere pittance— some fifteen thousand dollars, to be exact; what she needed most, he said, was to have her "wildbush" sucked, good and proper.

"She's partial to you, man." He beamed. "So just take her back to her van and ring her bell."

I hadn't figured on that. Generally, Charlie was first with any new girl. Had Juanita been physically attractive, he would have been. The fact is, I'd been thinking about Snake all the way home. But I didn't have much choice.

Juanita and I spent a long and active night in the van. And some of the next morning. She was eager, she said, to move in with the Family. That afternoon she made arrangements to give us her money. A week later George Spahn's four-thousand-dollar tax bill was paid in full.

9

Shortly after we returned from San Jose, Leslie Van Houten arrived at Spahn's in the company of Bobby and Gail Beausoleil. When Bobby and Gail split several days later, Leslie remained. She'd been there less than a week when she said, "Charlie is the most beautiful person I've ever met." One year later, she was arrested (and subsequently convicted) of murder.

By early October, three new girls had joined the Family—Leslie, Juanita, and Cathy (Cappy) Gilles, whose grandmother owned the Meyers ranch in Death Valley. Charlie began rapping in earnest about moving to the desert: "Out there," he said, "things aren't so crazy; we can have our children, and our children can teach us the things we need to learn. Out there, we're closer to the stars and to the land and to the spirit of life. . . . Death Valley, you know—it makes a lot of sense."

I didn't know until later that during our trip to San Jose, Charlie had been attempting to sell his music through a connection with Dennis Wilson and Dennis' agent, Greg Jakobson, without success. His impatience to leave Spahn's was born not only of undercurrents of animosity between him and the wranglers but because of frustrations with the music. Charlie believed in himself as a musician; and rightly so. The Beach Boys had already recorded one of Charlie's songs, "Cease to Exist," under the title "Cease to Resist." Music was, in many respects, his only legitimate vehicle for success in the real world. Even though he despised society, there was a part of him that sought success by its rules, if only to laugh in its face later. "Hey, man," he used to say, "some of those straight jokers are better con men than any I ever met in the joint. It's all the same, really . . . games. People mind-fucking each other for money and blood and calling it the golden rule. I tell ya, Paul . . . only the truth will set you free."

By the middle of October we had decided to go to Death Valley. But first Charlie wanted to center our energies and bring the Family closer together by taking one final acid trip before departure. He told me to "tune" the group, that it was a prelude to our journey.

At no other time did we prepare so elaborately for an acid scene. The girls made special garments—loose-fitting shirts and pants of velvet and silk; the softest, most comfortable clothing, embroidered with vivid designs of peacocks, sunsets, and flowers. We called them the no-sense-makes-sense clothes: shirts which had pocket flaps where there were no pockets, buttonholes where there were no buttons. Clothing designed for comfort and beauty and to free the mind.

We redecorated and rearranged the living room, placing couches all around the periphery, and mattresses on the floors. We covered the mattresses with a thick green satin carpet and scattered giant silk pillows everywhere. The girls made curtains out of satin and bought imported porcelain containers to hold zuzus and candles. They also purchased a filigreed waist-high hookah pipe, a Persian incense burner, and a golden hand-engraved goblet to hold our stash of hash and Colombian weed. After a week of "tuning," everyone was ready. Only Tex and T.J. and Cappy were absent. They'd gone north to bring back the bus.

My own feelings vis-à-vis Charlie and the Family on the eve of that trip had stabilized considerably. My bond to Charlie was strong. The pressures which had mounted following the first two months at Spahn's had been relieved by the trip north. I felt cleansed again, more in control. Still, Charlie remained an enigma. I loved him as a pupil loves his master. I saw his beauty and his wisdom, yet I had also seen the demon and would never forget it—believing too, at times, that the demon was not only Charlie's but mine as well.

The night we ate the acid it was windy. I recall this distinctly, since just before we dropped I went outside to smoke under the stars. The ranch was quiet, no sounds of cars or horses or birds. Only the wind blowing the eucalyptus trees and the brush along the hillside above the ranch house. I smelled the smoke coming from the chimney and went back into the house.

The Family sat in a large circle around the table, dressed in their bright silk clothing; some were barefoot, some wore handmade slippers. Charlie was clad in a scarlet silk shirt and was seated to the left of the woodpile we'd stacked beside the fire. Next to him on one side was Squeaky, on the other, Kim, then Sadie, Katie, Mary, Ella, Stephanie, Gypsy, Leslie, Juan, Juanita, Clem, Brenda, Snake, and Ouisch. The smell of lavender incense permeated the air. Charlie looked like some Eastern guru surrounded by his disciples. He smiled as I entered, then signaled for me to close the doors to the rest of the rooms. I did so, then sat down between Brenda and Snake while Charlie started rapping about karma and how you can make any kind of trip you want, so long as you listen to your love, do what your love says, and don't avoid it by running from fear. We sang a couple of songs; then I passed out the acid.

In the past, Charlie had generally taken less than the rest of us. He did this in order to maintain control and to orchestrate the scene. But that night, I'm sure he took the same dose as everyone else: two white double domes. We all dropped and within minutes started coming on. It was *very* strong acid. One tab would have been plenty.

I was strumming the sitar when the acid seemed to kick me in the face. I felt my cheeks flush, the skin tighten around my eyes. The notes from the sitar sounded like semitrucks rumbling through the center of the room. I glanced at Charlie; so did the others. We all saw the uncertainty in his eyes. He knew we were all in for a rough one. He asked Squeaky to get him a glass of soda water; she did, and he drank it down. But the look didn't leave his face, and it affected the entire group. Squeaky clung to Charlie's arm and tried to rest her head against him.

"What are you doing?"

"I'm hanging on to you."

Charlie shook his head, then after a long silence said, "No, I'm hanging on to *you.*"

As he said this I sensed the deeper implications of the remark. So did Squeaky. Charlie was being honest. He *was* clinging to Squeaky. She was virtually his number-one girl; she'd been with him from the beginning. No one spouted his rap better than she did; no one was more committed to him. She not only took care of George, but because of her rank with Charlie, she was inspirational to the rest of the girls. No one made love to Squeaky but Charlie. Charlie did need her. He *did* cling to her, even though clinging to anyone was against everything he preached. But at that moment, it became all too clear, at least to me (and to Squeaky)—Charlie was telling the truth. He *was* hanging on.

Squeaky freaked out. *"No, no!"* she insisted. *"I'm hanging on to you!"* Then she started flailing with both arms. Charlie grabbed her.

"No . . . no Charlie!" she screamed. *"It's not true,"* she bleated.

"Yes it is," he insisted.

She rolled into the woodpile and started kicking. *"Charlie . . . Charlie! It's not so!"*

Charlie watched for a moment before kneeling beside me. "Look, man . . . you watch her . . . whatever she does is on account of me." With that he changed his clothes and left the house. Everyone sat there in a state of psychedelic shock.

"Charlie . . . Charlie," they wailed. *"Where's Charlie?"*

I didn't have time to ponder. Lynn was cutting herself on the woodpile. Her arms and legs were gashed and bleeding by the time I pulled her away and got on top of her.

"Charlie! . . . No."

"It's okay, Lynn, quit fighting. . . . *Relax!"* I pushed her shoulders down. Her eyes were wide, the pupils dilated with hysteria. She looked into my eyes and started making strange faces—contorting her mouth in an almost demonic way. Unconsciously I responded by making the faces back at her; it was an instinctive action, yet it seemed to calm her down. Every nuance of expression in her face seemed to register in mine (I felt it), until we were flashing expressions in some kind of bizarre facial language. Gradually the spasms subsided. I relaxed my grip, trying to soothe her. "It's okay, Lynn . . . nice and easy . . . that's it." Then, without warning, she freaked out again, arching her back and kicking; deep guttural sounds emanated from her throat, sounds that were completely unintelligible. I muscled her down again and responded by making similar sounds, and once more we fell into a pattern of communication. Then her lower body began shaking—quivering in abrupt, spastic convulsions; her legs twitched and flopped on the floor as though charged with electricity. I was exhausted; it took all my strength to keep her down. I was ready to let go when her foot struck Kim, who was lying beside us, sending a visible current of energy into his body. He began to twitch and convulse.

Then he leaped up and raced into the bathroom. I heard a horrendous wrenching sound and the shattering of glass followed by the flow of splashing water. Kim had pulled the sink out of the wall and had smashed the mirror. Moments later he raced into the living room screaming at the top of his lungs, *"I'm the devil. . . . I'm the devil!"* I watched in horror as he crashed headlong through the front window and out onto the porch in a shower of glass. Everyone began screaming at once: *"Charlie . . . Charlie . . . where's Charlie?"*

By that time Lynn had wriggled away and was again thrashing in the woodpile; her clothes were half-torn from her body; her face and limbs were streaked with blood. But I just couldn't hold her any longer. Looking into her face had triggered my own reactive bank of subconscious impulses. I sat back and watched dumbly as she finally subsided in a quivering heap and began babbling to herself: "Charlie . . . Charlie."

Then Kim came sailing through the window again and landed spread-eagled on the floor. He got up at once and began ripping the tapestries from the walls and smashing glass out of the remaining windows with the heel of his hand. Sadie, meanwhile, had rushed into the bedroom to protect Zezos and Pooh Bear. "Get out! *Get out of here!"* I heard her scream as Kim stormed into the room. I started for the bedroom as Kim bolted out again, still screaming, *"Charlie. . . . I'm the devil . . . I'm the devil!"* I grabbed at him, but he tore free, then dove headlong into the fireplace.

"Jesus, Kim!" I raced over, jerked him out of the fire, and rolled him onto the rug. His eyes were wild— bald white and webbed with lines of blood. *"I'm the devil . . . the devil . . ."* he jibbered.

Hot coals burned on the rug; I glanced at Snake and she brought some water from the kitchen to douse the coals. She seemed the only sane person in the room. Suddenly Kim lurched away again and dove into the fire. Everyone around us was shrieking and freaking out. I yanked Kim out a second time and wrestled with him on the floor. *"Charlie. . . . Charlie . . . I'm the devil!"* It took all my strength to keep him pinned, and when I moved momentarily to give Snake room to get by, Kim broke away a third time and plunged into the flames.

It was then that everything seemed to slow down: time became elastic and incalculable. I looked at Kim in the fire and saw all around his body—conforming to every contour—a glowing force field—an aura. It had occurred to me in flashes while struggling with him earlier that he was *not* getting cut or burned! Not even his hair was singed. His body was totally protected by this force field.

For what seemed like an eternity I watched him lying in the fire, the flames spitting and flickering up around him. His legs were drawn up to his stomach, his body immersed in smoke. When I finally reached in and pulled him out, I saw that the force field had protected my hands. They were unmarked. As Kim lay on the floor, his frenzy subsiding, I obeyed an impulse and reached into the fire and withdrew a small handful of glowing coals. I gazed at them lying in my hands. They felt almost weightless, like a handful of dry cotton. I experienced sensation but no pain. Then a thought jolted me: "You idiot, you just burned the shit out of your hands!" As this notion claimed my mind, I could see the force field starting to change shape, I could see blisters forming, not on my hand, but on the aura itself, as though the blisters were working their way to the skin. As soon as I dismissed the thought, the aura returned to its original, miragelike shape. I tossed the coals back onto the fire as Charlie appeared in the doorway.

"Cool it . . . cool it. The cops are coming!"

Instantly all kinds of things raced through my head. I knew I was in charge. I thought of orders to give: "Hide the dope . . . grab your clothes . . . head for the trees." But each command, as I spoke it, became a question: What dope? We'd kicked over the table and scattered the contents all over the room; what clothes? They were ripped to shreds. If we ran for the trees, we might get shot. Then it occurred to me that I hadn't spoken any of these words, and that if we were arrested we'd be sent, not to jail, but to a mental ward. When I looked up, Charlie was gone and I knew that there were no cops, that he'd yelled in an attempt to restore some order. I found myself, suddenly, with my hand around my cock, muttering, "Can't we just make love?"

All around me people were going berserk. *"Charlie . . . Charlie . . . Where did Charlie go?"* Some of them were pummeling each other; others were throwing pillows; some were scratching and flailing on the floor like epileptics. It was complete and utter insanity.

"Charlie! Charlie!" the refrain rang out.

The words reverberated in my head. *"Charlie . . . Charlie."* Yet *I* had been responsible for the scene. *I* had struggled to keep it from running completely amok. *"Charlie . . . Charlie."* Pretty soon the name sounded absolutely foreign to my ears, like something from another language. "Charlie?" I muttered. "Charlie? Who in the hell is Charlie?" I flashed on the words: "All is one; I am you and you are me." Then, it struck me that no one else was standing; no one else even seemed real. "I'm Charlie . . ." I blurted. "I am Charlie."

The next thing I remember was slumping to the floor beside Snake. She'd put out the fires and had pulled Kim onto the couch. We sat with our backs against the couch, staring straight ahead. Stephanie and Ella were watching the fire. Clem was in one corner, his eyes half-closed, fingering the sitar. There were bodies everywhere. With so much commotion I hadn't really focused on my own mental processes. Yet, the instant I sat beside Snake, my mind began spinning like a projection reel: I saw countless past lives. I don't know if it was triggered by Kim's diving into the fire, but what I visualized was an eternity of death scenes: people expiring—in fires, battles, countless wars. I saw limbs being lopped off, heads falling from the chopping block; I saw shootouts, drownings, collisions—all manner of death. For a time it seemed purely sadistic; watching such carnage was no different from seeing the wind rustle the leaves; it was almost pleasurable. I watched it and it was all right. I watched it through the eyes of a cosmic and tranquil indifference. Yet, I was watching myself; these people were me in past lives, or perhaps all men in all lifetimes. With these scenes came the realization that the spirit feels no pain, that these deaths (as Charlie had said) were experiences in sensation—a form of transition. The spirit *didn't* die. Later I would attribute it all to the raps on ego-death—and letting go, which is what I did as I witnessed this slide show of lifetimes.

Moments later I was seeing myself again, this time as a man in prison. Charlie had always rapped about the joint, what he'd learned there, what it was like. I realized that I had lived many lives as a prisoner. I saw myself in prisons and dungeons of all kinds; some made of concrete and steel, some dry, some damp; some in the mountains, others by the sea. But inside they were all the same—dark, oppressive, and somehow terminal. All this I viewed with Snake beside me. Once, in the midst of it, I saw her reach for a cigarette. By the time she had it in her mouth, seconds later, I had lived out several episodes as a soldier. I'd seen myself in hand-to-hand combat with enemies of all colors and sizes, some on foot, some on horseback. Snake lit her cigarette and blew out the match. I put my head in her lap and closed my eyes. But I did not stop seeing this eternal story in my mind's eye —the odyssey and the inferno. It was endless and it was painless. Yet, paradoxically, I felt it deeply.

At one point, hours later perhaps, I sensed myself returning to the void. I saw the void for what it was—"a hole in the infinite." I saw it from all directions at once. I became total consciousness, experiencing perfect peace and absolute substance. The void was everything, yet it was nothing. It was solid, yet it was completely clear and open. It was the resolution of all paradoxes—boredom and exhilaration. It gave meaning to evolution, proved the wisdom of the inner quest. It revealed that self-awareness was meaningful only in terms of the struggle to attain it. The *process* was to be savored. Wisdom is never absolute except in the void. Life lies in its fluidity, in the process of change; suffering and joy; in an experience of the elements.

It was near dawn and the light of the new day was on the horizon. I sat beside Snake. Around us were ten others, an aftermath of survivors. I looked at them all: Snake, Brenda, Gypsy, Ella, Katie, Sadie, Leslie, Squeaky, Kim, Stephanie. I saw in their faces the essence of humanity. I saw perfection. Each face was a masterpiece, sculptured in flesh and bone. I saw them as children. I saw them as devils. Their ears seemed slightly pointed, their smiles twisted into beatific yet demonic lines which portended the gamut of human feeling and expression. I saw life and death, the paradox of the void. I saw in their eyes compassion, love, and the inscrutable indifference of the cosmos. It was as if we all sat perched on the highest peak of awareness and could fall from there into light on one side, and into darkness on the other. But at that moment, from the summit, we reflected perfection—all elements of our humanness and spirituality.

It must have been around ten o'clock when Snake brought me a cup of coffee and I walked to the window and saw Charlie outside asleep under a eucalyptus tree.

10

The freak-out changed my relationship to Charlie once again, though its impact, at the time, was more unconscious than conscious. While Charlie blamed the Family and the "uptight" vibes at the ranch for the craziness which erupted, claiming that he had no need to go through such "insanity" just because we did (thereby justifying his own quick and convenient departure), it was clear that he had failed to confront his own uncertainties and fears. He had violated his cardinal rule: "No one splits during an acid trip." In the meantime, I had unwittingly assumed leadership, moving from a role of passive submission to one of self-assertion. Both the choking scene and the freak-out were experiences I had learned from. I owed that to Charlie, or at least I believed I did. Charlie, on the other hand, had grown increasingly more frustrated, first because the Family scene was not coming together as he envisioned, and second because of his failure to sell his music. He was divided within himself; on the one hand he wanted a spiritual, communal life with the Family, with "nothing to do but make love." On the other hand, he sought success as a commercial entertainer, and wanted to influence the world with his music. We all believed the trip to the desert would resolve things. Charlie urged us to psych up for the desert. We did; most of us, anyway. All but Kim. For Kim the freak-out proved a violent and impassioned swan song. Shortly thereafter, he left the Family. Two days after his departure, the bus returned from San Jose and we began preparing for the journey.

After completely rebuilding the engine, we bought new heavy-duty batteries, rewired the electrical system, and rigged up large adjustable outside mirrors. We loaded the cabinets with spare parts, tools, and an abundance of dried foods. The girls redecorated the interior, painting the dashboard and replacing the curtains. As we worked, Charlie's mood became buoyant. Cappy had described her grandmother's ranch as a veritable paradise of orchards, vineyards, and magical beauty, a place where we might realize our spiritual goals and truly come together. Soon, everyone was sharing Charlie's enthusiasm. When word got out that we were leaving, the wranglers began coming around to inspect what we'd done to the bus. Benny shuffled in one afternoon, sipping some Jack Daniels: "Looks like a friggin' whorehouse," he quipped, removing his hat. "Cops are gonna shit if they pull you over and peek in here." He had a point; the interior was lavish to the extreme: a two-room salon with plush carpets, pillows, satin curtains, a low-hanging tassel-studded headliner, a gas stove, and a new refrigerator. We were ready.

On the afternoon of October 31, 1968, I observed Charlie sitting on the hillside above the ranch, smoking a cigarette. I waved at him and he waved back. Minutes later—it must have been about four P.M.—he came down from the hill and sauntered into the ranch house, grinning. "Let's git on out of here!" In less than an hour everything was packed and loaded: mattresses, blankets, clothes, musical instruments, food supplies, five cases of zuzus, a kilo of grass, and fifty tabs of acid. We all boarded the bus and Charlie fired up the engine. Tex cheered. "Listen to that baby hum!" Charlie cackled, and gave him a thumbs-up sign. Then he drove down the back road to the saloon and honked the horn. Squeaky and Juanita came running out and waved to us: we all waved

back. They were to remain behind to keep an eye on
George and the ranch.

Charlie headed along the boardwalk, honking at
Randy Star, who was ambling across the road carrying a
saddle. "Keep a tight asshole, cowboy," Charlie shouted
out the window. If Randy heard him, he didn't let on. We
swerved to the left and bounced on down the rutted
driveway along the corral gate toward Santa Susana Pass.
That's when I spotted a jack-o'-lantern perched on top of
a fencepost and realized it was Halloween.

We camped the first night in a canyon somewhere
in San Bernardino County, near the Cajon Pass. The following morning we took off at sunup drivin' north on
highway 395. The girls brewed coffee and served it
with sweet rolls and doughnuts. The sun was bright and
the air began to clear as we drove deeper into the desert.
The expansiveness of the terrain after so long in L.A.
was a real rush. I sat up front beside Charlie, who was
driving and smoking a cigarette. His hair was long and
disheveled, hanging across his shoulders in twisted
strands as he hunched over the wheel. He was ebullient as
Snake handed him a steaming cup of coffee.

He took a sip. "Out here," he said, swallowing, "we
got breathing room . . . it's alive. The sun can get to you
and there ain't no hassles with cowboy motherfuckers and
city rats. Look beyond that ridge . . . the way those
clouds are . . . looks like Malibu surf," he enthused.
"Yeah, here it's breathin', man; here our music can
breathe and our love can breathe, you dig it? . . . Hey,
Paul, we should have come to the desert a long time
ago."

When we got to Ridgecrest we turned west along
the Argus Mountain Range to Trona, then down into the
Panamint Valley: everyone was at the windows surveying the majesty of the landscape. The Panamints, eleven
thousand feet in some places, towered above the valley
floor like craggy prehistoric beasts. The sun blazed off
the land; heat waves slithered along its surface. I could
make out the timberline of piñon pine on the lofty face of
the range. An incredible panorama. Gnarled fingers of
basalt and granite seemed to cling to the valley floor,
claws of sediment clutching at us as we droned through

the vast immensity, singing songs and munching zuzus. Cappy had come up front to sit by Charlie and me to point out landmarks.

Catherine Gilles was seventeen, and slightly overweight, with a cute pixielike face and short flaxen hair. From the very beginning, she exhibited a strong commitment to the Family scene. Charlie liked her. In time, she would become one of Charlie's most capable and sequacious followers—even after he was convicted of the murders.

"What exactly did you tell your grandmother?" Charlie wanted to know.

"I just said me and some friends were going to come up and stay at the ranch."

"But you didn't say how many, right?"

"I just said some girls and me, mostly."

"What if she gets nosy and sends someone up to check?"

"She won't."

"Any other places up there?"

"There's the Barker ranch."

"What's the story on that?"

"I don't think anyone's there. . . . I'm not sure."

"It doesn't matter . . . we'll check it out. Hey"— Charlie grinned, putting his arm around Cappy—"this is God's country out here, you know it."

Cappy beamed.

"Hey, Paul, why don't you sing that song of yours about the crazy women in Peru. You know . . ."

Juan snapped his fingers. "Yes, I like dat song bery moch too."

Clem tossed me the guitar. Everyone clapped. Glancing at their faces, it was hard to imagine the freakout ever happened. Sadie sat near the rear of the bus nursing Zezos; Pooh Bear was asleep. Juan lay sprawled out on the floor, a languorous grin on his face, his stetson pulled over his eyes, a toothpick dangling from his mouth. The others sat huddled together beneath the satin canopy: Clem, Brooks, T.J., Ella, Stephanie, Ouisch, Bo, Juanita, Katie, Sandy, Brenda, Snake, and Tex. The windows were down; the heat was stifling. I took a sip of water from a canteen behind the seat, then sang the song. It was a song written by a high-school friend,

Rabbit McKie, one we'd sung together often before dropping out of school.

> *I am just a stranger here/ I come from down the*
> *road*
> *I did not come to ask you all to help me share*
> *my load*
> *I came to sing my songs for you*
> *And to tell you where I've been*
> *And maybe share a little time before I'm gone*
> *again*
>
> *I was born in California at a very early age*
> *My mother she was beautiful/ my father worked*
> *the stage*
> *But I could not seem to go along with all they*
> *had in mind*
> *So at the tender age of fourteen years, I left their*
> *house behind*
>
> *Oh, I was free to put to sea and it was nineteen*
> *and sixty-two*
> *So I went down a-fishin' tuna in the waters of*
> *Peru*
> *Oh, the sun it was so hot down there, it drove the*
> *women all insane*
> *And soon the salt of the seven seas was flowin'*
> *in my veins*
>
> *Now, I've seen the wall in Germany and I've felt*
> *it in the South*
> *And I've heard it said that freedom is just a ram-*
> *blin' at the mouth*
> *Yes, your masterminds and their dividin' lines,*
> *why they're just a passin' trend*
> *'Cause freedom is a song of spirit, written on the*
> *wind. . . .*

It was late afternoon by the time we drove through Ballarat—a one-store outpost in the middle of the valley floor. From there we proceeded south, deeper into the valley toward Golar Canyon, where we would begin our ascent to the Meyers place. Once out onto the alluvial fan, we started a gradual climb toward the base of the wash. The road was strewn with loose rock and in places was scarcely visible. Juan, Ouisch, Sandy, Snake, and Charlie climbed up on the front fenders while T.J. drove. Everyone was singing and drinking soda pop we'd purchased at Ballarat. The valley was incredible—silent and timeless—with nothing around us but the towering monolithic walls of the canyon and an endless expanse of desert. I sat in the back. The bus weaved and swayed; the gold tassels hanging from the headliner danced and reflected in the sunlight. Suddenly our vehicle seemed strangely appropriate for this desert pilgrimage, like riding on the back of a camel. I looked out the rear window at the rock formations, stark against the flat terrain. Joshua trees and mesquite grew in clumps along the base of the mountain; to the left the salt flats were interspersed with poppies, choya, and desert holly. From time to time something alive scurried across the road: a jackrabbit, a kangaroo mouse, and once an animal that looked like a cross between a raccoon and a squirrel. Cappy called it a ringtail cat.

Finally, we arrived at a plateau at the base of the canyon and parked beside the remains of an old ranch house. Only the foundations were visible. On the ground, scattered amidst the decomposition, were rotted jeep tires, hubcaps, scraps of bleached canvas, and several whiskey bottles.

"I don't think we better take the bus up Golar," Cappy said, standing beside Charlie. "It's too rocky."

"Yeah, looks like one mean-ass drive," Charlie concurred, gazing up the wash. "We'll park here and hike in. How long's it take to get up there?"

"Two hours, maybe three . . . if it doesn't get dark on us."

So the first of many treks up Golar Canyon began. Sadie and Mary carried their infants strapped to their backs. The rest of us grabbed armfuls of supplies—bedding, food, jugs of water, and packs—and started up the wash. A wind from the south had put a chill in the air and the sun was setting. Directly overhead, the clouds had elongated and turned crimson, appearing like disjointed entrails squeezed from the bowels of the sky. Within an hour it was downright cold, and we all put on jackets and sweaters. I was hiking alongside Clem and Snake, with Cappy just in front of us. The others followed, scattered

along the trail, some as far as a mile back. Halfway up,
the canyon widened out, becoming green with clusters of
mesquite. We filled canteens at a deserted one-room
shack Cappy called "the halfway house," then hiked beyond it onto the sloping flatlands where springs flowed
in from the surrounding hillsides. The rock formations became less severe, more rounded. In the distance the
mountains looked like scoops of melting ice cream. We
shouted down the canyon at the others, and they shouted
back.

At the top of the wash, we proceeded along a narrow road behind Cappy. She pointed out the Barker ranch
off to the right—a low-slung dwelling secluded behind a
stand of windblown cottonwoods and fronted by a grape
vineyard. But we didn't stop to check it out; instead, we
trudged another quarter mile to the Meyers ranch. Cappy had not exaggerated; the surrounding property was
lush with vegetation: salt cedar, tamarisk, fig, cotton-
wood, willow, and apple trees, and behind the house, a
rolling expanse of vineyards and wildflowers. The ranch
house itself was small and unpretentious, with a fair-sized
living room (fifteen by thirty), a fireplace, two small bedrooms, a tiny kitchen, and an outdoor bathroom just off
the back porch. The foundations of the house were made
of narrow-gauge railroad ties, taken years before from a
defunct Epsom-salts mine, then plastered over with stucco. It was a rustic, cozy little place and we moved right
in and built a fire before gathering around to eat zuzus
and canned fruit cocktail. By nine P.M. everyone was
asleep.

The following morning we were all up at dawn. The
girls made hotcakes and a huge vat of coffee and we sat
around the fire eating, while Charlie divided us into
scouting parties. All morning we hiked the roads and
trails through the mountains above the property. I went
with Clem, Sadie, and Snake. Around noon we hiked to a
promontory which towered over the ranch, and from
which, to our right, we could look out upon the floor of
Death Valley. To the right, the landscape fell away to
the expansive bleached white salt flats of the Amargosa
Valley. We could see the threadlike road to Shoshone and
Tecopa, and beyond it, the highway to Las Vegas; the
Great American Desert—three hundred and sixty de-

grees of tortured, tumultuous, serene, and undisputed wilderness. We couldn't have chosen a more scenic and strategic location.

Death Valley is starkly surrealistic. Ideas that would have seemed utterly inconceivable to me in West Los Angeles were perfectly understandable on a crystal-clear morning from the peaks of the Panamint Mountains. The desert is a ready-made acid trip. Perhaps for that reason the greatest visions of Indians and holy men have taken place on the desert. There has always been magic in the desert, and a good deal of myth surrounding the ambience of Death Valley. It has been called the hottest place on earth, devoid of animal life, vegetation, and water. Salt-infested pools and deadly gases, it has been said, fill the sand pockets of the valley, together with quicksands that lie across the bottomless salt marshes. Mules, it was once claimed, were the only beasts who could withstand the infernal heat. Not true. There was always life in Death Valley—animal life, vegetation, and human life. As a Family we came there looking for that life, an elemental life with which we had begun to lose contact.

Death Valley actually forms but one part of the Great Basin of the Great American Desert—an incredible arid trough spread over thousands of square miles. There are thousands of streams within the basin, but not one of them ever reaches the sea. The valley itself is actually the sink of the Amargosa River; most of it is below sea level. This is the land where the rivers are upside down, with stream beds on top and water beneath the sand and gravel. This phenomenon always perplexed Charlie, who, from the time we arrived, began speaking of "a hole" in the desert which would lead us to water, perhaps even a lake and a place to live. I remember days, after we'd been in the desert several months, when Charlie and I would walk the valley floor, along the borax flats, dry lakes, alkali washes, and salt sinks, looking for the "hole" —a subterranean world, a cave, a place where we might take the Family and make our home when "the shit came down." The idea of a "hole" was by no means a completely crazy one, since all water which flows into the valley, only to emerge elsewhere (as springs) out of pure bedrock, must go someplace. The entire mystique of sub-terranean worlds, infinite space, "magical mystery tours," "I am you and you are me," "No sense makes sense," and so on, was much more palatable in the desert am-bience. The cosmic vacuum of the desert was a perfect place to program young minds.

Shortly after noon that first day, everyone gathered at the top of Golar Canyon at the Barker ranch. Barker's, though less spacious than the Meyers place, was also built in the midst of dense, oasislike vegetation; at the time we arrived, it was in a general state of disrepair and the vineyards had all gone to seed—growing in a tangle around the house and up the latticework along the walls. It had a small living room, a bedroom, a bathroom, and a good-sized kitchen. It did not have a fireplace or electricity and relied on heat from a custom-made oil-drum stove, complete with small burners and an oven. Off to the right of the main ranch house was a bunkhouse made of railroad ties, which reminded me of the outlaw shacks at Spahn's. In general, the Barker place was funk-ier, more weatherbeaten, and somehow more conducive to the scene we had going. The place was completely de-serted except for an amiable, bowlegged desert rat and onetime prospector named Ballarat Bob, who sometimes slept there while wandering around the Panamints.

Charlie was still paranoid about staying at the Mey-ers place with so many people, particularly since Cappy's grandmother was under the impression they were all girls. When he asked old Bob if he thought we might move into the Barker place, the old geezer said he thought so, but that it might be a good idea, "jes' for the record," to speak with the owner, Ma Barker, who lived down the valley at Indian Springs. Charlie agreed, and the next morning he and I hiked back down the wash and drove to Indian Springs to talk to Ma Barker.

We found her easily enough in a small, weather-tight cabin surrounded by a flaccid chain-link fence. She lived alone most of the time and that morning was seated on her front porch dozing with a newspaper in her lap. Charlie wasted no time in laying his rap on the gray-haired, grizzled old gal.

"It's like Paul and me are musicians . . . you know, we done some music with the Beach Boys—and now we need solitude to do our music, get our own gig together. Up there on that mountain at your ranch . . . well, it's about as pretty a place to compose music as I've ever seen . . . right, Paul? And if we get lucky and sell some stuff, who knows, we might all get rich."

The old woman nodded, rocking back and forth in her chair, her eyes half-closed; a scrawny Siamese cat purred at her feet. Like George Spahn, she looked listless and torpid, but she hadn't missed a thing. She said she was more than willing to let us stay at the ranch so long as we kept her place in order and "fixed what needed fixin'."

"Why sure," she said as we were leaving. "That's fine . . . you just take care of my property and do some good songs . . . that'll be fine."

Charlie thanked her again and gave her a Beach Boys' gold record; then we split back down the Panamint Valley, stopping at Ballarat to buy soda pop.

During Charlie's rap with Ma Barker, I'd picked up the Las Vegas paper and had noted a reference to a racial incident in Haight Ashbury. The article stated that a San Francisco policeman had recently shot and killed a sixteen-year-old black kid who had allegedly pulled a gun on him. I took notice of the story only because the location of the shooting, just off Fillmore, was one block away from a place I had crashed at in the summer of 1967.

I mentioned the article to Charlie as we drove through the valley toward Golar Wash drinking our pop.

"Dig it, man," Charlie said, gesturing with one hand while steering the bus with the other. "This shit can't go on forever with blackie . . . pretty soon he's gonna revolt and start kickin' whitey's ass. I've seen it buildin' up for years. It was bad enough at Watts and San Francisco, but now that they wasted that jive-ass Martin Luther . . . well, that's a heavy number, man. I mean, you gotta figure whitey's karma's gotta turn one of these days . . . it's just a matter of time. The heavy dudes, though, are the Muslims. I've seen those cats in jail. They sit back real stoic like and watch and stay cool, you know. But they'll be the ones who bring the shit down. Yeah, it's gonna come down hard . . . a full-on war. And when it does, we're gonna be glad we're out here.

"The trouble with blackie is, he wants to fuck all the

white women . . . turn all the white babies brown." Charlie jettisoned the empty can out the window. "That brings a lot of shit his way. I mean, it was never meant that the races get mixed; that's what fucks everything up. That's what makes whitey mad. But it won't do any good, 'cause it's blackie's turn. His day, you know. Hey man, we don't want any part of that. It would destroy our whole scene."

I didn't pay too much attention to Charlie's racial rap; it sounded pretty farfetched. I knew he didn't like blacks. But with the exception of an occasional offhand slur or an old prison joke, he never really said much about "blackie." I never dreamed that in time the notion of a racial war between "blackie" and "whitey" would become the core of Helter-Skelter.

It was dark by the time we got back to Golar Canyon, parked the bus, and started our hike up to the ranch.

11

Death Valley marked a turning point for the Manson Family. It is not easy to make sense of what happened there. I can only describe my own experience of it. But I do believe that coming to the desert stamped the fate of the Family, and subsequently, the fate of its victims.

After living on the fringes of suburban Los Angeles, the solitude was a welcome change. The great expansiveness of the desert, honed by the silence, deepened the rapport we shared as a Family and also sharpened individual awareness. Within the magnitude of miraculous skies and limitless vistas, I felt closer to myself. Nearly every day I climbed the mountain above the ranch before dawn to watch the sunrise beyond the Amargosa range. I took a small thermos of coffee and something to nibble on, a doughnut or a piece of toast. Usually I had no more than sat down when the sun would appear like a great splintered gem blazing against the pinnacles and minarets of the Panamints.

In the beginning, life at Barker's strengthened our bond. We played nightly and our music got better. We began teaching the girls to sing harmony. Though Charlie was always the lead vocalist, everyone got involved in the music. Brooks and Clem played the guitar. When Bobby was around, he played too and sang background. I alternated, playing the horn and the flute. We spent hours practicing—refining old songs, writing new ones, rearranging medleys. Some of my fondest memories are of afternoons we spent under the cottonwoods surrounded by the mountains, singing—a natural cathedral, sculptured out of granite and sandstone. Nothing brings people closer together than their own voices in song. And our music, at least for a while, was good. Charlie was certain we would eventually be recorded by a major record company and that our songs, like those of the Beatles—the soul—would be an inspiration to what he called "the young love," the youth of America.

When we weren't singing or working around the ranch, we took small expeditions into the mountains and down the ravines, exploring the interminable maze of grottoes, fissures, passageways, and deep winding canyons. At night we often hiked up to the Meyers ranch and built a fire before gathering around to listen to Charlie rap. More and more he preached that there were no leaders, no rules, that all we needed was to submit to the cosmic vibrations around us.

"Out here, we are free. We've come to the void to listen to it speak. Now, we have to listen. There ain't no obstruction . . . nothing to lean on or hang onto. We got our music and our love and we just listen to that." Charlie usually sat in front of the fire with his legs crossed in front of him. He was often clad in Levi's, a plaid shirt, and heavy wool socks, his hair invariably curling around his head in tiny ringlets.

"Here, we have no leaders," he said. "I'm not the leader . . . how can I be the leader when I have to wipe your asses and get you a blanket? The leader is the slowest one among us . . . the slowest is always the leader 'cause we have to wait for him . . . he sets the pace. Pooh Bear and Zezos are the leaders, dig, 'cause they got us waiting on them . . . and that's the way it should be, for now, 'cause they can teach us . . . they can teach us not to think and to do what we feel and be on the point of what love is."

During the first month, we all felt good. Somehow the very act of coming to the desert as a Family was proof of a certain destiny. There was a genuine grandeur about it which gave us a sense of our own grandeur. It seemed that all our preparation and programming had been for a reason. We saw the desert as a reward; it was like coming to a new land, a new planet. It seemed inevitable. And somehow it validated Charlie even more. Like many spiritual leaders, he had led his followers to the desert. It seemed *right*. We had been through some of the heaviest group-therapy sessions imaginable; we had worked for months at "submitting," "letting go," shedding our egos. It had not been easy. These sessions continued in Death Valley, where the atmosphere was even more intense than at Spahn's. At Barker's we had little outside influence—no tourists, no wranglers, no machines. With infinity so close at hand, it was easier to give yourself. "Submit to the love," Charlie said. It was an alternative we didn't have to ponder. Certainly what we had come from as children was not all love—it was confusion, greed, pollution, and media programming; it was mass follow-the-leader since grade one; it was (and in most respects still is) mechanized, impersonal, decadent, spiritually impoverished. But we had come to the desert with Charlie. We had prepared, and it had come to pass. A Family of twenty-five, most of us from greater Los Angeles, products of the middle or upper middle class, sons and daughters of well-to-do and respected "pillars" of the American nightmare—twenty-five survivors from the bowels of the inferno, standing before a battered, twisted, high-powered ex-convict under the scorching sun of a timeless desert, looking for love. It was insane; yet, it was a fact: "no sense made sense." Certainly I had doubts; we all did. But man always feels doubt. In the face of the cosmos and his own glaring imperfections, what else can he feel?

Our initial euphoria, however, was short-lived. Gradually, things on a spiritual level began to degenerate. The group sex sessions became more strained and self-conscious. The very fact of being in the desert, where we anticipated such good results, made it worse. We all wanted so much to "make it" that we created further anxiety. Brooks, for example, just couldn't function. At Spahn's he could always go down to the corral, and his absence wasn't conspicuous. But at Barker's there was nowhere to hide; he had to take part in the sessions. It made him so overwrought at times that he'd roll up into a fetal position and just lie there quivering.

One morning he and I were standing by the woodpile talking. I was about to reply to a question he'd asked when suddenly his eyes rolled back in his head and his body stiffened. Seconds later he dropped, facedown and rigid, like a felled timber, striking his forehead against a log. Blood gushed from the wound, and Brooks didn't utter a sound. I thought for an instant that he might have put his lights out for good; but he finally managed to stagger to his feet and within a couple of hours was back at work chopping wood.

"Letting go of the ego" to Brooks was literally like dying; perhaps on an unconscious level, being in "Death" Valley made this death wish even stronger. Since there was no shit to shovel at Barker's, he assumed another "discontent" chore—chopping wood. From the day we arrived till the day we left, he was always at the woodpile chopping and stacking logs.

Another problem was supplies. It soon became apparent that with so many people to feed, it was hard to keep enough food on hand. Charlie was continually sending contingents to Las Vegas or L.A. to buy supplies and to bring back vehicles. Two days after our arrival, we sent someone down to bring back Juanita's camper. The following week, Bobby Beausoleil showed up with a girlfriend called Sweet Cindy. Each drove a run-down Dodge power wagon, donations to the Family. By the end of the first month we had four vehicles: the bus, Juanita's van (which we soon traded for a four-wheel-drive Jeep Scout), and the two power wagons. With so many expeditions to and from Barker's, we needed all the transportation we could get.

While everyone professed to love the desert (partly to please Charlie), it became clear that many were getting bored. Even Charlie seemed listless and irritable, and contented himself much of the time with lounging about in a hammock he had strung up behind the ranch house. In retrospect, I see it as a time of profound transformation. While Charlie appeared languid during the day, his nightly raps were invariably animated and inspired, their intensity augmented, it seemed, by the silence, the cold, and the intimacy we shared while huddled around the fire. Like everything, it was a paradox: in one sense Charlie became our source of entertainment. The longer we stayed in the desert, divorced from outside stimuli, the more convincing he became; the more we submitted. He had always preached the virtues of doing nothing. In time, we fell into a tempo of doing just that. A limbo.

We became as vacant as our surroundings. At night we sat around the fire watching him. There were moments when he seemed almost demonic, pacing like a caged predator before the flames, his hair long and scraggly, his eyes bright. Perhaps by submitting so totally we were trapping Charlie in a vacuum of his own creation. In the absence of everything, he became everything: wind, sand, sun, the cosmos itself. Yet, without feedback, he was completely alone.

He continued to proclaim the "beauty" of the Family; that we were all beautiful spiritually; that we had been guided to the desert to preserve that beauty and to strengthen ourselves for what was to come; there was a destiny at work which would see to it that our purpose was fulfilled. The desert, he said, would further purify our love and our bond, but at the same time would make us more vulnerable to evil. Society, he insisted, feared love and purity. "It's like that cat Billy Budd . . . he was beautiful but his love was too pure and they snuffed him."

If we were to survive the viciousness of the outside world and retain our purity, Charlie said we had to remain alert, stay hidden. I didn't really appreciate Charlie's application of this notion until one afternoon I hiked down Golar Canyon toward the halfway house and came upon Snake cowering beneath an outcropping of granite with her hands over her eyes and a feather in her hair. She looked up when she heard me approaching.

"Duck down, Paul!"

"What's going on, Snake?" I knelt beside her.

"They might see you," she said, pulling me toward her out of the light.

"Huh . . . who might?" I looked around, then at her. Her red hair was pulled over her face; she looked like a frightened child.

"The radar."

"What radar?"

She pointed to the sky. "If they find me, Charlie said they'd kill me . . . he said I was too beautiful and that they wouldn't let me live."

"Who's they?"

"The people."

It took me more than half an hour to coax her out of hiding and get her back up to the ranch. While the incident struck me as absurdly comical at the time, I realized that Snake was genuinely frightened. The next day she seemed in control once again, and I didn't think much of it. Snake was always a tough one, resilient both emotionally and physically. I figured Charlie was just bored and trying to amuse himself at her expense. But what was happening became clear to me in retrospect. Charlie was playing his games of fear manipulation, the same number he had tried to put on me. Once Charlie had instilled fear in someone, he devised a mechanism that triggered that individual's fear, then he used it to control that person and to titillate his own demonic power fantasies.

I saw even more dramatic evidence of this a short time later; this time with Squeaky. It happened one afternoon when Charlie and I took Brenda and Squeaky up to the Meyers ranch to make love before dinner. It was windy and the sand blew down the ravine and against the ranch house, sounding like rain. I was on one side of the fireplace with Brenda, and Charlie and Squeaky were a few feet away. They had just finished making love when Squeaky started to moan and convulse on the floor as if she were going into epileptic seizure. I flashed immediately on the freak-out scene at Spahn's when she had gone berserk in the woodpile. I was curious to see how Charlie would handle it.

"Charlie! Charlie!" she whimpered.

Charlie straddled her and grabbed her wrists. "Okay, Lynn . . ." he panted. "It's okay. Just tighten your fingers . . . if they want to tighten up like that, go on and tighten them . . . tight as you want . . . go on, tighten them good . . . yeah tighter tighter . . . come on, tight as you can."

Lynn's face was flushed and contorted, her breath came in short wheezing gasps, as she tightened her fists, still whimpering, her head thrashing from side to side.

"Okay now," he grunted, "just relax them . . . just a little . . . yeah."

The instant she began to relax, he told her to tighten them again. "Good. Now relax, tighten, relax. . . . Tighten . . . good, Lynn . . . relax, tighten."

By alternating commands he was gradually able to calm her down and work her out of the convulsions. Then he had her follow the motions he was making with his hands, until, finally, they both moved like one person. There is no doubt in my mind that Charlie had the knowledge to deprogram Lynn of that "condition." But he chose not to, preferring instead to maintain control over that mechanism, thus placing Squeaky in a position of complete dependence on him. Seeing this, I was later able to understand the desperation she had experienced during the freak-out when it became clear that Charlie (literally her savior) was in some respects more dependent on her than she was on him. I was also able to understand, for the first time, why no one but Charlie made love with Squeaky.

Two months passed. The games continued: games of concentration, submitting to the motion; letting go. I'd been in the Family half a year, and Charlie was still testing people's loyalties, manipulating their fears. Near the end of November he put me through another test.

It happened when Bobby Beausoleil came to the ranch with Sweet Cindy. Cindy was eighteen and extremely attractive, with reddish-blond hair and a curvaceous, compact body. Her large green eyes looked like a pair of Koh-i-noor diamonds. It was clear from the onset that she was not going for Charlie's rap. And this was unusual. Generally when Charlie laid his trip on a visitor, the person would wind up agreeing with him wholeheartedly (with twenty-five other people agreeing, it was hard to do otherwise). It got to be automatic; we'd all joke about how long it would take for the visitor "to fall into the hole," meaning to accept Charlie's trip without reservation. "Hole," in this case, meant "a hole in the infinite." It also had the connotation of "whole." Ironically, it had never occurred to us that falling into a hole could be considered a misfortune.

Cindy wanted to return to L.A. almost at once. But both power wagons needed repairs, and there were no other vehicles available. It was obvious that Bobby wanted to split too. Finally, Charlie got pissed off and said someone should walk them both to Ballarat, where they could catch a ride back to L.A. He looked at me, which meant I was to volunteer. It was nearly twenty-five miles to Ballarat from the ranch, and it was already late afternoon and getting cold. There was a pregnant silence while Charlie waited for my response. He knew I would go. My position in the Family was again being tested. Bobby and Cindy had no idea what we were in for. But I did; and so did Charlie.

The hike through Golar Canyon took about three hours. We reached the plateau at the foot of the wash and stopped to rest. It was dark—the night crisp, clear, and biting cold. Cindy pulled on a pair of wool mittens and zipped up her parka. Her hair was tucked inside a faded navy-blue sailor's cap. Bobby and I both wore army jackets and cowboy boots. But they didn't begin to keep out the cold.

"Jesus," he exclaimed, "it's freezing up here!"

"Yeah . . . yeah, it's a bitch," I concurred, trying to decide whether or not we should even try walking out. I looked at Cindy and she smiled. I could sense her relief to be on her way home.

"How far is it from here?" she chirped cheerily.

"A *long* way . . . let's get going."

We set out at a good pace, three abreast, along the valley floor, talking little to conserve our energy. The soberness of my attitude seemed to rub off. They knew we were not in for an easy time of it. A chilling wind banked off the canyon and funneled in at our backs. More stars appeared. It got colder, and gradually Cindy fell behind. We waited for her, then took off again, swinging our arms to keep the circulation active. Again she dropped behind and we waited.

"Come on, Cindy," I urged. "It's cold standing still . . . you have to keep up."

"Sorry," she gasped. "How much farther is it?"

"We just started." I gave them a swig of water and we proceeded.

Within twenty minutes Cindy was fifty yards behind us. Bobby was getting pissed off. We waited, leaning against a rock, beating our shoulders with our hands.

"Hurry it up, dammit!" he shouted when she came within hearing range.

"I have to rest," she panted. "God, I'm not used to this."

"Look," I said, "we'll slow it up and walk at your pace; the main thing is we stay together. How fast do you want to go?" We started off. "Come on, you set the pace, Cindy . . . and we'll stay together."

For the next two hours we maintained slow but steady time along the alluvial fan, our feet crunching against the scree-encrusted floor of the valley or sinking intermittently into the softer sand. We'd covered about a third of the distance when an ass-kicking wind boomed out of the canyon, flinging up sand and blotting out the sky. It was ice cold, howling like some demented being. We clung together with our arms across our faces and pushed on.

"I don't know how much farther I can go," Cindy whimpered.

"You'll make it," I told her.

A short time later she slumped to her knees. "I just have to rest. Can't we *please* rest? . . ." Bobby and I pulled her to her feet. Her teeth were chattering; her arms hung limply at her sides. I rubbed her arms, but my own hands were so numb I could hardly feel sensation in them.

"How fucking cold is it, you think?" Bobby marked time with his feet, keeping his head down to protect his eyes from the swirling sand.

"Come on, Cindy . . . you can make it . . . just keep. moving." I pushed her into motion. "Just one foot at a time . . . we'll get there."

We moved on. My hands and feet were completely numb. As we walked, I began to experience my own fatigue, and when Cindy again lagged behind, I gave up trying to hold onto her. Within an hour we had all separated and were walking single file—me, then Bobby, and finally Cindy. At a bend in the valley I turned around and looked behind me. I could barely make out Bobby's form against the desert floor. I lay down on a flat rock

to rest, putting my hands to my face. Then I sat up quickly and began clapping my hands together while kicking
one foot against the other. When the wind churned up
again, I lay down on the rock and closed my eyes.

For several minutes I lay there shivering, my flesh
icy, the rock digging into my body. Unconsciously I began muttering to myself. "This just isn't worth it. I might
as well just hang it up . . . let it go." The more I talked,
realizing it was a game I was playing with myself, the
more relaxed I became, the more I submitted to the
cold. "Submission is a gift. . . ." I chuckled to myself. The
rock seemed softer. My body began to warm up. It was
as though someone had opened me up and poured hot
honey-rum into my veins. I felt the presence of death
like a warm blissful whisper, as though the cold hard
night had turned into a caress. Charlie had rapped about
death being nothing more than "a release to love," and
that's how I felt. Yet, I was using that state to restore
my own energy. I knew I would not fall asleep. What
prompted me to move was the appearance of Bobby and
Cindy; instinctively and without a word I got to my feet
and we continued our trek to Ballarat. On the outskirts of
town we built a fire inside a deserted miner's shack and
watched the sun come up.

12

The subtlety of bizarre changes in the Family was
hard to determine, since everyone pretty much went
along with Charlie. Still, the focus and cohesiveness of
the scene had disintegrated. Most of the Family simply
weren't ready for the utter solitude at Barker's. Charlie's
own detachment was obvious.

One night during a rap, he paused in the middle of
a sentence and stared straight ahead, as though addressing a presence above our heads.

"I came to you," he said softly, his face wearing a
distracted expression, "as a deer in the forest. I came to

you with wonder in my eyes and love in my heart for you. For you were man and you were God and I could see it. I came to you with love. And you slaughtered me."

Though it didn't register consciously at the time, his statement was a prophetic one. It was the first sign that the flower child in Charlie Manson was dying, wilting away in Death Valley by day, freezing by night. Maybe the scorpion had returned to the valley of death where he belonged.

Then, all at once, things changed dramatically. Charlie returned from L.A. and a meeting with Dennis Wilson and Greg Jakobson to discuss the chance of our recording an album. He appeared agitated, yet enthusiastic. He said there was more violence in the city; that the blacks were on the verge of full-scale revolution. "It's just a matter of time," he declared. "The shit's gonna come down . . . it's gonna come down hard." What was different, however, was Charlie's attitude. Instead of advocating passive resistance, instead of seeking to remain aloof from the impending conflict, he began speaking of the Family's role in it.

"What we need to do is program the young love to split . . . when the scene comes down, they're gonna need someplace to go. Well, we got that place. We're here, and we can show the young love where to come. And we can show them with music."

Suddenly we were no longer "coming from nowhere and going nowhere," with "nothing to do but make love." Now we had a purpose. The timing was perfect. As things had started to fragment on one level, Charlie (perhaps unwittingly) had shifted gears, jolting us out of our passivity and indolence into an attitude of action. We had a responsibility to the real world. What we had worked to achieve at Spahn's—a level of psychic and spiritual freedom, a "oneness"—would be communicated to others. Since we had all tasted of city corruption and violence, we saw a virtue in leading "the young love" away from it. That's why we had come to the desert. The more Charlie talked about it, the more convincing it appeared.

I began flashing on the article about the cop who shot the sixteen-year-old black kid. I recalled what had happened in Watts and I remembered the rap of Black

Muslims in San Francisco. It hadn't been a year since Martin Luther King was gunned down.

Each time I went to L.A. from the desert to get supplies, I found myself scrutinizing the faces of blacks in the streets, looking for signs of discontent. Charlie had programmed us to see it. And we did. It's easy to project emotion into faces on the streets, particularly if that emotion is supposedly seething beneath the surface. Living in the desert, away from the frenetic pace of cities, only magnified our preconceptions and forebodings. Perhaps what Charlie saw in the faces of the blacks was the emerging (unconscious) violence of his own psyche. I'm not sure. But invariably people came back to Barker's muttering, "The shit's coming down, man . . . yeah . . . it won't be long now."

It got colder. Thanksgiving came, and we had a huge meal around the fire at the Meyers ranch. The next day it snowed. Brooks Posten chopped wood. So did I. In early December the weather drove us together in huddling, cuddling groups. To sleep, we packed side by side like sardines under blankets and sleeping bags; bodily friction was no longer a luxury; only Charlie's raps fired the air. Bundled in sweaters and a parka, he clomped the floor at night in his motorcycle boots, his hands thrust into the pockets of his jacket, his words crisp against the cold, his respiration visible white puffs. He no longer looked like the inspired, soft-spoken guru, but like a general briefing his troops before battle.

Now there was structure to what he preached. Everything that had seemed so nebulous before now had direction. Our songs reflected the change:

> *It's time to call time from behind you*
> *The illusion has been just a dream*
> *The Valley of Death and I'll find you*
> *Now is when on a sunshine beam*
>
> *So bring only your perfection*
> *For their love will surely be*
> *No pain, no fear, no hunger .*
> *You can see, you can see, you can see*

Naively, perhaps, we all thought Charlie was right, that we had a duty and that everything we had worked for could now be applied to our music. I've often wished we had recorded some of the sessions we did at the Barker ranch at the base of the mountains. We worked hard; hours and hours. And it showed. As a professional musician, I can say without reservation that what we were doing was as good as, and in most cases better than, some of the top-selling recordings of the day. Though Charlie had spoken to us of violence—the violence of the revolution—there was never any talk of *us* doing anything but music. We had yet to hear the words Helter-Skelter.

In mid-December Charlie sent out two contingents from the ranch, one to Sacramento, one to Los Angeles. The Sacramento group, which included Tex, Sadie, T.J., Katie, Stephanie, Ella, and Leslie Van Houten, went to buy zuzus from a candy connection on the outskirts of the city. We were all pretty much addicted to zuzus and Charlie wanted an excuse to put the bus on the road again. He didn't like leaving it parked unattended at the foot of the wash. Meanwhile, I was to take Snake and Gypsy with me to Los Angeles to buy supplies and to go to Spahn's, where Gypsy would take over "George duty" for Juanita. After that, we were to rendezvous with the candy trip in Malibu.

The first night in L.A. I went with Snake and Juanita to Westwood Village to see the Beatles' film *The Yellow Submarine;* afterward we visited a friend of Charlie's in Topanga Canyon, who asked if we'd heard the Beatles' *White Album,* released just days before. When we said no, he played it for us. The following morning I called Charlie and he said to come back by way of Vegas and to trade in Juanita's van for a jeep (which we eventually did). By the time we finally got back to Barker's, Charlie had gone to L.A. to meet the candy run. He too spent the night in Topanga and heard *The White Album.* After that, things were never the same.

Two days later, Charlie drove the bus back from L.A. Not wanting to leave it at the foot of Golar Wash, he decided to bring it all the way to Barker's by taking a back road on the far side of Death Valley through Shoshone and Furnace Creek, then down a horrendous twisting, rock-strewn gorge. By the time he arrived, the bus was a wreck. The outside dual tires and the mufflers had been ripped to shreds, gouged by the rocks; the interior was also torn up by a cord of wood that had broken loose and had battered everything. It sounded like a tractor as Charlie drove it behind the ranch house and parked. It was New Year's Eve, 1968, and "colder," T.J. quipped, "than a dead celibate's nuts." But Charlie was fired up. *The White Album* had turned his head around.

That night we all hiked up to the Meyers place and built a roaring fire. Everyone was back. We had a full supply of food, candy, beverages, and enough wood to keep the fire stoked and blazing. Charlie was completely energized; his mood charged everyone. It was like a ritual gathering of some desert tribe to make New Year's resolutions. A ceremony before the fire. The flames reflected in Charlie's eyes as he spoke:

"Are you hep to what the Beatles are saying? . . . Dig it, they're telling it like it is. They know what's happening in the city; blackie is getting ready. They put the revolution to music . . . it's 'Helter-Skelter.' Helter-Skelter is coming down. Hey, their album is getting the young love ready, man, building up steam. Our album is going to pop the cork right out of the bottle."

Two days later, Charlie and T.J. split for Los Angeles to try to negotiate with Dennis and Greg Jakobson. Greg was married to the daughter of onetime comedian Lou Costello and had some good contacts in the record business. He had met Charlie in May of 1968 and had always encouraged him with his music. Charlie didn't need much encouragement. By that time, he was determined to get our album on the market.

Charlie's burst of energy seemed to revitalize everyone from the stupor of winter cold. While he was gone we all listened to the album over and over, particularly to five songs; "Blackbird," "Piggies," "Revolution 1," "Revolution 9," and "Helter-Skelter." Sitting high in the Panamints around the fire, the songs did seem strangely prophetic. We listened to "Helter-Skelter," to the discord and caterwauling of "Revolution 9," which ends with machine guns firing and people screaming in agony as though it were the end of the world.

Indeed, at that point Charlie's credibility seemed indisputable. For weeks he had been talking of revolution, prophesying it. We had listened to him rap; we were geared for it—making music to program the young love. Then, from across the Atlantic, the hottest music group in the world substantiates Charlie with an album which is almost blood-curdling in its depiction of violence. It was uncanny. By then, we had all made some uncanny discoveries together; journeys to inner worlds, to planes of consciousness, to the great wilderness of Death Valley. We had submitted to wildernesses within ourselves; we had experienced ego deaths; we had watched each other "letting go," submitting to fear, releasing to the love which was Charlie. Few of us doubted Charlie's power. He had alluded often to his being a spiritual medium, a "hole in the infinite," a latter-day Jesus Christ. Why not? On the eve of the New Year (1969), the rest of the world seemed no less insane.

From the day I joined the Family, Charlie referred to the Beatles as "the soul," and later even called them part of "the hole in the infinite." Certainly the group had affected (and directed to some extent) the early Family philosophy; their album *Magical Mystery Tour* set the tempo of our entire trip during the early days: the idea that life is what you make it; that you're free to be what you are, so long as you submit to the forces inside you: "turn off your mind, relax and float downstream." Charlie believed in the Beatles and we believed in Charlie. By the time *The White Album* was released, with "Helter-Skelter," both Charlie and the Beatles had been more than validated in our minds.

Around the tenth of January T.J. returned from L.A. in the jeep. I was working with Brooks and Clem, stacking wood alongside the ranch house. We watched T.J. park the jeep and hike up the trail, his head warmed by a snow-white stocking cap, his newly grown beard billowing out from his face like a swarm of bees. He was out of breath by the time he reached us.

"Charlie . . . says . . . we should all come to L.A.," he announced, trying to catch his breath. "He's got a place in Canoga Park where we can stay." T.J. looked at me. "He says you should pick someone to watch this place and for the rest of us to boogie on down there today." He fumbled for a cigarette in his shirt pocket, then extracted it from the package with his lips. "Motherfucker . . . it's cold," he muttered, offering us a smoke. He struck the match and cupped his hand around the flame. "Charlie says we got to get closer to the action for a while. Hey, the shit is really coming down . . . Charlie says he's got a deal lined up with some guy named Melcher."

By three that afternoon we were packed and on our way—all but Brooks and Juanita, whom I asked to stay at Barker's to keep an eye on things. With the big bus out of commission, we took one of the Dodge power wagons and an old vintage pickup we had acquired from someone in Las Vegas. At ten that night we pulled into Los Angeles and drove to the house Charlie had rented.

The Family's new residence was a two-story house at 20910 Gresham Street, in Canoga Park, just two blocks from the DeSoto Plaza and Junior's Market, and less than twenty minutes away from Spahn's. Suburbia—a tree-laden middle-class neighborhood full of kids, tricycles, and dogs, mellow enough when compared to L.A. proper, but hectic after living in the desert. But it was warm. No one complained about that. The house, made of stucco and redwood, had been painted a bright canary yellow. It was bigger than Barker's (four bedrooms, a spacious kitchen, a small dining area, and a huge living room set off by a concave brick fireplace) and sat on a good chunk of land, most of it in the back and all of it lush with pepper and eucalyptus trees. The front yard was divided by a walkway leading to the porch, which bisected a dichondra-and-crabgrass lawn. Two full-grown pepper trees graced the front yard with swaying branches and clusters of dried leaves. To the right of the house was a large two-car garage, and in the back, an empty toolshed.

Charlie had immediately dubbed the place "The Yellow Submarine." From there, he said, we would remain "submerged beneath the awareness of the outside world" while working on our music.

Things got more intense, Charlie's raps more elaborate and graphic: "You know what's gonna happen one of these nights . . . the blacks from Watts are gonna break into the houses of some rich white piggies in Beverly Hills and start wasting them . . . you know . . . and it ain't gonna be very pretty . . . like they'll be vicious . . . they'll chop them up and mutilate them and fling blood around; then whitey is gonna retaliate . . . he'll go into the ghetto and start shooting blacks. I can see it happening. Then, blackie will go on TV and appeal to the government. 'Hey, look what you've done to my people.' And the war's gonna start, man . . . it's gonna be worse than any war this country ever knew, 'cause it's gonna be here on these streets in these cities and it's gonna come down hard. It's gonna be a war between whitey and the Uncle Tom niggers . . . for keeps, 'cause this war has been a long time comin' . . . the slaves are gonna have their day. But dig it, the smart ones will be the Muslims, 'cause while the shit's comin' down they'll be hiding in their basements with all kinds of weapons and strategies, and when the time is right they'll come out and finish off what's left of whitey. That's why we got to get our scene together and get back to the desert.

"We gotta be ready," he said, "to save the babies . . . there're gonna be lots of homeless babies from this, and we got to take them with us. So we're gonna need vehicles to transport people . . . dune buggies, motorcycles, and good maps."

The more he rapped, the more we sensed the impending holocaust. I remember sitting in the living room beside Snake and Clem and looking out the window, wondering if the violence would reach us. We listened to *The White Album* for hours, to "Revolution 9," the gunfire and the screaming. It gave me chills. Meanwhile, we practiced our own music for hours, wrote new songs to operate beneath the level of people's awareness and to program those "who were *one* in their minds," to come to the desert.

> Everyone who is a One
> Is looking for the last door
> So if you are a One, my friend,
> You don't need to look anymore
>
> And everyone who is a two
> Knows there's nowhere else to go
> So get on down that road, my friend,
> Let it go, let it go, let it go!

The more Charlie talked about revolution, the more we agreed. We had been conditioned "to agree," to accept and submit; we had also learned that often just agreeing was enough, that if Charlie saw you were willing to experience something, it would not be necessary to actually do it. At times I felt Charlie was merely testing us, gauging our reaction to his gory descriptions. Later, when he started talking about mounting machine guns on the roll bars of our dune buggies to defend ourselves against the pigs—"while the guys drive, the girls can man the machine guns"—it sounded pretty farfetched and I felt often that he was playing games. When people said, "Yeah, sure, Charlie, far-out," subconsciously they were playing the "old" games without really digesting what he said. Yet, they agreed.

It may well be that in time, with so many people going for his rap, Charlie became a victim of his own imagination—perhaps the power of all that agreement created a reality, until ultimately he really believed he was destined to engineer a race war.

One day in mid-February around ten A.M. Charlie asked me to ride up to Spahn's with him in the jeep. I grabbed a handful of plums from a bowl in the kitchen and followed him out to the car. We drove to the end of Gresham Street and turned left on Variel, then took the back road over to Topanga Canyon and proceeded north. It was cloudy and overcast but Charlie seemed as loquacious as ever.

"I want to see how things are shaping up at Spahn's . . . talk to Juan and get a little scene going there again. I'd like you to bullshit with George while I look around."

"Sure."

When we passed Devonshire, then crossed the intersection at Chatsworth, Charlie pointed to a black guy on the sidewalk with a white girl; they were holding hands.

"Dig it, man . . . that's why blackie's been so pacified . . . still got a handle on whitey's women. He's up in Haight Ashbury now raping the young love, expending all his energy. But now that the young love is starting to split, he's gonna get real frustrated, you know. And that's when he's gonna blow it."

Just before we reached the foothills, Charlie stopped at a liquor store and ran inside to buy some doughnuts; he was already eating one when he climbed back into the jeep and handed me the package. I took a doughnut as he Brodied out onto the highway, then turned onto Santa Susana Pass Road.

It was good to be out of the congestion. Though Spahn's is just five minutes away from the business district of the San Fernando Valley (about eight miles off the freeway), it lies in the foothills and gives the illusion of total isolation. We wound along the base of the foothills past the railroad tracks, then accelerated up the hill toward the curve where Clem and I, months before, had totaled Dennis' Ferrari.

"Hey, man," Charlie said after a long silence. "Speaking of young love, how about you hustling some new blood? You know, maybe enroll in that high school. I see some fine-looking girls walking to school in the morning. Can you dig that?"

"Sure, why not . . . maybe I can get my diploma!"

Charlie chuckled. "Yeah . . . get educated . . . study the mystery of history, and the ramis-jamis . . . and in the meantime, we'll call it the in-between time. Then, on the other hand, of course, you have a ring." Charlie looked down at his left hand, the middle finger of which sported a turquoise ring. "Now," he went on, "take the toad's toenail . . . pretty, ain't it—bleep, bleep—ride in a jeep."

We turned in at Spahn's and drove alongside the saloon and parked. Tommy Thomas emerged from under the building, barking, and Charlie stooped to pat him. Moments later, Randy swaggered out of the barn, and when Charlie shouted, Randy waved back and smiled.

"Look, he's grinning," Charlie said through his teeth, still grinning. "Must have taken a good shit for himself."

"What's happening, Shorty?" I greeted Shorty Shea as he came out of the tack room behind us, carrying a saddle and a handful of bridles.

"Not much. Howdy, Charlie . . . where you guys been? . . . Oh, yeah, Death Valley. . . . Squeaky says it's pretty nice out there."

"Colder than a well digger's ass at night," Charlie quipped.

"I bet." Shorty gave Charlie a long expressionless look, then hoisted the saddle to his shoulder with a grunt. "Got to get these horses saddled and ready to go." He ambled off toward the corral, where Larry and Juan Flynn were saddling mounts for a gang of tourists. Juan had moved back to Spahn's to work full time for George as a wrangler. He showed up on occasion at Gresham Street, but infrequently. Juan was one of the first to start drifting away from Charlie's orbit. Charlie sensed this and wanted to find out why.

Charlie slapped at a fly on his cheek. "Same old shit

. . . got to submit to these poop-butt motherfuckin' flies. Go on up and check George out, will ya, Paul? I want to look around a bit, then I'll be up there."

I called Tommy Thomas and he trotted ahead of me up to George's house. I knocked and the bell sounded.

"Come in, come in," he shouted. "I'm blind as a bat, can't see a thing."

I went inside and sat down at the table next to George. Gypsy winked from across the room; she was doing the breakfast dishes. I asked George how things were going and he told me that a few months back Charlie had given him the money to pay the taxes (money the Family had gotten from Juanita) but that the government wanted more all the time.

"Hell, if it keeps up, I'm gonna have to sell this place off. If it wasn't for Ruby Pearl, nothin' would get done."

"What happened to Dody?"

"Hell, they come and got her . . . dragged her off to some funny farm up north. Damn shame, is what it is . . . she never done nothin' to hurt anybody."

"Who ya got living in the back ranch house?"

"Some fella and a gal and a baby . . . fella says he's James Dean's brother . . . damned if I know . . . but they're okay . . . pay right up."

A few minutes later Charlie came in. Gypsy poured us all coffee and Charlie bullshitted with George about the business of running a ranch. Soon Charlie was crackin' jokes and both he and George were laughing uproariously.

"Damn," Charlie gasped. "All that laughin' makes me fart, George."

"Nothin' wrong with that," George snorted. "You know the old sayin' . . . a fartin' horse will never tire, a man who farts is good to hire."

After we left George's, Charlie grabbed his guitar from the backseat of the jeep and we walked up the trail to the outlaw shacks. We sat on the steps a while and talked, then Charlie started to play.

"Just like when you first come to Spahn's," he mused. He began singing nonsense songs and I joined in; he'd do a verse, then I'd join in; then I'd do one and he'd sing along. In a matter of minutes we were in perfect syncopation, anticipating each other with almost absolute precision. Since the day I met Charlie, we'd always had this uncanny sense of timing; it was like complete psychic harmony. It was always there, and it seemed to amaze Charlie as much as it did me.

What Charlie and I achieved during these duets is what he sought to bring together with all the Family on all levels—a single flow of energy; such complete submission to impulse that all energy became a single force unto itself. This was a profound concept, one I came closest to experiencing when we did music together. While it tied me very closely to Charlie, it also linked him strongly to me.

Suddenly he set down the guitar. "Hey, man," he said, "take my hand." He held out his right hand.

"Rub it . . . go on, pretend I'm Snake." He sniggered.

I rubbed his hand with the fingers of my right hand.

"Do it again . . . keep doing it . . . yeah, wait." He pulled his hand away. "Dig it, never make the same motion twice. Vary it, you know." He took my hand. "Rub it like this, then change it, improvise, get the feel . . . you see. It's like music, man, you change the beat, you feel it, you tune into the soul. Hey, it's like making love. You can't just bang away—bang, bang, bang, with no rhythm, no sense of surprise; it ain't the meat, it's the motion. That's where it's at with anything that's got some soul. But you have to let it flow . . . let it be what it is, 'cause it's all one rhythm. Hey, you ever seen motion like this?"

Charlie began moving his hands like a belly dancer's, weaving them around, under and over each other. "See," he said, "no two motions alike . . . every motion its own . . . pretty soon they go by themselves, you know. Look at the motherfuckers, they're alive!"

Later we walked back to the ranch house to say good-bye to George and Juan. When we passed Randy on our way out, he waved.

"Take it easy, Paul . . . Charlie."

"Hey, don't step in any horseshit," Charlie bellowed.

Driving back, Charlie told me the vibes seemed okay at Spahn's. "George ain't no problem. Gypsy and Squeaky take good care of him. I want to start stashin' some vehicles and parts up there, put some campsites along the creek, you know. Maybe we better check back on the Fountain too, see what those crazy bastards are doing."

As we turned off Santa Susana, Charlie asked if I

wanted to hear a song he'd just written, and without waiting for an answer, proceeded to belt it out. The song, "The Eyes of a Dreamer," a fast-moving ballad, was one we would later record on our album; it said a lot about Charlie during those days before "the holocaust."

> *It's all in the eyes of a dreamer*
> *It's all in the eyes of a man*
> *All the things we've done in life*
> *And all the things we planned*
>
> *Can the world be sad as it seems*
> *Where are your hopes, where are your dreams*
> *They're in the eyes of a dreamer*
> *In the eyes of a man*
>
> *All the songs have been sung*
> *And all the saints have been hung*
> *The wars and cries have been wailed*
> *And all good people have been jailed.* . . .

Charlie glanced over, grinning; he had both hands on the steering wheel; his head was tilted back, his hair flowing. "Dig this next part."

> *The moment is ever constant in the mind*
> *Everywhere I look the blind lead the blind*
> *Here's your chance*
> *To step out of time*
> *There ain't no reason and there ain't no rhyme*
>
> *For the trouble you bring*
> *Is the trouble you bring*
> *And a thing is a thing*
> *Is a thing, is a thing.* . . .

It was two o'clock by the time we got back to the house. I had Stephanie draw me a bath, then I changed clothes and drove the BSA bike I'd just acquired down to Birmingham High to enroll.

13

Living in the midst of the San Fernando Valley heightened my desire to return to the desert. The tragedy of city life is that you forget what fresh air and real color are; everything is shrouded in gray. Color and fragrance are muted to the point of extinction. I envied Juanita and Brooks being left in the desert and recalled Juanita's rap about Mexico. She spoke of the small tropical villages she had lived in; of all the smells and colors, and how she missed the fresh fruits of the marketplace: mangoes, papayas, coconuts, pineapples. Her words prompted memories of my childhood in Lebanon. By comparison, L.A. seemed dead.

"Charlie's right," she told me. "L.A. is intense. It's doomsville."

Life in the Yellow Submarine *was* intense. There always seemed such urgency in the air: we had to be ready when the shit came down. Instead of rejecting the real world, we were forced, at least temporarily, to become part of it. Charlie began, gradually, to recruit a more macho element to assist us—mechanics, bikers, and ex-cons—who could score and repair dune buggies and Harleys, vehicles we needed for the desert. While he rarely allowed these guys into the inner circle of the Family, he kept them around, enticing them with girls and dope.

One of the new breed was Bill Vance (David Lee Hamic), an ex-con and friend of Charlie's who had recently been released from prison. Through Bill we got access to the Gresham Street house. Bill was a hulking six-footer in his late forties, with short brown hair, brown eyes, and a battered face. His nose looked like a disjointed mountain range. He'd done time with Charlie for robbery and assault, among other things, and was the first of Charlie's new recruits. Bill hit it off with Ella right away, and Charlie used this liaison to his own advantage. Within a week after our arrival, Bill had arranged for Sadie, Ella, Stephanie, Katie, and Mary to work as topless dancers at clubs in the valley. To buy vehicles and out-fit them properly, we needed money. The girls went to work willingly.

Karate Dave was another "heavy-duty" recruit who joined us during that period. He was twenty-six, a Viet-nam vet, and tough as nails. He had a plastic elbow (a vestige of his battlefield experience) and carried himself with an air of cold and utter confidence. Dave wasn't big (five-nine, 160 pounds) but was built like a gymnast. While he seemed to like Charlie, he never tried to in-gratiate himself. He was in it strictly for the goodies—all the women he could handle and what promised to be some excitement.

Through Dave and Bill, others were enlisted to help prepare for Helter-Skelter: guys to score motor parts, camping gear, tents, and building supplies; guys who could later work around the clock on various projects at Spahn's and who knew nothing of the inner workings of the Family; men who were content to do what they were told to do in exchange for sexual gratification and good weed.

Not long after we met Dave, two new girls joined the Family, a petite, hippie brunette from Canoga Park called Crazy Patty, who immediately traded her VW for a dune buggy, and a buxom, gregarious brunette runaway named Barbara Hoyt whom Charlie assigned to Karate Dave. Barbara had a round, moon face, a disarming snaggletoothed smile, and huge boobs. She fell right in with the tempo of things at Gresham Street and eventually moved into a tree house in the backyard with Dave.

Charlie's finesse in handling such diverse elements was extraordinary. While laying out his spiritual rap on the Family, creating a reverent, almost sacred feeling of brotherhood and intimacy, he was able to bullshit with the macho brigade in their own language, bringing them close to our scene but not close enough to really under-stand the subtleties of what was happening. While his female flower children made love to rednecks and ex-cons, Charlie continued to woo the establishment of the music world—Dennis Wilson, Greg Jakobson, and Terry Melcher, (Doris Day's son), who he hoped would give us the break we needed. And all for a single purpose: Hel-ter-Skelter. By the end of February 1969 we considered ourselves a band of tuned-in, spiritually hip revolutionaries—destined to make a mark on a decadent, disintegrating civilization.

By then my stint as a student at Birmingham High had come to an end. After two weeks of classes, I'd gotten bored, but not before luring several attractive girls to Gresham Street to get loaded and make love. While none of these girls ever joined the Family, my success pleased Charlie.

"Motherfucker! Those little gals just love your ass!"

Meanwhile, we practiced our music daily. Within a month of our arrival, we'd purchased all new sound equipment and two new guitars. Through Dennis and Greg we lined up recording sessions at Brian Wilson's studio. But none of them went well. Charlie liked to improvise, even during live recordings, and it just didn't work. Invariably, our best sessions were outside the studio, in a relaxed atmosphere. Charlie wanted Terry Melcher, the owner of a record company, to come and hear us at Gresham Street. "All we need," he said, "is a chance . . . one break and we get this album together . . . it's gonna happen, man!"

Charlie told us he thought it happened when Melcher promised to come to the house one evening and hear us. We cleaned the place thoroughly and set up the instruments and equipment in the living room. The girls prepared vegetables, lasagne, green salad, French bread and freshly baked cookies. Then they rolled some good weed. We waited. All afternoon we waited. When Melcher didn't show up (or call), Charlie was seething. "That motherfucker's word isn't worth a plugged nickel."

Preparations for Helter-Skelter accelerated. By the middle of March we had purchased three dune buggies and three Harleys. We kept the dune buggies at Spahn's and the Harleys in the garage at Gresham Street. Charlie also bought three hundred dollars' worth of topo maps so that we could chart a road to the desert—our own road—beginning behind Spahn's in Devil's Canyon and running through the Simi Valley (bypassing highways, over and under culverts) and out to Death Valley. At night we'd lay the maps out in the upstairs bedroom and plot out the road. I still have memories of Charlie pacing back and forth over the maps. "We're gonna need more Harleys . . . we'll need enough so that we can all ride together; like one person, like one mind, so that when it comes time to turn, we'll just turn together, without speaking, you know. We'll move like a flock of birds, instinctively and with precision."

For hours we labored over the maps, pinpointing potential command posts and campsites along the way. By the end of the month we had the road pretty well laid out.

We began making sorties into Devil's Canyon, scouting out the terrain in our dune buggies, plotting the road. It was a trip—racing over the sand dunes, looking out across the great expanse of the Simi Valley, sensing that the time was fast approaching when we would put our program into action.

At night, after the evening meal, Charlie rapped about our need to be unified: "Let go of the ego, let it die; just turn off your mind. Hey, things haven't changed; it's just that now we move with the time; now we got to make our scene of service. Yeah, there's gonna be some shootin' and dyin', but that's not new. There's always been times in history when a lot of people die, and it don't have a thing to do with right or wrong or wing and wang . . . or diddly shit. It's beyond all that, 'cause the cosmic wind blows over the universe and man just reaps his karma whether he likes it or not.

"Hey, the Beatles have tuned in to it. They've been taping into the vibes for a long time. Look at their songs: songs sung all over the world by the young love; it ain't nothin' new. It's all been written down. It's written in the good book, in Revelation, all about the four angels programming the holocaust . . . the four angels looking for the fifth angel to lead the people into the pit of fire . . . right out to Death Valley. Yeah, it's all been written down, so we might as well submit to it. It's all in Revelation . . . Revelation is now! The Beatles are now! It's all in black and white, in *The White Album*—white, so there ain't no mistakin' the color—it's all in the words and the music. So listen and pay attention."

Charlie spent hours quoting and interpreting Revelation to the Family, particularly verses from chapter 9:

> *And the four angels were loosed*
> *which were prepared for an hour*
> *and a day, and a month, and a year,*
> *for to slay the third part of men. . . .*

And the fifth angel sounded,
and I saw a star fall from heaven
unto the earth: and to him was
given the key to the bottomless pit.

The implications were clear: the four angels were the Beatles, whom Charlie considered prophets for what was coming down. The fifth angel was Charlie. "The third part of men," he said, was the white race, those who would die in Helter-Skelter. The passage "And he opened the bottomless pit . . . And there came out of the smoke locusts upon the earth; and unto them was given power as the scorpions of the earth have power" was not only a reference to the Beatles (locusts) but implied that the power of scorpion (Charlie was a Scorpio) would prevail. In describing the locusts (Beatles), Revelation said, "their faces were as the faces of men," yet "they had the hair as the hair of women," and wore "breastplates of fire," which Charlie said were their electric guitars. Charlie read on: "And it was commanded them that they should not hurt the grass of the earth, neither any green thing, neither any tree." Charlie maintained that cosmic wrath would only be leashed upon men and not on nature; that when the holocaust was over, the natural beauty would remain, and the world, at least in the desert, would be like Eden again. And we'd be the survivors, ready to start a whole new scene.

"When all the fightin's over, the Muslims will come in and clean up the mess . . . 'cause blackie has always cleaned up whitey's mess. But blackie won't be able to handle it and he'll come over and say, 'You know, I did my number, man . . . I killed them all and I'm tired of killing. The fightin' is over.' And that's when we'll scratch blackie's fuzzy head and kick him in the butt and tell him to go pick the cotton."

Charlie never hid his racial prejudices. And blacks weren't the only ones he chided. He made jokes about Jews, particularly old Jewish men who lay around resort hotels with their comical penguin bodies, buying and selling humanity as though it were a commodity. He told Tex that Hitler was just a tuned-in dude who leveled the karma of the Jews. Charlie razzed the cowboys and Okies for their redneck shortsightedness, yet his own prejudices often coincided with theirs. He said priests were the biggest hypocrites of all. "Always walkin' around talkin' about life and love and the beauty of God. Dig it, all they ever wear is black; black! They walk around like the fucking sky just fell on 'em. Their faces never see the sunlight. They look like zombies, man; morticians. They preach love but they never have a woman. Yet, those poop-butt motherfuckers got the gall to tell you what life is about and how you should repent and all that shit. Hey, if anything is a sin, it's those assholes."

Later, people would ask me how a man like Charlie Manson could *ever* be considered Christlike. How could he ever get *that* close to people, so close they spoke his rap and thought his thoughts. The answer is simple, really: he listened to them, each of them. He concentrated on what they said. He sympathized with their problems, knew their idiosyncrasies. He allowed them to express all their fears, hopes, aspirations. Seemingly, he did not judge, he merely listened and focused all his attention on them. He became friend, brother, lover, and father. He gave himself in a way that perhaps no one else ever had, particularly in the beginning. Ironically, few people ever really pay attention on that level. He taught the girls not only to love their minds but their bodies and to use them without inhibition. What he had started at Spahn's, he continued at Gresham Street. He was always changing the motion, remaining unpredictable.

At times he'd gather us together to preach about the psychology of women. Though he'd be addressing the girls, everyone was present.

"Dig it, this is a planet of women . . . the men are just guests here. I mean, everything is set up for women; they pretend it ain't so, but it is. They're the mothers, the ones who bear the life of new generations. It's like they have the greatest creative energy going for them. But they need the seed of man, dig. It's up to man to bring woman to life and to tap into her energy. Women need to be loved, and we should love them, not as little boys but as men. The trouble with society is that women have made little boys out of men. Mothers have cut the balls off their sons before they developed their sexuality . . . left them boys instead of men. That's why women today are not satisfied . . . they want men but all they find are little boys.

"We have to treat our women like women but also

like daughters. We gotta cultivate them like a garden of flowers so that they give us life, so that when we tap into them we will become energized. Women are like batteries that gotta be charged. We give to them and they give back to us. It's like money in the bank. Women are cosmic creatures, beautiful and strong. But they also got a streak of the witch in them. All of them got it. They're dangerous, dig; they can't help but want to cut your balls off. That's their game; sad but true. Hey, look at all the dudes running around without balls! Women got the motherfuckers. Still, we got to love them; they're our daughters, our power. But we can't be goin' on their trip. If you do, why you just wind up singing those high notes yourself, dig; it's a game; it's always been a game."

It was clear that Charlie feared losing control over his women. As a child who had been beaten and deserted by his own mother, his fear and paranoia were to some extent understandable.

He spoke like a pimp. There was never any doubt that the girls *belonged* to him and that their favors were a gift, not from them, but from Charlie. "Your love is my love," he would say. "It's all one love; when you love someone, I am loving them; we are all loving them."

Regardless of the mechanics (and theory), it worked; the girls in the Family adored Charlie; he knew each of them—their hang-ups, their likes, dislikes, phobias, their tastes in food, sex, music, their backgrounds—everything. Whenever someone appeared who might cause a problem to our scene—a narc, redneck, probation officer, anyone from the straight world—Charlie knew immediately which girl would be best suited to neutralize that person. He was masterful at this; to do it, he had to know his women well.

Standing beside Sadie in the kitchen one night at Gresham Street, I listened while she told Patty: "Charlie is the only man I ever met who is complete. He will not take back talk. He will not let a woman talk him into doing anything. He is a man." Months later, after her capture, Sadie was asked by the authorities if she thought Charlie was an evil person. She said, "By your standards of evil, looking at him through your eyes, I would say yes. Looking at him through my eyes, he is as good as he is evil, he is as evil as he is good. You could not judge the man."

Even when Charlie was gone, the intensity was almost the same: the only rap, Charlie's rap. Sadie, Squeaky, Tex, Clem, Mary, Brenda, Ella, Bo, Snake, Cappy—everyone spewing the same line: "Hey, it's coming down . . . get ready, Helter-Skelter is coming down." I remember Squeaky standing before the fireplace urging us all to forsake our games and ego trips. "We have to flow with the love!" she wailed in her high-pitched voice. "We have to let the love happen. Charlie is our love, and we are Charlie's love. It's all one. It's all happening now . . . so just let it go . . . just drop it . . . let it die . . . die, motherfuckers! Let it die!"

Sometime in March, Charlie began sending people out on *creepy-crawly* missions around Canoga Park. The idea was to enter someone's home at night and to move about from room to room without being detected. "When it comes down, we got to be prepared to save the babies. It might mean some sneakin' and peekin' around . . . takin' some chances." While I never went on any (breaking and entering) creepy-crawlies, I heard reports from those who did; everyone seemed to enjoy it. Snake said it was like going out on Halloween and taking your treat without ever knocking on the door. Only months later would it become clear that these exercises were dress rehearsals to murder.

One night, shortly after Sadie and Ella had gotten home from dancing at a bar in the valley (it must have been around two A.M.), Charlie ordered them to go with Tex, Clem, Mary, and Bill Vance to creepy-crawl a couple of houses on Variel Street. Within five minutes they were on their way. Bill, an expert when it came to breaking and entering, had taught most of the girls how to remove screens, slip locks, avoid watchdogs, and to implement the tools of the trade: penknives, razor blades, bobby pins, pieces of wire; he also showed them the best places to look for valuables. No one liked to steal more than Bill, and no one in the Family was better at it.

Around four P.M. the following day, Charlie asked me to take the jeep and drive Sadie to work at the club. Sadie had slept all morning; she was in good spirits as we pulled out of the driveway. "Hey, Paul, see that place?" She pointed to a white stucco house set off the road near the corner of Variel and Gresham. "That's where we went last night, through that window . . . that one, see, next to the garage . . . walked right by this guy and his old lady, then right into the kitchen and had some orange juice and cookies. Then we split. They didn't even twitch. We didn't take anything—except for Bill; he grabbed a couple of credit cards for Charlie."

Everything was for Charlie; every thought, action, gesture. It now seems hard to imagine that one person could hold such sway over so many. And in retrospect, it became clear that no one was more dominated by Charlie than Sadie. Had someone told me as we drove toward Canoga Park that in less than five months she would commit one of the most heinous murders imaginable, I would have thought him mad. I had made love with her; I had helped her give birth. In group sessions I'd related to her as a brother and a father. I had sensed a childlike quality in her and a hardness born of deep anger. But I never thought her capable of murder.

When we got to the club, just off Devonshire, I stopped in the parking lot near the rear entrance. Sadie kissed me on the cheek and hopped out. I watched her trot toward the door just as two guys in business suits emerged. They ogled her as she passed them.

"Nice ass," one of them muttered.

"Yeah, and she can move it . . . I saw her dance in here last week."

At that instant both men looked up and saw me as Sadie shouted, "See ya, Paul."

"That your girlfriend?" one of them asked.

"Yeah."

"Nice."

"Yeah."

14

Where the eagle flies
We will lie under the sun
Where the eagle flies
We will die . . . die to be one

The nights are so dark
And the wind's so cold

Love's fire is burnin' . . . and you can't grow old
Livin' with the poison ones
Sun-in with the Devil's sons. . . .

—from a song written by Charles Manson,
summer of 1969

The more involved we became in Helter-Skelter, the
harder it was to see anything else. Momentum carried us
along with Charlie. To say no would have been to violate
all that we had worked to achieve. Even when Charlie's
raps became more militant (I shuddered at some of his
descriptions), it all seemed to fit with his earlier statements regarding death. We'd been programmed to think
of death in a cosmic sense, knowing that the spirit never
dies. We'd all experienced countless ego deaths and had
watched each other experience them. We *knew* that life
was merely a series of transitions in consciousness. When
Charlie got into elaborating on the blood and gore of
racial war, we all considered it a kind of therapy he was
putting us through. At least I did. Blood and carnage
were as much a part of life as anything else; the media
were filled with it, seemed to thrive on it in fact. So long
as we had no karmic connection with it, so long as we did
nothing to cause it, we could view it without judgment.
And at that point, there was never a hint that we would
have any part in killing.

The emotional impact of living in the center of Los
Angeles after months of relative isolation (at Big Sur,
Spahn's, and Death Valley) also served to validate Helter-Skelter. For nearly two years we'd been completely
removed from TV sets, radios, newspapers—all contact
with the outside world. Our reality had been primarily
Charlie and his teachings. Our heads had been filled with
Charlie and all his intensity at a time when he was more
positive. Then, suddenly, we found ourselves stranded in
the midst of civilization again, blaring billboards, buying
and selling, TV newscasts reporting what seemed to be
nothing but violence and bloodshed: Vietnam body
counts, riots in the streets, student demonstrations, and
Richard Nixon's jive.

Around the first of April we began gradually to move
out of Gresham Street and back to Spahn's. Conditions
were crowded in the Yellow Submarine—too many peo-

ple, too many vehicles and motor parts; too many paranoid vibes. By that time we had acquired, in addition to the dune buggies and motorcycles, a milk truck and two diesel semitrucks, one of which had already been parked at Spahn's. We had also accumulated a stack of unpaid electric, water, and telephone bills, and the collectors were beginning to hound us.

Since we couldn't move back to Spahn's *en masse*, without causing suspicion, we had to do it a little at a time. We started by establishing a campsite in the ravine just below the ranch. Charlie and I purchased several parachutes from a surplus store in Los Angeles; after dyeing them green, we converted them into tents beneath the oaks. Meanwhile, we began remodeling the saloon into a kind of nightclub where we could set up and perform our music and store our instruments. We knocked out the back partition behind the stage, painted the walls and ceilings black, then bought strobe lights and white Styrofoam balls to hang from the ceiling. It was trippy—like showtime at the Griffith Park Observatory. Finally we set up our sound equipment and instruments on stage, and began, at night after the tourists had split, to hold jam sessions.

Sometime in mid-April we made a final exit from the Gresham Street house. Charlie had T.J. pull one of the semis into the driveway. We loaded everything inside it: Harleys, VW engines, a big diesel motor, countless dune-buggy and jeep parts, and all our belongings. Then we drove into the mountains of Mulholland to a mansion off Kanan Road, overlooking the sea. Charlie had learned that the rock group, the Iron Butterfly, had recently moved out and were on vacation. We moved in. Bill Vance broke the lock on the gate and hooked up the electricity. We spent nearly two weeks in the mansion, making music, planning strategy, and hiking around the hillside to plot the rest of the road. Charlie insisted we have access to the sea and to the desert and that the two roads be joined. According to Revelation 10:2, "He set his right foot upon the sea and his left foot on the earth."

Around May we left the mansion and moved back to Spahn's, staying in the campsites so as not to disturb George and the wranglers. Charlie kept two girls with George at all times and told the old man we'd be helping out with wrangler chores. George said he was much obliged.

Once at Spahn's, everything was geared to Helter-Skelter and moving back to the desert. The acquisition of a huge open-topped semitrailer bed (which we covered with tarps) gave us additional space to store parts, to work on the motorcycles, and to sleep up to fifteen people. We had mechanics rebuilding Harleys, diesels, and dune buggies round the clock. We paid them, and paid them well—in money, dope, and all the sex they could handle. Meanwhile, the tourists came to ride horseback, look at movie sets, and talk to the wranglers, who went about the business of tending George's stock. Pearl showed up daily to see George, balance the books, and make sure everyone was on the job. At noon each day the cowboys generally gathered to eat lunch and bullshit. They got to know the mechanics and Bill and the sundry motorcycle types who began appearing with greater frequency. While they never became chummy with the bikers, they did share a languorous tolerance that allowed our work to continue. The days got hotter, and sometimes the smog seeped out of the valley and reached up into the foothills. The smell of horseshit permeated the air, and as always, the flies had the run of the place. Shorty and Randy continued to bad-vibe us, but not enough to alter the momentum of what was coming down.

. It was during this period that we met Danny De Carlo, a tough, booze-addicted biker, who, at the time, was treasurer for a motorcycle gang known as the Straight Satans. Danny was a fast-talking, earthy little dude (five-eight) with a thick black "waterfall" hairdo, dark, direct eyes, and a passion for "beer and broads." He invariably wore the full Levi's garb (with "Straight Satan" embossed across his jacket) and boots, and walked like a Hell's Kitchen hoodlum. He had a good sense of humor, a quick wit, and while blinded by his own prurient inclinations, he was, as the saying goes, nobody's fool. He later told authorities that his rapport with Manson was enhanced by the fact that he (Danny) could satisfy Charlie's girls sexually, thus taking the pressure off Charlie. While this was pretty farfetched (Charlie only allowed Danny access to certain girls), Danny did acquire the nickname "Donkey Dan"—a tribute to his "size"; it was a sobriquet he was proud of.

We'd met Danny just before leaving the Gresham Street house. Charlie cultivated him for his knowledge of bikes, his street savvy, and because he could keep things copacetic between the Family and outsiders who sometimes showed up to make trouble. Charlie seemed to like Danny (he was always more favorably disposed to smaller guys) and saw to it that Danny got rewarded. Danny had recently separated from his wife and was invariably hot to trot. Sherry, a new girl, and Ouisch were virtually given to Danny in exchange for his talents as a mediator and mechanic and his knowledge of firearms.

De Carlo was born in Canada but had been given U.S. citizenship after serving in the Coast Guard as a weapons expert. When it came to guns, Danny knew what he was talking about. His father sold firearms for a living, and Danny had dismantled, repaired, and fired all kinds. By then we were beginning to accumulate a small arsenal, which Charlie insisted we'd need for defense purposes while convoying people to and from the desert. Through various sources—most of them ex-cons—we had purchased several small-caliber handguns, two twelve-gauge shotguns, a Schmizer machine gun, and a thirty-thirty. We also began carrying buck knives around the campsite. It was later that summer that Charlie acquired a sword from the then president of the Straight Satans, a guy known as "Eighty-six George." George had come to Spahn's to convince Danny to leave the Family; not only did he fail in that effort, but wound up being conned by Charlie. Charlie offered to pay one of George's traffic tickets in exchange for the sword—a twenty-inch razor-sharp weapon, the top of which had been honed into a fine and delicate point. Approximately two months later, Charlie would use the same blade to slice off Gary Hinman's left ear.

By the end of May the girls were designing buckskins—all-purpose, combat-ready clothing which would last indefinitely and be conducive to life in the desert. At the same time, Tex, at Charlie's suggestion, began constructing a Family shelter across the road from Spahn's, a place to hide and store supplies in case of emergency. Tex worked on the project for several days, using two-by-fours and slabs of plywood ripped off from a nearby construction site in the valley. The shack he built was small (fifteen by twenty feet), yet well-designed, almost like a lean-to, with one side fronting on the slope of a ravine, with a small window facing the creek bed. In it we stocked provisions, camping gear, dried foods, and several handguns. The Family called it the Helter Shelter; Charlie referred to it as "The Just-in-Case Place."

In the midst of these preparations, Charlie moved about like a seasoned field general, giving orders. We set up base camps in the creek bed and explored the mountains around Spahn's so that we knew every hill and gully. We took dune buggies and Harleys into the canyons and worked on the road. At times Charlie would order us to evacuate one campsite and set up another. It was like commando training. We began to feel like a well-trained band of guerrillas. Meanwhile, our mechanics worked on the vehicles, and our girls continued to dance topless and to bring home fat paychecks to cover our burgeoning expenses. At night we played music in the saloon and sang the songs of revolution.

Charlie continued to make trips to L.A. to confer with Dennis and Greg. Despite earlier frustrations, he had not given up trying to get our album recorded. We had spent hours making tapes and wanted to get them heard. But Charlie's anger at Melcher hadn't subsided. I didn't learn until later that he had finally gone to 10050 Cielo Drive (the scene of the Tate murders) looking for Melcher, only to learn that Melcher and his then girlfriend, Candice Bergen, had moved to Malibu. It was during this visit to Cielo Drive that Charlie met the owner of the house, Rudy Altobelli, who was then living in the rear cottage and who later told authorities of Charlie's visit and that it was quite likely that Charlie, on his way in, had seen the occupants of the main house: Voytek Frykowski, Abigail Folger, and Sharon Tate. Charlie never went back to Cielo Drive, but on August 9 he sent four people there to pay a visit; Tex Watson, Susan Atkins, Patricia Krenwinkle, and a new girl named Linda Kasabian.

Linda was the epitome of the young flower child, on her own since sixteen. She'd traveled from the East Coast to California during the summer of love ('67) in search of spiritual fulfillment; she'd lived in Taos and Seattle; she'd worn flowers in her hair at Haight Ashbury; she'd crashed in cheap hotels and communes and had taken psychedelics in quantity before coming to Spahn's late that summer with her two-year-old daughter, Tanya. Linda was five-one and petite, with long light brown hair, green eyes, and a soft, clear speaking voice. When she met Charlie, shortly after I left the Family, she was nineteen and certainly no novice to the jargon of the time. Yet, she fell for his rap hook, line, and sinker. One month later, he sent her to kill.

As things became more fragmented, Charlie's bitterness and frustration surfaced with greater frequency. He began spouting "death to the piggies," and quoting from the Beatles' album. He said we had to work faster; once again we took our group to a studio for a recording session in the valley, but things fell apart; Charlie got pissed off at the technicians and we split. One evening, a short time later, we were practicing in the saloon. Charlie was sitting on a stool in front of the mike, with Bobby to his left, playing the drums. Tex and Brooks were behind Bobby playing steel guitars. I was on Charlie's right doing vocal accompaniment. Behind us, the girls were singing background. During a break, Charlie suddenly stood and demanded that Brenda sing.

"Sing what?"

"Anything, just sing."

"But . . . what do—?"

"Goddammit, sing!" Charlie walked over and yanked her hair.

"Ahhh."

"That's a sound . . . now, try something else." He jerked her hair again.

"Oweee."

"Good . . . now, sing."

She sang.

Cleanliness became a real problem; with no access to indoor facilities, we were forced to go for days without bathing. We all rinsed off in the creek regularly, but it was hard to stay clean. People have been led to believe that the Manson Family was "dirty and unkempt," but this was not the case. Up until the summer of 1969, Charlie demanded good personal hygiene, and that clothes, food, musical instruments—everything—be kept orderly. But living at Spahn's like commandos made it impossible to maintain these standards. The natural, easygoing rhythm of life we had enjoyed gradually became too diffused and disjointed, and finally, decadent. With bikers and hippies and strangers coming and going at all times, there was little opportunity to put the old scene together. Still, there were moments—those nights when the girls made meals at the campfire and we sang songs and Charlie rapped. Those nights were soothing and I remember lying beside Snake in the tent listening to the crickets and wondering what the future held for us. I made love to Snake a lot during that period. It was one experience that always felt *right*. With Snake I shared a kind of inner harmony that sustained me even when things started coming apart. It was not that Snake and I spent a lot of time together or that we consciously cultivated a "special" friendship; it was just that when we were together, it *was* special. It was something neither of us talked about, but it was there from the beginning, from the day I arrived and Charlie sent her to seduce me by the same creek bed, just one year before.

Months later, lawyers, law-enforcement authorities, and friends would ask me why, when things had degenerated so, I remained with the Family. What needs did the Family fulfill? Why didn't I split? It's hard for people to understand what deep needs *were* met by the Family. I can only say that living day in and day out with a group of people with whom you've shared all manner of experiences, without inhibition, binds you deeply. It wasn't only Charlie. I was close to everyone. It gave me a feeling of security against the impersonality of the world. I felt we shared more than any genetic family; we shared a kind of communication that is rare between people. The Family met many needs: sexual, spiritual, communal, recreational, artistic. We were brothers, sisters, fathers, mothers, lovers to each other. We were one. It was a hard thing to let go of, even when it all faltered. Rather than leave it and invalidate all that was good, it seemed easier to ignore or refuse to acknowledge the changing vibes, the degeneration. I had experienced fears before, and they had been dissipated through confrontation. Charlie taught me to submit to these changes. I had endured the choking, the freak-out, and a good deal more. Plus, if Charlie was right and Helter-Skelter was coming down like he said, I needed him and the Family to survive.

But others, too, were feeling the change. One afternoon I was hiking up from the campsite toward the saloon. Charlie had asked me to help the mechanic assemble a new Harley. I'd just reached the saloon when Bo came up and started walking with me. She wore a full-length gingham dress and was barefoot. Her face was smudged with dust and she'd lost so much weight that her eyes seemed enormous. All of us had begun eating less; with no place to cook but the campfire, it was difficult to prepare meals for so many, so that we resorted to living off sweet rolls and cakes, which we continued to get in quantity from our bakery connection in Santa Monica. One look at Bo and I knew she'd been crying.

"What's the matter, Bo?"

"I don't know. I just feel . . ."

She stopped when we reached the semitruck, and the mechanic, a guy we called Turk (a friend of Bill Vance's), stuck his head out of the trailer. "What's happening, Turk?"

"Did De Carlo ever bring them plugs?"

"I don't know."

"Shit." Turk wiped his forehead with a greasy rag, then stuffed it in his back pocket. "Where's Charlie?"

"Down at the corral, talking to Tex."

Turk jumped out of the semi and trotted toward the corral.

When he was out of earshot, Bo told me Charlie had scared the shit out of her. "Charlie said when Helter-Skelter comes down they'll come looking for me, and if they find me, they'll chop me up. He said blackie's gonna terrorize everyone. He said they're gonna smear the piggies' eyeballs on the ceilings and paint the walls and floors with blood."

I knew what Bo was feeling. I had experienced Charlie's demonic side. Yet, I did not want to acknowledge it. I wanted to move beyond Helter-Skelter; to go back to the desert. But things only got worse. And my own fears and uncertainties became apparent to Charlie.

One night, not long after my conversation with Bo, Charlie asked me to go with him to Canoga Park to pick up some girls. He said we needed to relax and have a good time. I'd worked all day with Turk and Tex, helping pack and assemble parts so we could transport them to Barker's.

I'd crashed out in the semitrailer in my sleeping bag and had just dozed off when Charlie woke me.

We took the milk truck and drove down to Topanga Canyon Boulevard, then turned left on Chatsworth. Charlie was talkative, but I sensed that some of it was put on, that he was trying too hard to be "his old self." Somewhere near the Topanga Plaza, near Gresham Street, we pulled up alongside some girls in an MG and started rapping with them; but they weren't interested, and when Charlie got belligerent, they flipped us off. Minutes later, it seemed, we drove by the Gresham Street house and turned left on one of the cross streets. About halfway down the block Charlie spotted a truck parked in someone's driveway, a big heavy-duty Dodge ambulance-weapons-carrier. He stopped the milk truck and turned off the ignition.

"Hey, brother . . . we could use that truck, you know. Why don't you hot-wire it and take it back to the ranch?" Charlie's eyes drilled mine, but he kept right on talking. "Just drive it directly to the campsite, load up with supplies—food for Juanita and Brooks, some tools, and a little dope—then take a few girls and head for the desert. Don't wait for nothin' . . . just load it and get on down the road. After you check on things at Barker's, come back in the pickup."

All that went through my mind as Charlie spoke is difficult to recount. It lasted just a split second, but during that time I experienced an involved process of assessment. I'd known troubles with the law, but always for minor offenses. I'd never stolen a vehicle. Yet it wasn't the stealing that made me hesitate; it was a composite of feelings brought on by the changing vibes. Though Charlie had not indicated directly that we would have anything to do with perpetrating violence, it was clear that we were preparing for it. I was divided in myself; part of me had begun to doubt Helter-Skelter. Yet, if it was really coming down, I didn't want to be left out; I wanted to survive, and to do so, I needed Charlie. On another level, I saw his request as another personal challenge; he had sensed my wavering state of mind and perhaps thought it time to test me again.

"You're not gonna say no, are you?"

I grabbed a piece of wire and a flashlight from under the seat. While Charlie waited, I trotted up the road to the driveway. The front end of the truck was less than ten feet away from what looked like an open bedroom window. Moving quietly, I found the hood latch and slowly raised the hood. The truck had a starter button in the cab, so all I had to do was hot-wire the ignition. It took just seconds for the motor to fire. As the engine turned over, a bedroom light came on. I leaped into the cab, slammed it into reverse, and backed into the street before ramming it into first; I burned rubber for about fifteen feet and then I was in second and flying by Charlie, who was still parked. He gave me the okay sign and a big grin as I roared by, turned right, and headed for home.

At the intersection of Devonshire and Topanga Canyon I tromped the brake to avoid running a light. As it was, I overshot the crosswalk and had to back up. As I did so, a squad car eased up alongside me. I looked straight ahead, my heart pounding. Then I took a deep breath and glanced down at the cops.

"In a hurry, are ya?"

"Kinda . . . yeah."

"Well, slow down, partner, you'll live a whole lot longer."

When the cops turned left, I headed north on Topanga, then hauled balls up Santa Susana Pass to where the road ended. I parked on the shoulder, then clambered down the hill to the campsite and woke up the Family.

15

"Hurry up, goddammit!" I urged. "This fucking truck is hot."

It took no more than half an hour for us to load up with supplies: food, clothing, and several empty five-gallon drums. By the time Karate Dave and I and several girls pulled back onto the highway, it was about four A.M. The girls were still in their nighties and T-shirts and were excited as hell. I sensed their eagerness to be leaving for the desert; or was it my own projected delight?

Dave and I sat in the front with Brenda between us. Dave wanted to drive, so I rolled a couple of joints and passed them back through the curtain behind the seat to Ouisch and Cappy. The back end of the truck, though spacious, was cluttered with pieces of hose, bricks, sacks of cement, and three or four well-stocked toolboxes. The girls pushed the stuff to the rear and sat in a circle just behind the seat. It was a beautiful dawn, and I rolled down the window to enjoy the fresh air as we droned north through Antelope Valley.

For some reason I flashed on Brooks Posten, who was then at Barker's with Juanita. In my mind's eye the changes in Brooks somehow reflected the changes in the Family. During our stay at Gresham Street, he had come down several times to play music and get in on the L.A. scene—preparation for Helter-Skelter. But each time, he became more and more "zombied out," more incapable of functioning, as though everything inside him recoiled and degenerated, rendering him almost catatonic. There were periods at Gresham Street, generally following one of Charlie's grisly raps, when Brooks would go upstairs and remain in the bedroom for three or four days, coming out only to use the bathroom or to drink water. Intermittently he'd be able to function in the music scenes, but his participation, relative to everyone else's, was marginal; that's why, for the most part, Charlie kept him at Barker's. In retrospect, it became clear that Brooks's experience in the Family was, at the deepest levels, a "death trip." Subconsciously, and in part because of his own deep-seated guilts, he had given himself to all that was negative in Charlie. Were it not for his stints in the desert and his discontent duty—chopping wood, and earlier, shoveling shit—Brooks might not have survived.

I smoked the last of the roach Brenda handed me and rolled up the window.

My feelings that night were even more confused. On the one hand, it was exciting ripping off the truck and running from the law. And I enjoyed playing commandos on the outskirts of L.A. But the changes in Charlie were scary; there was the sense of something being terribly *wrong*; like the presence of terminal illness before it's been diagnosed. I had sensed it for weeks but had repressed it. And I tried to dismiss it again as we sped along toward Mojave. Being on the road, going *away* from Charlie, made it easier to rationalize my deepest feelings. As I talked back and forth to the girls and to Dave, I found myself looking forward to the desert and to chopping wood with Brooks.

But that didn't happen. Just outside Mojave, Dave shouted back at the girls, "Stash the dope; the heat's on our ass." Moments later we were pulled over by a highway-patrol unit for having no rear license plate, something no one had noticed in our eagerness to split.

One of the two cops scanned Dave's driver's license with a flashlight, then shone the light on me and Brenda.

"Hi," Brenda said cheerily, waving her fingers.

"You people want to get out of the truck, please?"

"You mean all of us?"

"Yeah, all of you."

Dave got out, and Brenda slid out behind him. I followed. Then the curtain parted and Snake's shapely leg appeared as she climbed over the seat. She wore nothing but a T-shirt and her underpants, and the young cop who had opened the door to begin a search stood back and gaped. Then came Sandy, Ouisch, Cappy, Bo, Sherry, Sadie, and Crazy Patty.

The cops exchanged glances. While the older one eyeballed the girls with feigned nonchalance, the other searched the van top to bottom. He didn't find any dope but he did uncover a license plate behind the back seat. After running a check on it, they took us all to Mojave. Dave and I were separated from the girls and spent what was left of the morning in a communal drunk tank. The next day they took me to L.A. county jail in a sheriff's bus and booked me for suspected auto theft. I didn't know what had happened to Dave or the girls. Two days later I was released. Apparently the truck had been stolen several times and they could find no registered owner. When I got back to Spahn's, the girls were there. So was Dave; he had climbed out the bathroom window in Mojave during a court recess and had escaped the same night. A week later, Dave left the Family, and I never saw him again.

Returning to Spahn's so suddenly, after anticipating a stay in the desert, made me even more aware of how degenerated things had become. Charlie was angry that we had not gotten there with the truck. Two weeks earlier he had sent another supply run to the desert, but the truck had broken down on the road and had to return. Charlie's face reflected the tension; his capacity for patience, which had once seemed infinite, had all but disappeared. Walking around Spahn's in the midst of a conglomeration of people—mechanics and motorcycle types, ex-cons and curiosity seekers—began to unnerve me. There was never a time when the Family was together as one unit; the communal acid trips and therapy sessions were a thing of the past, we were always disjointed, off on separate trips; when we were together, there was no longer a feeling of unity; there was only confusion and Charlie's cryptic, acidic spiels about blackie and the shit coming down. I found myself alone more, roaming around the ranch in a state of detachment. I began violating Charlie's rules, eating meat and smoking pot during the day, like a child defying his parents. I did it unconsciously; yet, I flaunted it.

One afternoon in late June I found Charlie standing outside the saloon talking to Squeaky. When Squeaky walked back up the hill to George's, I approached Charlie. He stood leaning against the building fingering his beard; his eyes were glazed. He didn't see me until I was right beside him.

"What's happening, Paul?" He put his arm around my shoulder and gave me an affectionate squeeze.

"When are we gonna go, man? . . . We gotta make it to the desert. Sometimes I think we'll never get out of here. . . ."

As we walked together toward the corral, Charlie still had his arm around my neck. "You're right, brother, dig it. Helter-Skelter is ready to happen . . . it's gotta happen soon. All the piggies are gonna get their jolt of where it's really at. We have to stock supplies at the desert and be ready to boogie . . . I don't know why we can't get a truck up there. It's startin' to piss me off."

We stopped at the corral gate and looked in at the horses. Charlie climbed up and sat on the top rung of the fence, looking down at me.

"I'll tell ya, blackie never did anything without whitey showin' him how."

I looked up at Charlie, and he winked. "Helter-Skelter *is* coming down. But it looks like we're gonna have to show blackie how to do it."

My blood ran cold. The words echoed in my ear.

"*Show blackie how to do it!*" I knew exactly what Charlie meant. All the horror I had been sensing flooded my being; it was like an instant nightmare lived out in silence. I did not look at Charlie, but gazed straight ahead at the horses, motionless save for their tails, which flicked intermittently at the flies. In that instant I flashed on the choking scene and the look on Charlie's face. I saw Brooks Posten lying prone on the floor of the Gresham Street house. I saw the faces of the girls: Squeaky, Sandy, Ella, Sherry, Mary—all of them rapping out of the void of what remained of them, rapping all that was left: Helter-Skelter.

Without looking at him, I muttered, "When are we going to the desert?"

"I'll tell ya what we're doing." Charlie hopped down from the fence and stood beside me, looking up toward the saloon. "We're gonna load the fucking semi full of dune buggies and Harleys and we're gonna take them to the desert; we're gonna stockpile supplies up there right away."

As he spoke, I felt a vague sense of reprieve, that if I could go to the desert it would be okay, that if I just got out of there, everything would work out. I did not want to think about Charlie's remark. Up until that moment, I had gone all the way. I had believed in the beauty of what was once a reality. I had faced my fears, suffered countless ego deaths. I had loved Charlie and the others (I still did). I had done everything asked of me—pilfered credit cards, conned people, played the games. I had begged, borrowed, and stolen for Charlie. I had even seen and believed in qualities which seemed Christlike. I had submitted, accepted, and flowed with the love. I had said, "Yes, I am you and you are me. We are one." I had swallowed Helter-Skelter. I had done everything to promote it. But unlike Sadie, Katie, Squeaky, Clem, and Tex, I had never really "ceased to exist." And now from the deepest center of my self there was something that said, "No, good God, *no!*"

But it was all on the inside; it was all happening away from Charlie's eyes. At that moment, I feared Charlie. But part of that fear was that he might be right; that Helter-Skelter was inevitable and that despite its horrors, we had to go through with it. I was equally afraid of myself, of the part of me which had become him. I didn't really know who I was. I had little control. What moved me was an instinct to escape.

Charlie put me in charge of organizing the expedition to the desert. I went at it with gusto—getting the mechanics to finish their work and load up the supplies. It took several days to complete the work and get the Harleys and dune buggies ready for the trip. Sometime around the first of July, in the evening, we began hoisting the machinery onto the semi. I supervised everything, saw to it that the vehicles were well-secured and that all supplies were accounted for. It wasn't until most of the loading had been completed that Charlie informed me I was to remain at Spahn's.

By nine P.M. everything was ready. I trudged dejectedly back to the other semitrailer to tell Charlie. The trailer had become a central headquarters for the Family during the latter part of June; with all the parts and supplies pushed off to the sides, there was enough room to seat the entire Family. As usual, Charlie sat at the head of the group on a small stool, rapping out instructions, while Sandy, Ouisch, Mary, and some of the others were sewing buckskins.

"Hey," I called in, "ready to go."

Everyone filed out and gathered around Charlie in front of the saloon. Danny De Carlo and Bill Vance were lashing rope around the tailgate of the truck. "I need a couple of girls to go along with me," Charlie said. All the girls jumped up and down. "Take me . . . me, Charlie!"

"What is this?" Charlie barked. "Am I some kind of schoolteacher or something?" He ordered Ouisch, Stephanie, Snake, and Brenda to get in the truck, then moments later drove out the driveway and disappeared down the road. What I felt then was a combination of confusion, anger, depression, and fear. After they had gone, I walked up to the outlaw shacks alone and sat on the steps. For some reason I thought of my old girlfriend Mona, a pretty blonde I'd known in Topanga Canyon before joining the Manson Family. In retrospect, I realize that this thought was not so unusual; unconsciously, I was grasping for a way out, even if it meant returning to my past.

But I didn't have long to ponder the situation. In

less than half an hour Charlie was back; he said the trailer wouldn't trail the truck and had to be rerigged. He was furious.

"Goddammit, we just *can't get* a motherfuckin' truck up to Barker's!"

I stood beside Brenda and Bo, near the rear of the rig.

"Look, Paul," he barked suddenly. "Take Danny's pickup and run some of these supplies up to Brooks and Juanita. They're gonna wonder what the hell happened to us. He can use your truck, huh, Danny?"

"Be my guest."

I was delighted! "I'm gonna need someone to go with me." As I said this, the girls began to fidget and edge forward, wanting to go but afraid to speak up for fear Charlie would object. At that point, it became all too clear just how hung-up they were, how dependent on Charlie. Only moments before they'd reacted like a bunch of eager kids; now they were mute. Charlie saw it too and fell into a rage.

"Motherfuck! What's happening around here? Everyone has to ask permission to breathe!"

I didn't wait for him to finish. "Come on, Bo . . . you go with me."

Charlie didn't say a word as Bo and I climbed into the cab of Danny's truck. There was a rule in the Family that only girls carried dope, and since we were taking some seeds up to Brooks and Juanita, we needed a girl to go along.

Charlie told me to deliver the supplies, stay a couple of days, and then come back to Spahn's. I drove out the highway and headed for the freeway.

Danny's truck had been recently tuned, and I tromped on it. The more distance I put between myself and Spahn's, the better I felt. Bo, meanwhile, had begun to whimper and then to cry. It was nothing new for Bo. She seemed to have a predisposition to tears; it was her way of handling stress. During earlier scenes in which she became the center of attention—going through some ego death—her emotional output was extraordinary. All you could do was let it run its course. But I knew from our earlier conversation what she was feeling. At one point she put her head on my shoulder and clutched at my arm.

"Come on, Bo . . . Jesus . . . what's wrong?"

"I feel heavy things coming down. It scares me. Charlie scares me."

I didn't say anything. I just put my arm around her. Neither of us really knew how to handle what was inside us; we'd both been so heavily programmed by that time that all natural impulses were trapped, blocked off. The desire to escape, to run, was being satisfied by being on the road. Yet, deep down, we were both tied to Charlie in ways we couldn't begin to understand. We had come to believe in Charlie so deeply that truly doubting Helter-Skelter was impossible. Helter Skelter *was* coming down; our life at Spahn's—disjointed, confused, fragmented— was an expression of it; it *was* happening. Charlie was causing it. There was more fear than before. Charlie had always told us fear was good and that we should submit to it. I remember the night he took Bo before the mirror and made her look at her body; I had learned that there was truth in his words: "Face your fears"—that by confronting fears I had gained knowledge. Had Charlie sensed my feelings, he would probably have told me that fear of violence is just another fear—that death is merely a release to the love. "Dying," he had said, "is something like orgasm . . . it leaves you in a state of calm, a state of bliss." The implication was that he had died before.

Inside, I was torn, my thoughts divided from my emotions. My instinct was to run, and I was running, so that looking out the window that night made me feel hopeful. But I was still locked into the programs, still a part of Charlie. I found myself rationalizing his words: "We're gonna have to show blackie how to do it." Maybe there was another way of showing him; maybe he meant something else. Charlie is a man of love; we are all submitting to his love; Helter-Skelter is to program the young love to come to the desert. I remembered the good scenes—feeling close, being loved. Outside, the night seemed infinite, opening wider as we drove on. I pushed harder into the center of the night, with Bo beside me, wanting to feel free, wanting to send my spirit beyond the horizon, sensing that if we could just go faster it might happen. But physical freedom was not enough; my insides were tied to Charlie and the Family in ways I hadn't begun to sort out. I found myself latching onto phrases Charlie had taught us, like, "I am you and you are me," and "No sense makes sense." My mind would rest on one thought until another thought emerged to replace it; then another and another, until it felt as though I were going mad. It was as if my being had been inhabited by so many contradictions that all thoughts and feelings—the very flow of my blood—was blocked. Who was I? What was left of me? Only the highway, straight and nearly empty of traffic, provided the illusion of direction and freedom. Yet, while all this raged in my psyche, I found myself soothing Bo with words which came from still another part of myself.

"It's okay, Bo . . . we're on a good trip now. We're going back to the desert, just you and me . . . no bad vibes there . . . just the desert. Look at the sky, Bo."

We watched the sun come up just outside Ballarat and stopped there to buy coffee. By eight that morning we were hiking up Golar Canyon toward the Barker ranch. Somehow, climbing the rocks lessened the tension, as I scrambled ahead of Bo, stopping every few minutes to wait for her. The closer we got to Barker's, the faster I climbed. I found myself again anticipating seeing Brooks. I didn't know why. It wasn't as though Brooks and I had ever been close. But I believe, looking back, that I envied his being in the desert, away from what was happening. I also made a subconscious connection between Brooks's "zombied-out" state while at Gresham Street and what was coming down in the Family. My urgency was also prompted by the fact that in less than a month's time we'd sent three expeditions to the desert. None of them had arrived.

We rested midway up the canyon, then completed the hike without stopping.

When we reached the gate in front of the ranch, Brooks appeared on the porch.

"Hey Paul!" He called something into the house, then came bounding down the hill like a frisky goat. He wore Levi's, a loose-fitting T-shirt, and worn-out Hush Puppies. I'd never seen Brooks move that fast or with as much agility. I couldn't believe it was the same person. His blue eyes were clear. There was color in his cheeks. Even his shaggy blond hair looked healthy. He gave us both a warm hug.

"I was hoping they'd send you," he said.

"Hey, man . . . you look good! This desert life must agree with you . . . what you been eatin'?"

"I've been climbing mountains." He glanced over his shoulder toward the ranch house. "Met this far-out old prospector dude . . . he's a trip."

"How's Juanita?" Bo wanted to know.

"Okay. She's up there making some vegetable concoction. We got a little garden going."

While Brooks spoke, I saw a man step out of the bunkhouse and sit down on a rock just outside the door.

"What's goin' on at Spahn's . . . how's Charlie?" Brooks asked both questions at once.

My answer was automatic and only half-conscious. I was still watching the man on the hill.

"The shit's coming down."

"Comin' down fast," Bo added.

"Hey, that's him." Brooks's eyes followed my gaze. "Let's go up, then I'll help you bring in the supplies." As we walked up the trail toward the house, the man stood up and lit a cigarette. He was of medium height, had short salt-and-pepper hair, and appeared slightly overweight. Dressed in Khaki pants and a plain short-sleeved shirt, he looked like the classic redneck pig, and I found myself growing suspicious as we approached him. Still, the transformation in Brooks was a strong recommendation of this man.

"What's this dude's name, anyway?" I muttered under my breath as we drew closer.

"Paul . . . Paul Crockett."

Part
Three

The Power
of
Agreements

16

Wildflowers were still blooming in July, and the vineyards were green; there was fruit on the apple and fig trees and a rich yield of boysenberries behind the bunkhouse. It felt good standing in the sunlight with Bo, beside Crockett and Brooks. The mountains were a blue-purple against the sky. Everything seemed alive and measureless; a breeze funneled down the canyon, blowing over the garden. Even the heat felt clean. I could smell coffee brewing in the kitchen.

We'd been there just moments when Juanita burst out the door to give Bo a big hug; then me.

"God, Paul, don't you guys ever bathe anymore?"

Crockett grinned. "Yeah, ya are a little ripe-smellin'."

Bo and I exchanged glances. Neither one of us had bathed for days. She wore what she'd worn a month ago —tattered tight-fitting Levi's and a filthy green blouse which clung to her small upturned breasts. I was in buckskins. I'd worn them since we came to Spahn's, and they were smeared with grease from hours spent working on engines. Still, Crockett's remark pissed me off.

Juanita gushed on about how well the garden was growing and how good she felt. And there was no denying it, she did look robust and energized; and somehow, prettier. Both she and Brooks seemed to reflect the vitality of the surroundings. I glanced suspiciously at Crockett, who stood to my left beside Bo, a cigarette dangling from his lips, his eyes on the mountains. When Juanita asked us inside to eat, we followed her—Brooks, Bo, then Crockett. I walked behind Crockett, scrutinizing him, wondering what he had done to bring about such profound changes in my friends.

The ranch house appeared unchanged, except that

they'd moved the big dining-room table into the center of the living room. Juanita brought in a steaming pot of beans, and moments later a tin piled high with freshly baked cornbread. Bo followed with coffee. Bo and I ate ravenously while Brooks told us of their latest mining ventures and how much work he was doing. I'd never seen Brooks so voluble and enthused. He mentioned Bob Berry, and when I asked who that was, he told me it was Crockett's partner. I understood by an exchange of glances between Brooks and Juanita that she and Berry had something going. Crockett, meanwhile, sat directly across from me, chain-smoking Pall Malls and playing solitaire, raising his eyes only on occasion, to let the smoke clear so he could see the cards. I got the impression Brooks was trying to entice him into the conversation, but all he got out of the stoic miner was an occasional "yeah," "uh-huh," or "nope." I found myself watching Crockett's thick, gnarled fingers manipulate the cards as he laid out his hand.

Looking at Crockett, you had the feeling he belonged to the desert; his skin was weathered yet resilient, like a reptile's. His face looked like the craggy wall of a mountain, as though it had been eroded and sculptured out of rock; it was hard to imagine that such a face had ever been young. His gray eyes were deeply set beneath a prominent thick-browed forehead, his nose beaklike and commanding. A strong, well-formed jaw accentuated the sensitivity of his mouth, which was full and all the more intriguing because he seldom opened it, at least during the first few hours we were there. Yet there was something tangibly solid about the man. He was *like* a mountain; you *felt* his awareness.

Later, while Brooks and I hiked down the wash to bring up the supplies, I asked him about Crockett; that's when Brooks told me that he and Juanita weren't going back to the Family.

"What do you mean? Helter-Skelter is coming down. You can't bail out!" As I spoke the words, I felt detached from them.

"Me and Crockett got a scene going here. I mean it, Paul, this dude is far-out; he's taught me a lot. I feel good. I want to stay feeling good."

"But what about Charlie? . . . What about the Family?"

"What about them?"

"What are you gonna do when Charlie comes up and finds out what's goin' on?"

"He can't."

"He *can't!*"

"Crockett put up a psychic barrier to keep him out; no one can come up here unless they have true love in their hearts."

I flashed on all our failed attempts to send supplies to Barker's. I pictured Charlie pacing back and forth in front of the saloon, cursing; I thought of Crockett playing solitaire. I said, "Come off it, Brooks!"

At the base of the wash we unloaded the pickup. Brooks helped me strap a pack of canned goods to my back; then he handed me several canteens. He hoisted his pack to his back and adjusted it. We began the climb back up the wash. Months before, Brooks could barely climb the wash without a pack; now he was moving like a mountain goat. I told him to slow down.

"What about Helter-Skelter?" I asked.

"Let Charlie worry about it . . . I'm not."

"The shit is coming down, man . . . it's heavy!"

"Not up here, it ain't."

"Hey, you're letting this old mumblefuck miner turn your head around."

"Yeah, I guess I am."

Though I wasn't cognizant of it at the time, Crockett was well prepared for my arrival; he'd heard much about me from Brooks and Juanita. They had told him that I was close to Charlie, one of the few people who could "get things done," who didn't-seem to be totally under Charlie's domination. By the time I got to Barker's, Crockett had been there nearly two months, long enough to become deeply intrigued by the story of Charles Manson, his Family, and what they called Helter-Skelter. He'd taken a liking to Brooks and wanted to help him break away from an influence which had obviously been destructive. When he met me and found that I too was riddled with Charlie's programs and viewpoints, he let it be known that he could teach me "things." But he never came out and said it; he never preached. That was Crockett's beauty as a teacher: he seldom told you anything; he merely suggested ways you might discover yourself.

But it didn't happen right away. I was suspicious of Paul Crockett. What could he teach me? He was old (forty-six), had short hair, never smoked dope or took drugs, and he spoke like a hick—the epitome of everything I had been programmed to despise. He was a redneck and a pig. At that point I figured if any teaching were to be done, it would be me educating him, clueing him on Helter-Skelter. Brooks, I figured, was easy prey—so spaced-out that anybody could teach him anything. Brooks and I had always been on opposite ends of the spectrum in the Family—Brooks at the bottom, shoveling shit, me at the top alongside Charlie, getting my fill of all the goodies and privileges. In coming to know the two of us, Crockett was given a gander at the whole spectrum of Charlie's program. Not only that, in Bo and Juanita he had discovered how the same programs worked on the girls; everything that came from their mouths was in some way a part of Charlie's rap. But I figured (as we climbed the hill) that Crockett, too, would fall "into the hole," once I set him straight.

Paul Crockett was born on February 24, 1924, at 9:30 P.M. in a little town called Ada in the state of Oklahoma. He was less than a year old when his parents moved to Texas, where he grew up with no recollection whatever of ever having been in Oklahoma. Though his mother was a schoolteacher and his father a Methodist minister, Crockett never took to institutions, religious or secular, preferring instead, as he used to put it, "to figure things out for myself." He left home at the age of eighteen and joined the Air Force to become a navigator and an officer. He was sent to the South Pacific, where he flew in fifty-two combat missions, concluding from the experience that war only proved "what fools men are." When they told him he could become a captain before his twenty-first birthday if he'd stay on, he asked if he had a choice. When they said yes, he resigned and came home.

It was after his combat experiences that he began asking himself serious questions about life and its purpose. The influence of his father and mother had inspired a thirst for knowledge, yet he could not come to grips with accepting the word of others. While working at a variety of jobs—construction, bicycle repair, manual labor—he began reading: novels, philosophical works, theology, books on Eastern religions; the Bible, Gurdjieff, anything he could get his hands on. Later he would say that reading gave him a lot of data to work with but that gaining knowledge came from doing—from integrating and accepting his own experiences; he found too that there were many experiences that simply couldn't be explained "in normal ways."

He used to tell the story of the day his brother pushed him out of a car while going down the highway. "We were doin' about seventy. . . . As I was fallin', time seemed to slow down. I could see the pavement and the rocks along the side of the highway. I pulled my arms in close to my body. My whole body seemed to be enclosed in a kind of cloud. A couple of times I stuck my hand out away from my body, but I pulled it back quick because it hurt when I stuck it out there. When I finally came to a stop in the gravel along the roadside, I'd skidded about fifty feet. Except for my hand, which had a gravel burn on it, I wasn't even scratched. Hell, I just stood up and dusted off my clothes."

One of the biggest influences in Crockett's life was a man he met in Carlsbad in the early fifties—Dr. S. L. Bailey: "Old Doc Bailey was the first man I met who could answer some of my questions. When I first met the Doc he was into what he called concept therapy and conceptology. He was working with a woman named Ruth Drown, who had developed the Drown Radio Therapy— a method of measuring the energy flow in the body by taking pictures with this little box. The AMA saw the box and called it a fraud, so that's what the Doc called it, 'the fraud.' But it worked. It had all kinds of dials and it measured energy frequency in any part of the body. Like if you had too many positive electrons in a certain gland or in the bone marrow, you'd tune in on it. Then, by puttin' your hand on the electrode plate and turning the dial very slowly back and forth and always keeping in touch with it—not too fast or too slow—the flow of electrons would either come to the body or go out of the body to give you the balance you needed.

"At the time I met the Doc, I had a problem which stemmed from one leg being shorter than the other, or at least that's what I'd been led to believe. Over the years it had gotten worse, till it hurt so bad at night that I couldn't sleep. And when I did sleep, I was so stiff in the mornin', I couldn't move. It got so I stayed awake all the time. I went all over creation tryin' to get helped; to orthopedic surgeons, neurosurgeons, and even out to the Bradshaw Clinic. They took X rays and said my body was calcifyin' . . . that the pictures showed I was turnin' into bone; not long after that I met the Doc and ended up gettin' treated by him and his machine for the next nine years until my body and my mind were pretty well cleaned up.

"I saw the Doc help a lot of people . . . a lot of people in all kinds of pain would come and restore the balance and take away the pain. He had a hell of a followin'. You could hardly get into his office, there was such a crowd there. It seemed impossible . . . but to me it was a reality. I saw it work.

"But it wasn't the machine; it was the Doc's way with people; he got them to agree to really want help and to set about it systematically. He was positive and he was truthful, and from him I learned to trust and know somethin' of what I was. . . . Then, one day, the old Doc shook hands with me and said, 'Well, I think I got you in good shape.' I wondered what he was shakin' hands for, then about two hours later some friends come and told me he'd just dropped dead. I thought: Well, hell . . . first time he shakes hands with me in nine years, then he goes and dies. I didn't know what to make of that."

After the death of Dr. Bailey, Crockett studied other disciplines, including Scientology, theosophy, and the doctrine of the Rosicrucians, utilizing precepts that he could use in his own life. "But I was never willin' to sell myself like most of them groups want you to do. . . . I might agree to do certain things for a certain period of time, but when that time was up, I was on my way."

In the late sixties Crockett became interested in mining and got into a joint venture with a couple of friends. They traveled through the Southwest looking for gold, silver, copper, tungsten, titanium, and anything else that had a market value. Then in March 1969, Crockett and a friend named Bob Berry came to Death Valley to explore the mining possibilities in a place they'd been the previous summer and knew was rich in gold: Golar Canyon. There he met Brooks Posten and Juanita.

More than a year later he described his feelings in an interview: "I'd never run into a stranger situation; talkin' to this kid disturbed me. He kept tellin' me about life and love and that to be free you had to submit to love; he talked about karma and psychic balance, and a lot of what he said was perfectly true and beautiful. It really intrigued me. But the words he spoke were not from him; they come outta him, but they were from another source . . . from a man he called, Charlie. I began to wonder where the kid was . . . where was *his* personality. It seemed hard to believe that anyone could be that heavily programmed. He told me about the Family, the girls, and about this holocaust, this Armageddon that was gonna happen, Helter-Skelter. I got real interested. I wondered about this guy, Charlie. . . . But mostly I liked Brooks and wanted to get him straightened out. It seemed like a good time to use the knowledge I had gained in a positive way. I'd only figured on stayin' in Golar Canyon a couple of weeks. I wound up stayin' eight months. It seemed like I'd found another kind of gold worth minin'."

During dinner that first night I laid out my rap on Helter-Skelter, trying to convince Crockett what I felt to be "the truth." That the shit *was* coming down, that we were on the verge of an all-out race war, and that the survivors would wind up in Death Valley with Charles Manson. Part of what I said was motivated by my belief in Charlie and Helter-Skelter; but I also considered it a personal challenge to convince this old mountain goat, Crockett (in front of Brooks and Juanita), what the real score was. To me Crockett was an adversary. I could see that he had all but succeeded in prying Brooks and Juanita away from the Family and everything we had worked so hard to achieve. Despite my own forebodings and misgivings, I had made an incredible inner investment in the Family. My loyalty to Charlie wasn't dissolved; I felt I owed him a lot. He trusted me, depended on me.

During the course of the meal I held forth without pause. No one could get a word in edgewise . . . and it was good. I rattled it off like a well-rehearsed soliloquy while the others ate. Crockett listened, looking up at me from time to time and nodding his head. Then at last he finished his meal and pushed his plate away from him and lit a cigarette.

"The way I see it," he said, "Helter-Skelter is only

coming down on you and Charlie—in your head. . . . If you think Helter-Skelter, well, that's what's gonna happen. If you put your attention on that, well, then that's what you'll get. For me, well, there ain't no such thing."

With that, Crockett took out his cards and began to play solitaire.

Later that night, Bob Berry returned from Las Vegas with supplies; Juanita greeted him warmly at the door, and after he had been introduced to Bo and me, she brought him a cup of coffee. Bob was about thirty—five-six, stocky, and muscular. He had short dark hair and rather coarse features. He looked more like a cowboy than a miner, and like Crockett, was not one to talk much. Whenever Juanita showed him affection in front of us, he'd blush and try to appear indifferent. He and Juanita were staying together in the bus, where Bob claimed they were on "mountain-lion watch." Brooks later explained that they'd spotted a few cougars around the ranch and that Bob used this as a pretext to go up there and sleep with Juanita. For a conservative guy like Bob, running into a sexually liberated member of the Manson Family, especially a gal like Juanita, whose appetites were voracious, was better than discovering gold. He hadn't finished his second cup of coffee when he said it was time for him and Juanita to go back "on watch."

The next day I hiked with Brooks and Crockett into the high country above the ranch to dig some rock out of a gold mine they were working, called the Gold Dollar. I was still battling with Crockett in my mind and refused to work with them. While they dug, I sat on a promontory overlooking the Panamint Valley. But I could hear Crockett instructing Brooks on the techniques of digging rock: "No . . . not like that . . . like I told ya, sometimes ya gotta talk to these rocks . . . ya gotta talk them right out of there. It ain't how hard ya hit it, it's the way ya hit it. . . . It's like a vibration . . . the right vibration . . . ya tap in the right place, ya talk to it, and it comes out . . . comes out so's the ore's not all busted up and destroyed. Ya pay attention and ya get the feel. Ya work together . . . with it, not against it."

That night Crockett asked me if I wanted to play some attention games with him and Brooks. We were all seated around the table after dinner. Bo and Juanita had gone with Bob Berry down to Ballarat; the ranch house

was quiet and the table was cleared c..
filled with Crockett's cigarette butts.

"Okay, now, let's start it out like this. W..
to put your attention on something, ya do it . . . .
put all your concentration on it. Then when I tell
take it off and put it someplace else, ya take it off and put
it on whatever I tell ya. . . . Got it?"

I nodded.

"Okay, now look there at the doorknob . . . focus on it
. . . put all your attention on it."

Brooks and I gazed at the doorknob.

"Keep your mind on that . . . only that."

Moments later, Crockett told us to take our attention off the doorknob and put it on the ashtray. We did.

"Now take it off the ashtray and put it on that chair."

After about fifteen minutes I interrupted him. "What
the hell kind of game is that?"

"Attention game. Ya do it for hours and hours over a
period of time, and it will build up your powers of concentration. It will rehabilitate a facility inside ya that
most people have forgotten how to use . . . a power. Ya
see, most people know how to put their attention on
things, but they don't know how to take it off . . . they
don't know how to reject things. Your attention is a part
of you: it's what you extend as a spirit; if ya got it all
stuck out on different things, ya don't have all your
energy with ya. But if ya learn to take it off, ya keep all
your energy intact. It grounds ya in the moment; it keeps
ya conscious."

What Crockett said reminded me of Charlie's rap
about "coming to Now." But Crockett made it more understandable. Had I not been so spaced-out and open to
such thoughts because of my experiences with Charlie
and the Family on LSD, I might have shut him out.

"People know how to accept but not how to reject.
To reject, or take your attention off, doesn't mean ya have
to dislike or put value on what you're rejecting; it means
simply that ya reject it; ya take your attention off. Most
people can't reject without disliking or evaluating what
they reject . . . but if ya dislike it, ya really don't reject.
Fact is, ya might as well accept it, 'cause it's a part of ya."

We began playing the game again, and I really got
into it. Before I knew it, two hours had gone by. I wanted
to keep playing, but Crockett was tired. He took his pack

...son
...khouse to sleep. Brooks
...ere to wait up for Bo.
184

...was on Crockett like a tick, asking
...questions, then trying to answer them
...in what Charlie had told me. He listened and
...about his work, digging rock, asking me to get out
of his way, saying very little. We hiked all over the
mountains that day, and I wound up carrying back a pack
full of rocks. That night while we "high-graded" the rocks,
separated the ore from the waste, Crockett started rapping about agreements.

"Everything that *is*," he said, "*is* by agreement. It's
the same as your attention. When you agree to something, ya tie up your attention in it . . . and attention is
spirit, the matrix of creation. People agree to things all
the time—implied agreements, all kinds of agreements.
. . . Ya say you'll be someplace at a certain time without
really meanin' it; ya don't go, but ya don't take down the
agreement either, so that part of your energy is strung out
. . . lost in that agreement. Had ya rejected it outright, ya
would not lose the energy. But people wind up leavin'
their attention buttered all over creation . . . through
agreements. Ya get my drift?"

I nodded. Crockett was coming on pretty strong, yet
what he said made a lot of sense to me. Though I didn't
know it at the time, he was preparing me to see enough
so that I might *reject* Charlie's trip.

But as he spoke, it got even heavier. "Look at it this
way: we live in an electronic universe. Agreements are
circuits made up of psychic energy; circuits can short out
or blow if you're not careful, but the power of agreements extends beyond that. Everything ya see around ya
is a product of it—this table, the house, my body, your
body. What holds all that in place is the force of agreement. Ya agree it's there, and so do I. In that sense it's
a reality. It's been made that way through millennia of
time . . . through this process."

"You sure you never took LSD?" I asked.

He shook his head.

"You mean *everything* is by agreement. . . . Charlie
says everything is in your imagination."

"Yeah, that's kind of how it is . . . but it's there because we agree to it . . . and it's been agreed to by the

spirit of people for years. It's a legacy, an agreed-upon reality, but there is another reality . . . when ya look at it from that reality, an astral reality, everything is just tiny particles of light being held together by electromagnetic lines of force. You can't put your hand through a wall, because you've agreed it's solid and that it's there. But on another level, you *can* put your hand through it . . . it is light, it is penetrable. But only on this higher level of reality which is a truer reality . . . it's only because people have gotten so far away from the true reality over thousands of years that they find this hard to see . . . to see it ya have to overcome the power of agreement of millions of people and thousands of years."

Many who have taken acid have had glimpses of this other reality Crockett spoke of. I knew I had, many times —times when solid objects start moving and become transparent, times when "the normal way" of seeing things suddenly lost its validity. Charlie had spoken of these things, but he had never explained them so that I understood. Often when I had asked Charlie questions he had answered by saying, "If you don't know, there's no telling you. You either know or you don't. If you ask a question, the answer is in the question . . . therefore, you do know." I saw that line of reasoning as a strength in Charlie. Later, in retrospect, I viewed it as his way of copping out.

For three days I wandered around the mountains with Crockett and Brooks; listening to Crockett had put me in a state of confusion. I knew I had to go back to the Family. I felt my obligations to Charlie; I found myself repeating *his* programs in my mind. Brooks asked me to stay with him and Crockett; he said Crockett would help us get our own musical scene together; he claimed Crockett (who never played music in his life) had taught him more about music than anyone else. Paradoxically, what drew me to Crockett was his indifference; he wasn't really trying to influence me or to convince me. He didn't tell me anything unless I asked him. What he did advise was *not* to *believe* anyone. *"Find out* and *know* for yourself." If I wanted to play the attention games, I was welcome; if not, that was fine. Brooks, however, did urge me to stay. He wanted company. His memory of Charlie and the Family was not that short; the more people he got to "agree" with Crockett, the stronger that reality became too. "Come on, Paul, I talked to Bo. She says she'll stay if you do."

After just two days I had begun to see Crockett's influence on Bo; it wasn't that he spent a lot of time with her, but when he was with her he was completely focused and attentive. And he treated her with a sincere and genuine human reverence, or, as he put it, "like a lady." Ironically, Crockett was deeply imbued with a sense of manners and propriety where women were concerned. "I think the beauty of women is about as close to truth as a man can get," he once mused. His impact on her was overwhelming. She began smiling, and I realized when I saw her smile—Bo had the kind of smile that when you saw it you felt like someone turned on a light inside you —that I hadn't seen her that happy since the first summer at Spahn's.

One night after dinner I went out on the porch and Bo followed me. Her hair was washed and coiled in a braid on top of her head. Her face seemed rounder and more childlike. I sat down and leaned against the wall of the ranch house, and she sat beside me.

"What are we going to do, Paul?"

"We got to go to Spahn's."

"I don't think—"

"The shit's coming down, Bo. . . . Dammit! We got to go back. I told Charlie we'd be back. I got to return Danny's truck."

"Do you want to go back?"

"No, but I got to."

"Why?"

" 'Cause Helter-Skelter is coming down."

17

The following morning at breakfast I told Crockett we had to go back. I half-expected him to ask me why, but he didn't.

"When ya leavin'?" was his animated response; he almost seemed glad.

"After we eat." I glanced at Bo, and she looked down at her plate.

Crockett asked me to pass him the sugar, then told Brooks to hurry so they could get to the mine before it got too hot. Bob and Juanita came in and sat down.

"See any mountain lions last night?" Crockett quipped.

"But I don't want to go," I blurted suddenly. "I like it here. I'd like to stay."

"Then what's the problem?" Crockett wanted to know.

"It's Charlie and the Family. . . . I can feel it in the pit of my stomach. I got to go back, but I really don't want to."

Crockett sipped at his coffee; then he looked at me. "What kind of agreements ya got with this man?"

"Agreements? . . . I don't have any agreements." As I spoke the words it dawned on me what Crockett was driving at—what he'd been driving at for the past three days. I realized that I had all kinds of agreements with Charlie. I'd agreed to Helter-Skelter; to spending the rest of my life—even eternity—with the Family; to Charlie's philosophy, to all kinds of things.

Crockett leaned back in his chair and rolled a cigarette from a can of Bugler. "Why don't ya go down and ask Charlie to release you of all yer agreements, then you'll feel free to do something else."

"Think he would?"

"How the hell do I know? Ask him and find out."

I watched as Crockett exhaled two streams of smoke through his nose. "I will," I said.

"Ask him to release me," Brooks said. "Me too," Juanita chimed in. "And me," Bo sputtered, setting down her cup.

After breakfast Crockett and Brooks walked Bo and me down to the mouth of the wash and helped us load the pickup with mining tools Crockett wanted dropped off in Ballarat.

We climbed into the cab and fired up the engine. "Hurry back, Paul," Brooks said.

"Yeah," Crockett said with a grin. "I got a bunch more games we kin play out here."

It takes ten hours to drive from Golar Wash to Spahn's ranch; that's a lot of time to think. It sounded easy: "just ask Charlie to release you of all your agreements." But would he? What would he say? Just what agreements? Did it mean rejecting everything? Did I *want* to reject everything? Could I? Could Bo or Brooks or Juanita? Was Helter-Skelter real or was it all in Charlie's head? Was Crockett right: that if we put our attention on Helter-Skelter, we would make it happen? Reject, release, take your attention away. It sounded good; but it wasn't that simple. For more than a year I'd been programmed to do the opposite, "to relax and float downstream," to "cease to resist," "to submit," to be one with Charlie's love. The closer I got to L.A. the more apprehensive I became. Bo slept most of the way but woke up near Saugus to express her own apprehension, her fear of Charlie. "I don't know if I can do it, Paul. How can we tell Charlie we want out? And if the shit comes down, what are we gonna do?" By the time we drove into Spahn's I had decided, not that I would leave Charlie (I was incapable of making that decision), but that I wanted the option to be able to leave if I so desired. In order to do that I knew I'd have to do as Crockett suggested.

Spahn's Ranch at night was generally quiet; the flies disappeared; so did the tourists. The wranglers went home. Walking along the boardwalk, I sometimes had the feeling that the hillsides were closing in. If you stopped in one place and listened you could hear the crickets, and intermittently the horses would snort and raise a ruckus. With the lights on—the lights from George's house, the saloon and tack room—the movie sets looked even more authentic. Living on a movie set, you develop a consciousness of acting. That's how I felt the night Bo and I drove onto the property, like an actor waiting in the wings to speak his lines.

It was dark, probably around nine P.M. when I parked Danny's pickup beside the corral, and, seeing a light coming from the semitrailer bed, walked over there with Bo. I could hear Charlie's voice as we approached. I glanced at Bo, then climbed the stairway, pulled open the flap, and went inside.

Charlie was seated on a stool at the head of the

trailer, facing me from behind a low table. A gooseneck lamp to his right illuminated his face; nearly all the Family was present and sat in front of the table and along the sides of the trailer on mattresses; in one corner behind Charlie was a mattress on which Pooh Bear and Zezos were sleeping. Charlie grinned and got to his feet as I entered with Bo right behind me.

"Hey, brother, welcome back! Hi, Bo."

We greeted everyone and Charlie sat down, still smiling. "How's things going at Barker's?"

"Good."

"Brooks and Juanita?"

"They're doin' fine." I leaned against the side of the trailer with Bo beside me. Snake and Ouisch sat directly in front of us.

"So are we, brother. Danny just delivered a whole shitload of dune-buggy parts; Clem's bringing in a rebuilt engine for the big semi. We're ready now . . . ready for Helter-Skelter."

Before Charlie could say another word I broke in. I heard myself speaking, but it was as if I had no control over the words.

"Hey, I found out why we had all that trouble getting our shit up to Barker's ranch, why we had them breakdowns and busts."

Charlie gave me a quizzical look.

"There's this old prospector up there, a guy named Crockett—a far-out old dude—said he put a psychic gate across the canyon. No one can get in unless they have true love in their hearts."

Charlie sniggered. "Oh, yeah. So what else is new?"

"No much, 'cept I'd like to ask you something." I felt Bo flinch.

"Anything, brother."

"I'd like to be released of all my agreements."

The eyes of the Family turned on me.

"Me too," Bo said.

Charlie's hesitation was only momentary; *his* eyes were hard on mine; then he laughed. "Agreements? Oh, sure, brother, I release you of all agreements."

"Brooks and Juanita too," Bo declared, her voice barely audible.

"Sure . . . sure . . . I release you . . . ain't no agreements." As Charlie spoke, I felt all his attention directed on me; but he didn't break stride, he went right on talk-ing about Helter-Skelter and what was coming down and that it wouldn't be much longer before we'd be going to the desert. It's hard to tell what Charlie was thinking, but what I had said clearly disturbed him. He may have thought that I was testing him, and probably figured, rather than start a scene in front of the Family, he would confront me later—which is what he did.

Just minutes after the gathering in the trailer ad-journed, Charlie came looking for me. I had left the trailer and walked down to the saloon to see if my BSA was still parked inside the door. I found it under a canvas tarp and wheeled it out on the boardwalk to check out the ignition switch. When Charlie knelt beside me and asked what I was up to, I told him I wanted to take the bike back to Barker's and use it to shuttle supplies up the canyon.

"Yeah, sure," Charlie said, dismissing my remarks. "What's all this talk about agreements . . . who's this guy Crockett?"

"Just a guy that's livin' up there with Brooks and Juanita . . . him and a friend named Bob. They're mining gold up behind the ranch." I stood up, and Charlie stood beside me.

"What are they, pigs?"

"Naw, Charlie . . ."

"They been fillin' your head with this agreement stuff . . . what's that supposed to mean?"

"It just means I don't want to get hung-up, man. I want to feel free to come and to—"

"You are free . . . anyone hangin' onto you?" Char-lie's voice tightened. "I don't see any chains on you; look, brother, I'm one guy who knows what free is . . . and what it isn't. We're all free here . . . we're not locked in the joint or in the heads of those straight piggie ratfuckers from Bel Air. We're free to lead the young love when the shit comes down. . . ." He flicked the hair from his eyes. "Yeah . . . yeah . . . maybe you're right . . . maybe we have been a little hung-up . . . waitin' around . . . but the time's comin' . . . it's now, man. We're gonna have to show blackie how to do it; then we go to the desert . . . and there ain't no psychic gate that's gonna keep us out."

Charlie rubbed his hands across his face; his eyes

were bloodshot; he looked frazzled and wrung-out. He said, "Get some sleep, brother . . . that's a long drive."

I got the BSA running, then grabbed a parachute out of the trailer and hiked up to the outlaw shacks. I'd no more than wrapped myself up inside the chute when I heard someone coming, then a voice.

"Paul . . . Paul . . ."

It was Snake.

"Yeah . . . over here."

I could see her figure silhouetted in the doorway as she stepped inside, then walked over to the corner of the room where I'd laid down. She lay beside me and I put my arm around her.

"You're leaving, aren't you?"

"I guess so."

"Why?"

"I'm not sure. I don't—"

"But Helter-Skelter is coming down."

"Yeah."

Snake took off her dress and crawled inside the chute. Her body was cool and firm. She told me the scene was getting heavier but that Charlie had said it "wouldn't be long." She said too that she had missed me. I knew Charlie had sent her, but it didn't matter. What I had going with Snake didn't depend on Charlie. We made love and talked and listened to the crickets. Holding on to Diane Lake, her beauty, her innocence, was like holding on to all that was left of the Family—wanting to keep it and preserve it, but not being able to.

I slept only about four hours. By sunrise the next morning I was riding my BSA through the Antelope Valley, bound for the Barker ranch. It was July 11, less than a month away from the Tate–La Bianca murders.

I arrived at Barker's late in the afternoon and slept all that night and most of the next day. When I woke up and staggered into the living room around five P.M., Crockett was sitting at the table playing solitaire.

"Coffee in there," he muttered. "Hot."

I went into the kitchen and poured a cup, then walked in and sat down across from Crockett.

"Where's Brooks?"

"Beats me."

Crockett finished the game and grinned. Then he scooped up the cards, stacked them, and stuck them back in the box he kept in his shirt pocket. He lit a cigarette. "Well?"

I told him what had happened with Charlie and that I wanted to stay at Barker's for a while. I told him I didn't know whether I was leaving the Family for good but that I wanted my freedom and I wanted to learn some things from him, maybe about mining . . . maybe about music.

"What can you do?" he asked at last.

"What do you mean?"

"What are ya good at?"

"I can hustle."

"You kin what?" Crockett squinted.

"I'm good at hustling things. . . . I can *get* things."

"Ya mean *stealing?*"

"Naw, I don't have to steal."

"Kin you *hustle* some food? We need supplies . . . it means driving to Vegas."

"Sure . . . sure . . . no sweat."

"Good . . . you kin take Stanley's truck."

"Who's Stanley?"

"Bob Berry's brother; he loaned us his truck. It's down at the base of the wash."

"Green pickup?"

"That's it." Crockett got up and fished inside his pants pocket. He pulled out some change and handed it to me.

"That's all the money I got."

"Twenty-nine cents! Gee, thanks!"

"And no stealin' . . . just hustle."

"What about gas?"

"Some gas drums in back of the truck, enough to get ya there." Crockett handed me the keys and we walked to the front gate. I told Crockett I'd be back in a couple days with all the food he could handle. Then I started down the canyon.

I found the truck at the base of the wash and drove it to Ballarat; from there I traveled by way of Shoshone, then cut across the Pahrump Valley to Vegas on the Blue Diamond Road, arriving late in the afternoon.

Coming from Death Valley into Las Vegas is like leaving one dream to enter another—an oasis or nightmare, depending on your point of view. At night, from a distance, it seems like one of civilization's crowning achievements; on closer inspection it's nothing but a surrealistic mirage. By day it looks like what it is: a string of casinos and motels flanked by run-down suburbs and a man-made lake. It has a border-town ambience and enough vice to soak blood out of a turnip. A safe way to come to Vegas (and the way many people leave it) is the way I arrived—broke. It was dark by the time I entered a casino on the strip and "cashed in" my twenty-nine cents for a quarter. With it I played a slot machine and lost before adjourning to the parking lot to sleep in the pickup.

I spent the next day hustling food. First I hit the supermarket garbage bins and salvaged a few canned goods; there was some fruit and very ripe avocados, but without ice they would never survive the trip back. After that I cleaned up in a restroom and began a door-to-door campaign soliciting donations in food for a needy group in the desert. I got all I could handle. By eleven A.M. my truck was loaded with vegetables, fruit, boxes of cereal, spices, and poultry. I had three live chickens, a rooster, two watermelons, and two dozen eggs. That afternoon I drove to Shoshone, listening to reports of the Chappaquiddick incident on the radio. The following morning I gave a guy a chicken to fill my gas tank and headed for home.

Four hours later I parked the truck at the base of the wash. After loading all the food I could carry in a makeshift backpack, I stuffed two chickens in my shirt and started up the gulch on my motorcycle, eager to show Crockett what I'd gotten and slightly vexed (at myself) for undertaking the project without some assistance. I was chugging at a good clip along the alluvial fan, my mind on Crockett and Charlie and all the changes that were coming down, when I hit a rock. The chickens squawked raucously as I flew ass-over-elbows and came down nose-first on the rocks. Cursing, I got to my feet and began hobbling around to retrieve what I could— boxes of dried food, cans, fruit, and a few eggs that had miraculously survived. I finally managed to corral the chickens, one of which was only half-alive, and laboriously made my way up the wash on foot.

Crockett and Brooks were on the porch when I got there, Brooks strumming the guitar, Crockett playing solitaire.

Brooks came running down to meet me. "Hey, you okay?"

"Yeah . . . take some of this shit, will ya?"

Crockett greeted me with a bemused smile. "Did okay, huh?"

"Yeah." I slumped to the porch and leaned against the wall. "Dumped my bike down there . . . still some stuff in the truck."

"I'll go down." Brooks grabbed a pack from inside the house and started toward the wash.

"Hurt?" Crockett wanted to know.

"Yeah . . . yeah. I hurt," I said sharply, clutching at my ribs.

"Wanna fix it?"

"What you got in mind?" I retorted sarcastically.

"Know a game."

"Shit."

"Come on." Crockett got up and walked into the ranch house. I followed him.

For the next half-hour we played his game. He instructed me to sit across from him at the table.

"Now, ya just pick a spot in the center of the room, an imaginary spot, and put all yer attention on it. Got it?"

I nodded.

"Just concentrate on that spot . . . good. Okay, now, where did it happen?—the accident. Put yer attention *there* . . . visualize it . . . see it?"

I nodded. I could visualize the rock clearly. I saw the bike.

"Now come back to the center of the room."

Again I focused on the imaginary spot.

"Now, where did it happen?"

"On that rock."

"Put yer attention on that rock." Several minutes went by. "Now, come back to the center of the room. Now, where did it happen?"

Each time I focused on the scene of the accident, I saw more. I reexperienced the pain as the bike twisted and I brushed the handlebars, then came down on my ribs. I felt my face scrape the ground, and the chicken beneath me.

"Now, come back to the center of the room."

Again and again we repeated the exercise, and each time I saw more.

Finally Crockett said, "Well, where are ya now?"

"I'm at that rock."

"Well, I told ya come back to the center of the room . . . why don't ya just leave that experience there and come on back here?"

I looked at Crockett. Then I rubbed my hands across my ribs. I lifted up my shirt and checked my side. I felt no pain at all. There was only a small welt on my left shoulder.

"When an accident happens," Crockett explained, "and pain comes on, ya have a tendency to reject it, 'cause no one wants it. But once it's there, ya can't *really* reject it; ya have to experience it. It's like trying to un-experience something that already happened."

As he said this I remembered times on acid, during a bad trip, when I saw something I didn't want to see and tried to unsee it. It didn't work.

"So if that happens and ya feel pain later—if ya carry pain ya didn't completely experience at the time—that pain is locked in yer mind, so ya got to go back and re-live that pain in its proper time and space, focus on it so that you can leave it there where it belongs. It's just a way of makin' ya conscious . . . only reason ya had the spill in the first place was most likely that ya weren't there . . . yer head was someplace else . . . maybe thinkin' about me up here in the shade . . . huh? It's a hundred and twenty-five degrees today, ya know?" Crockett grinned.

I picked up Brooks's guitar and went back out on the porch. Crockett's words on pain reminded me of what Charlie had said about fear—"you have to accept your fears and experience them . . . so you can go beyond them." Lessons I had learned in the Family were proof of that. Much of what I had experienced in the Family prepared me for what Crockett was soon to teach me. But there was a difference between Charlie's teachings and those of Crockett: while Charlie asked that we *accept* and submit to *his* love, *his* will (without thinking), the assumption being that he was *truth*, Crockett demanded that we *discover* for *ourselves* what that truth was by being totally conscious. "Ain't nothin' I can tell ya, only thing I can do is steer ya in a good direction; it's yer eyes and ears and attention that got to do the findin'."

Charlie asked that we submit to him (be uncon-

scious); Crockett, that we listen to ourselves and be conscious. What Charlie sought to create were extensions of
himself (I am you and you are me); what Crockett encouraged was the opposite—the discovery of individuality.

That night at dinner I told Brooks and Crockett I
was staying. A few days later I headed back to Spahn's to
pick up my belongings. I found the mood even more chaotic and foreboding. What had evolved into a bad dream
was about to become a nightmare.

18

I arrived at Spahn's late in the afternoon and parked
behind the tack room. It was hot and muggy; the wranglers were just quitting for the day. I recognized Shorty
and Randy with their backs to me, standing with Pearl by
the corral. I waved but Pearl didn't look up. I had an
impulse to go down and say good-bye, but decided against
it. Danny De Carlo was sitting in front of the saloon
drinking a beer when I walked up. Ouisch squatted beside
him, embroidering one of Charlie's shirts.

"How's the Great American Desert?" Danny hoisted
his beer in greeting.

"Hot. Hi, Ouisch."

"I'll drink to that . . . want one?"

I shook my head. "Charlie around?"

"Went to Malibu to pick up Bruce," Ouisch said
cheerily.

"Davis?"

She nodded.

"Where's he been?"

"England . . . studying Scientology." She moved away
from the door as I went inside. "What are you up to,
Paul?" she called after me.

"Just come to get my boots and drop off my buckskins."

"Hey, De Carlo!" I heard Bill Vance's voice from
the semitrailer. "You gonna lie on your butt all day or
give us a hand with this carburetor?"

"Just like the fuckin' army, ain't it," Danny muttered as I came out with my stuff. He drained the dregs of the beer, then picked up the rest of the six-pack and sauntered off toward the semitrailer where Bill, Turk, and another mechanic were standing. Ouisch followed him.

I tossed my gear into the back of Stanley's pickup, then trotted toward George's place.

"Hi, Paul." I heard the voice and turned to see Sherry and Pooh Bear step out of a tent set up on the site of Dody's old lean-to. Then Sadie, Snake, and Brenda appeared. They were all dressed in Levi's and wore buck knives strapped to their waists. I walked over and peeked inside the tent just as Charlie and Bruce Davis wheeled into the yard in the milk truck and parked at the side of the saloon.

As they got out of the truck Charlie said something to Bruce and he walked off toward the corral. I went down to meet Charlie. As always, he greeted me warmly, putting his arm around my shoulder.

"I'm glad you're back . . . real glad." Charlie wore buckskins, motorcycle boots, and a hunting knife strapped to his left hip. "Man, you know you're breakin' my heart. What's happening with us?"

"Nothin'. It's just I want to stay out at the ranch for a while."

"With that guy Crockett?"

"He's there."

We walked along the boardwalk.

"Do me a favor. Stay the night . . . stay in the tent. Did you see how I got it all fixed up over there? It's real nice . . . great place to make love . . . you can just stay in there, you know . . . Snake and Brenda are there."

"I got to—"

"Hey, haven't I always given you everything I got? Everything . . . all that I have is yours, man!"

I glanced at the tent and saw Snake standing in the doorway. She waved. We walked over to Stanley's truck and Charlie leaned against it, his eyes on me. He sensed then, I think, that I was really leaving, and might not come back. It must have been heavy for him. I'd been a mainstay, someone he could depend on. I reflected the flower child in him; now I was checking out. Bruce Davis, it appeared, had already assumed my position as second in command.

"What about our music, man . . . what about Helter-Skelter, the revolution?"

"I'm still into the revolution, but . . . this isn't how it used to be . . . all these other dudes, everyone strung out all over the place. Where's the love? . . . It just isn't the same."

Charlie's voice was suddenly hard.

"No, it ain't . . . man . . . the shit's coming down. The love thing is over—it's Helter-Skelter now . . . and don't you forget it. And when it happens, we're comin' to the desert—*all* of us."

"Yeah, Charlie." I climbed into the truck. "But with Crockett at Barker's, you can't get up there."

Charlie's eyes flashed. "You just watch me, brother."

At that moment I had no idea how dangerous a game I was playing. I swung the truck around and headed for the corral; that's when I spotted Juan Flynn leading a horse up from the creek. He called to me, and I stopped the truck. Dressed in a pair of Levi's, cowboy boots, and his battered straw hat, his powerful upper body delineated with sweat, Juan cut an awesome figure in the afternoon sunlight as he approached the truck.

"Where 'ave you been, Paul?"

"Barker's."

"For good, huh?"

"I don't know . . . scene here is getting freaky."

The expression on Juan's face acknowledged his agreement. "Hey, Bo and Stephanie left too . . . T.J. has gone, Karate Dave. Last week some black dudes come here looking for Charlie . . . he say he's going to cut them up."

"When you comin' to the desert?"

"Maybe soon . . . I have work here."

"Guy out there I want you to meet."

Juan stepped away from the truck and I headed for the highway, shouting to Shorty as I passed the corral. He waved his hat. It was the last time I was to see Shorty Shea. As I reached the Santa Susana Pass Road, I switched on the radio to find some music. I don't remember the exact date, but it had to be around the twenty-fifth or twenty-sixth of July, approximately one week before Charlie sent Bobby, Sadie, and Mary to Topanga Canyon to murder Gary Hinman.

By then I was beginning to consider Crockett a man I could learn a great deal from; also, unconsciously, I was priming Charlie for a confrontation with Crockett. By lauding Crockett's powers, I was building my own strength. My direction, however, was by no means certain; it was more like drifting out of one orbit into another, being drawn, half-willingly, half-unwillingly; I saw the potential for growth through Crockett's games of attention and consciousness. I had seen it work following my spill on the motorcycle. Afterward I had told Crockett, "I want to learn how to do that. I want to learn the laws of healing. Can you teach me?" But he had not committed himself; he had said only that it takes time. We had made no agreements; he knew that my ties to Charlie were deep, that it would take a long time to free myself from them. Part of what drew me to Crockett was that he did not press me. Unlike Charlie, whose ego demanded that he be the center of attention, always talking, selling his rap, Crockett felt no such need. His powers were silent and unspoken, like those of the desert.

For the next two weeks Crockett, Brooks, and I were together constantly. We rose early, hiked up to the mines, and worked several hours before trudging back with backpacks loaded with rock. Later, with mortar and pestle, we crushed the rock, separating the gold from the quartz base. This physical labor worked wonders on us. Within a relatively short time we were lugging out sixty and seventy pounds on our backs while scaling some of the steepest and most treacherous mountains in the Panamints; that kind of work and danger (one false step and it's 250 feet into oblivion) forces you to concentrate, to be there, to "come to Now." Everything we did, Crockett did with us; his body seemed indefatigable. It vexed me to see a man I considered "old" bounding up and down those trails without effort while I was exhausted.

We planted more vegetables—tomatoes, lettuce, squash, melons, onions, carrots, beans; we rebuilt fences, refurbished the bunkhouse, and laid a new floor in the kitchen. In the evenings we played concentration games for hours, learning to be silent yet in full communication with each other. Gradually my senses revitalized. I found myself aware of sounds and smells and changes in air currents; we could hear people coming through the canyon long before they reached the base of the wash. There were many occasions when Brooks and Crockett and I would look at each other simultaneously, acknowledging that we heard Bob and Juanita driving back from Ballarat hours before their arrival.

The desert lends itself to psychic phenomena; you become aware of plants, rocks, mountain peaks, lizards, insects; with everything so open and delineated, it's as though each entity is given its own special place in the cosmos "to be," and you begin to respect that space, that organism, and the vibrations it contributes to the whole of the surroundings.

At no time did we smoke dope or use drugs of any kind.

I began to understand how Crockett *could* put up a psychic barrier on the entrance to Golar Canyon. Once when I asked him about it, he said, "Well, we have created a beautiful place here . . . a good life; we've agreed to put our attention on what we have. We don't want no one comin' in here to mess it up. Unless people come with true love in their hearts, well, it don't make any sense us havin' anything to do with 'em." When Brooks asked Crockett what love was, he said, "Love is just allowing someone to be . . . the granting of beingness."

Crockett wasn't a musician, but he agreed to help Brooks and me with our music; he said it was important we had a goal and that music was a good one. The only instrument we had with us at the time was Brooks's guitar (and it had only four strings). So I cut a piece of bamboo and made a flute and taught myself to play it. In the evenings we sat outside on the porch and played. Crockett told us to project our music to the surroundings.

"Play to them rocks up there . . . play to the trees . . . project your sounds to what you see around you so they can feel it too. Sounds are just vibrations of feeling, and if you give them spontaneously and consciously, well, then, I don't see why you can't make beautiful music. There ain't no formulas for music . . . no set ways."

What Crockett said about music was very much like what Charlie taught us—to improvise and be loose, to tune with the flow of energy and just use the instrument to project it. But Crockett said more.

"The rhythm of life," he insisted, "can be understood

in terms of cosmic octaves . . . in laws of seven . . . the scale. All life is conditioned in action. It's no accident, ya know, that the word *do* is the same word as the first note of the musical scale, do. The scale begins with do and ends with do, and that, ya see, is the very pulse of life. Like they say, 'the beat just goes on.' When you play music 'consciously' with this kind of awareness, ya realize what power it really has. It's like them walls of Jericho . . . music brought them right to the ground.' Music can bring down a lot of walls. It's the harmony ya make when ya mine ore out of the mountains . . . that clear precision of sound that lets ya inside the mystery. Ya hit that pick just right, and the sound takes ya right up the musical scale to the jackpot."

One evening around six-thirty I was by myself on the porch. Crockett and Brooks were up at the mine, and Juanita and Bob were in the bus. I was playing my flute, trying to project the sounds across the garden and beyond it to the fig trees. I was completely absorbed in the sounds and the touch of my fingers on the stops. But I noticed a lizard at the far end of the porch basking in the last of the sunlight, and after a time he crawled over to me and just stayed there by my leg while I played. A little while later, he crawled up on my leg, just tilting his head from time to time. Finally he crawled up my arm and across my hand and out onto the flute, looking into the holes, curious, I guess, as to where those sounds were coming from. It was only when I moved my hand and started laughing that he shot down my arm and dropped to the floor, before crawling through a crack in the porch.

Sometime around August 3, Stanley Berry, Bob's brother, drove up to the ranch to tell us he'd located a good mining prospect in the Muggillon Mountains in northern Arizona and that we should go down there and check it out. We talked it over one evening during dinner and decided to make the trip. Stanley left the next morning, saying he'd meet us in Kingman at his brother Tom's place and that we could start from there. We left two days later.

We stopped in Las Vegas to buy supplies and a few mining tools. Bob drove while Juanita and Crockett sat with him up front. Brooks and I rode in back. The drive from Vegas past Lake Meade is a scenic one, and after days of hard work, Brooks and I were enjoying it. We sat on a mattress with our backs against the cab of the truck discussing the prospects of a meeting between Charlie and Crockett. I asked Brooks if he thought Charlie and Crockett would get along.

He shrugged. "I doubt it . . . but I'd sure like to see them together. I think Big Paul would blow Charlie's mind."

"Charlie says he's comin'."

"Yeah, when Helter-Skelter comes down . . . he'll be tryin'."

"Think Crockett will ever agree to that?"

"Told me he wants to meet Charlie *sometime*."

"Charlie might blow Crockett's mind."

"Yeah."

At that moment, both Brooks and I turned around to see Crockett looking at us through the rear window. He had a big grin on his face.

For the next week we waited for Stanley. While Brooks and I roamed around Kingman, Crockett stuck pretty close to Tom's, reading and playing solitaire. But he was getting angry. By the end of the week he was arguing with Bob.

"Don't your brother know what a telephone is?"

"He'll be here," Bob said.

"We'll wait one more day."

"I said, he'll be here."

"After tomorrow, I won't."

On Saturday, August 9, 1969, while Brooks, Crockett, Juanita, and I drank iced tea and watched a late TV report on the Apollo 11 first moon landing, which had taken place the week before, Tex Watson, Susan Atkins, Patricia Krenwinkle, and Linda Kasabian paid a visit to 10050 Cielo Drive in Bel Air to do a job for Charlie. The following morning at breakfast we saw another news broadcast describing the slaughter of five people and an unborn child; Crockett was seated at the table across from me sipping his coffee. Brooks was to his left, and Bob and Juanita were still in bed. The newscaster had finished his brief report, closing with a remark about how bloody the murders had been and that Roman Polanski, the husband of Sharon Tate, had not been available for comment. Crockett lit a cigarette and looked at me, exhaling as he did so. "Wouldn't it be somethin' if old Charlie did that."

I looked at Brooks, who was wiping egg from his platter with a piece of toast. "Naw . . ." he said, "no way."

But Crockett's crack bothered me. My first impulse was to call him on it. Where did he get off saying a thing like that? He didn't know Charlie. He didn't know the Family; he was just a wise-ass miner with a big mouth and a lot of games. Yet, when he said it, a chill ran through my body.

"What's the matter, Paul?" Crockett asked.

"Nothin', except you got a rotten sense of humor."

In retrospect, I see my reaction to Crockett's remark as an expression of my own uncertainty. Had I truly believed it impossible, I would have forgotten it at once and regarded it, as Brooks had, as a bad joke. Yet, in some respects, Crockett was indirectly attacking me. Since Charlie and the Family were one, any comment regarding Charlie was applicable to us. If Charlie's trip had become murder (which I wouldn't consciously allow myself to believe, despite his talk about showing blackie), then all of us were in some sense a part of it. Months later, I would ask Crockett about the remark. He said he remembered making it but that he hadn't really *thought* it was true. "It's jest that sometimes somethin' comes into yer head and ya say it and it don't make any sense and ya don't really believe it but still ya say it. It's kind of an impulse. I've found that sometimes them impulses are right and sometimes they're not, but I like to give 'em a chance. Fact is, I never thought of old Charlie as a murderer until I finally come up to him face to face."

The next day, when Stanley failed to show, we loaded the truck. Bob got angry and said he and Juanita were going back to Barker's to get their stuff and split. Crockett said that was a fine idea.

In Vegas we bought a newspaper, and that's when we read about the La Bianca murders. According to the article, the police did not believe the Tate and La Bianca murders were related; the article said further that a suspect for the Tate murders was in custody. It did not say that on the door of the refrigerator in Lino La Bianca's house two words had been written in blood: Helter-Skelter.

From Vegas we drove across the Pahrump Valley into

Shoshone. Bob stopped so that Juanita could buy some cigarettes. Then we filled up with gas and headed north. We weren't twenty miles out of town when a sheriff's patrol car screamed down upon us and nearly ran Bob off the road. Two khaki-clad officers leaped out of the car with shotguns.

Moments later we were all lined up along the roadside with our hands up. The shorter, stockier cop waved the shotgun at us; he looked like a madman.

"Don't any of you move, by Jesus, or I'll blow your goddamned heads off!"

19

August 1969 will always remain indelible in my mind: the Tate–La Bianca murders, the bloodcurdling fruition of the Manson nightmare, demons unleashed from the bowels of a diseased man in a diseased society. In August 1969, at a rock festival at Woodstock, 400,000 gathered to listen to a moving expression of a generation's agonized feelings for its country—for the gulf between the flower children's aspirations and the harsh realities of what was going down in America. I felt the harshness that morning while gazing down the barrel of Don Ward's shotgun.

Don Ward was short, balding, middle-aged, and built like a fireplug. His reputation as a lawman had spread far beyond his legal jurisdiction in the valleys around Shoshone. I'd never met him before that day, but I'd been told once in Tecopa that "old Don Ward is a little bit o' hell." He was that morning. When Bob asked him what was going on, he waved the barrel of his shotgun up under Bob's nose.

"What's goin' on is that this gal"—he pointed at Juanita—"about two months back, she gave my niece a marijuana cigarette!"

"I didn't even—"

"Yes, ya did!" Don bellowed, his face turning a vibrant crimson. "My wife runs the drugstore in town and she seen ya. Now, you just listen: there's six kids in Shoshone on pot. And I know where it come from—from that goddamned ranch up by Golar Wash. If I ever hear of it happenin' again, ever, I'm gonna come up there and clean that whole place out!"

"Don't threaten us," Crockett said. "It isn't necessary, and you won't like it." Ward glanced at Crockett as the other cop handed him I.D.'s taken from our wallets.

"It might have been necessary a couple of months ago," I added, "but it isn't now . . . you can search the truck."

"I know what I can do!" Ward barked. "And I know this gal was passing out marijuana."

"Not anymore," Juanita said. "Things are different. I'm married now . . . this is my husband."

Bob's head spun around as though he'd been punched

"I.D. says you're Wildebush and he's Berry. Well, we don't go for them back-porch ceremonies around here."

"Well, we're *getting* married."

"Ain't that swell."

Ward returned the I.D.'s and told us to scram. "If I hear of any more funny stuff going on at that ranch, there's gonna be some heads rollin'."

By noon the next day Bob and Juanita were packed and ready to go. We helped them transport their stuff to Bob's truck at the foot of the canyon, wished them luck, and watched as they drove out across the valley. It was the last I ever saw of Juanita Wildebush.

During the next three weeks Brooks and I worked daily with Crockett—climbing mountains, digging, studying the terrain. The exercises he put us through were strenuous. With full packs, he had us running up and down the steepest trails time after time without resting, while he ran with us, suffering as much as we did. "Keepin' up with two twenty-year-old kids ain't that easy."

One afternoon, while Brooks cleaned up the ranch house, Crockett and I went out to work the Gold Dollar. On the way back from digging (our packs filled), Crockett suggested we play follow the leader. "Ya just do what I do." With that he took off down the trail at a trot. I followed him, stepping where he stepped. When we got to the bottom, he turned around. "Now, let's run back up.

You go first." I was beat but determined to keep up with Crockett. I took off up the trail with him right behind me. By the time I reached the top, I was panting. But I'd no more than paused to catch my breath than Crockett whirled around and started back down again; wearily I trudged after him, trying to keep pace, trying to keep from falling on my face. By the time we reached the bottom, I was gasping for air. "Okay," he said, "one more time." I couldn't believe it! Instinctively I turned and started back up, but my breathing was coming too hard, I just couldn't go on. I was angry and exasperated. Midway up, I'd had it and was ready to cuss Crockett out. When I whirled around, he was right behind me, grinning. I don't know what I intended to say, but all that came to my mouth was a long wheezing "Youuuuuuul!"

As I gasped out this word, Crockett stopped in his tracks, still grinning. I looked at him dumbly, half-dazed.

"What happened to all that heavy breathin'?" he asked.

As he spoke I realized that my panting had stopped. I was calm, collected, and breathing evenly. To me, the experience was almost revelatory—off and on for years, I'd practiced yoga, trying to learn to control my breathing and energy flow. This new discovery elated me.

"No need to keep on breathin' like that once ya stop workin'," Crockett remarked. "Most times people get to breathin' hard and let the momentum of it carry 'em when they don't need to. . . . Let's head back and get something to eat."

I followed Crockett up the wash, feeling suddenly more centered and in tune with my body than I ever had squatting on a yoga mat.

"Ya know," he said moments later, "one reason you work so hard is that you never learned how to walk."

He pointed out how I dragged my feet instead of walking with my knees raised and my steps following each other in an even rhythm. "Walking shouldn't be work, it should be like floatin'. Tell ya what, pretend you're walking four inches off the ground. Ya just do what I do, make every step a different step, never take two steps alike. Ready?" I nodded, and Crockett strode forward, stepping to the left, then to the right, up on a rock, down on another, walking on his toes, then his heels, on the side of his foot—taking long strides, then short ones, then a series of tiny steps. We must have looked like a couple of spastics winding our way up the wash. But in time, during the days that followed, this exercise helped me gain an awareness of walking, and I learned to move with an easy stride that took much of the tension out of the exercises.

Crockett used to say that the body is the temple of the spirit and that the way the body moves is a reflection of the spirit. "The spirit moves the body and the muscles in a beautiful way. It don't mean the spirit has to stay in the body, but mostly it does, and the way I see, it deserves a nice ride. Spirit," he said, "occupies no time and no space. It can postulate, and perceive what it postulates." But getting in touch with it, he insisted, was impossible unless one was tuned in to the body. "It's like all that yoga . . . gettin' the body lined up so's the spirit can move around some and be in touch with other spirits, other forces."

Charlie's views on the body's importance in sex closely paralleled Crockett's. Charlie had said that what made sex "a spiritual trip" was spontaneity—"Change the motion, change the rhythm," or as Crockett had put it, "Never make the same step twice." It was a way of getting free, aligning the body with the spirit, and in so doing being in touch with the greater energies around you.

"Sometimes," Crockett said, "you hear people say that mind and spirit are one. But it really ain't like that. A better way to look at it is to picture a man riding in a carriage. The carriage is the body. The spirit rides in the carriage. The mind is the driver sitting on top. The emotions are the horses pulling the carriage. The brain is the reins between the mind and the emotions. The mind, the emotions, and the body are all vulnerable to distraction, laziness, habit, misdirection. I mean, you just can't let that carriage go along on its own momentum and think your spirit is okay. Ya got to be aware all the time. That's why we keep on carryin' heavier loads and climbin' steeper trails—to keep our awareness keen. It's like ya told me Charlie said, 'Come to Now.' Well, that's right, where the spirit is concerned, Now is a twenty-four-hour-a-day proposition."

Perhaps the heaviest experience of that summer happened around eight-thirty one night when it started to rain. The three of us were sitting in the bunkhouse playing bridge. A couple of my friends—a man and his wife—had come up to the ranch that day and were sleeping in the bus with their little daughter. We were in the midst of the game, joking about how we had made it rain (it seldom rains in Death Valley in August) just by postulating it in our minds, when I remembered I hadn't taken the mattress up to the bus for my friends to sleep on. The mattress was still leaning against the wall of the bunkhouse.

"That floor gets pretty hard," Crockett said. "Why don't you run the mattress up to 'em?"

"Rainin' too hard now."

"Naw, the rain will stop when you go outside . . . long enough for you to take it up there and come back."

Brooks and I both looked at Crockett.

"Well, are ya gonna do it?" he asked me.

"Sure . . . sure." I grabbed the mattress and ran through the open door. The moment I stepped outside, the rain stopped dead. Flabbergasted, I hurried up the hill to where the bus was parked, left the mattress, and trotted back to the bunkhouse; it couldn't have taken more than forty seconds. Not one drop of water fell on me. Yet, the moment I stepped back inside the bunkhouse, it started to pour.

Crockett was grinning from ear to ear.

"How the hell did you do that?"

"We did it," he said.

"How?"

"Well, you saw everything I saw—you tell me how. . . ."

"But how did you know?"

"Sometimes ya just know things."

"It doesn't make sense," I said.

"Postulate and perceive," Brooks declared.

By that time Brooks and I were firm believers in Crockett's powers. The stronger his influence, the more anxious we were that he meet Charlie. We hadn't seen a newspaper in weeks and knew nothing about developments in the Tate–La Bianca investigation, nor that Spahn's had been raided (on August 16), the Family arrested for possession of stolen vehicles, and later released. We asked Crockett to agree to see Charlie, but he wouldn't until he was ready, until his own curiosity about "this guy Charlie" got the better of him.

A few days later, Brooks and I were in the garden

picking vegetables while Crockett sat on the porch whittling on a piece of wood. The air was still; yet, I heard something—a low rumbling sound which seemed to be coming from some great distance.

"What's that noise?"

Brooks looked up.

"Hear it?"

"Yeah, I hear something. Sounds like a motor . . . someone coming up the valley."

For three days we heard the sound—a low, ominous vibration, a kind of psychic rumbling that seemed to echo through the canyon. But no one came. Finally, one evening after hiking back from the mine, I asked Crockett what it was.

"Your friend Charlie," he said solemnly without looking at me. "I lifted the gate. Wish I wouldn't have. Listen to it . . . sure ain't the sounds of harmony, is it?"

Sometime around noon the following day, Brooks and I looked up at the same time. We were seated at the dining-room table across from Crockett.

"You smell that?" I asked.

"Yeah . . . somethin'," Brooks mumbled through a mouthful of cornbread.

Crockett sniffed. "Smells like a combination of honey . . . and pussy."

For some reason the association struck me. "It's Brenda . . . goddamn, it's Brenda!"

Two hours later, a bright yellow dune buggy pulled into the yard, and Brenda, Tex, and Bruce Davis got out.

"Here they are," Crockett declared in a monotone as Brooks and I walked out onto the porch.

Brenda waved. "Howdy," she called out.

I waved back and walked down the path with Brooks, my eyes on Tex Watson. I could hardly believe it was the same person. He looked like a zombie. His face was unshaven; his hair had grown several inches and hung over his eyes. The clothing he wore—Levi's and T-shirt—was filthy. His vapid stare unnerved me. Like Bruce, he carried a sheathed hunting knife, and I noted when he stood aside to let Brenda out of the dune buggy that a shotgun and a box of shells were lying on the seat.

Bruce was no less grungy, yet he seemed more

alert. There were open sores, like boils, on the side of his neck and on both arms. Brenda, meanwhile, though she appeared slightly emaciated, was enthusiastic and greeted Brooks and me with a hug, as Bruce hopped out of the jeep to deliver Charlie's message:

"Charlie's down at Sourdough Springs . . . says if he has your *agreement*, he'll come up." By that time Crockett had ambled down from the house.

"Sure," he said, "send him up."

While Bruce drove the dune buggy back down the wash to relay the message, Brenda and Tex followed us inside the ranch house. Brooks brought out a plate of cornbread and a pot of coffee. When I got up to go to the kitchen, Crockett followed me, leaving Bruce with Tex and Brenda. Brenda was rapping on about Helter-Skelter and how they were ready to move everything to the desert. I heard her mention something about Bobby and Mary, but the words were unintelligible. Crockett walked up beside me to say that Charlie was playing "fear games" and to keep my cool.

Less than an hour later Charlie drove into the yard behind Bruce with a full contingent of girls: Squeaky, Sandy, Ouisch, Snake, Sherry, Cathy, and Gypsy. When I went out to greet them, Charlie gave me a big hug, but his eyes were scanning the ranch house. "Where's this guy Crockett?" he asked almost at once.

"Come on in and meet him."

It must have been about four when we all gathered in the ranch house around the table. Crockett sat at one end playing solitaire, Tex at the other, beside Snake and Squeaky. Charlie, meanwhile, paced nervously around the room, casting an occasional glance at Crockett, while declaring that the movement of guns, jeeps, dune buggies, and supplies to Death Valley had begun. At one point Charlie came up behind Brooks, who was seated beside Crockett, and pulled out his hunting knife. He jerked Brooks's head back and laid the blade against his throat; he spoke to Brooks but looked at Crockett.

"You know, Brooks, I should cut your throat."

"Right, Charlie," Brooks said jokingly, as though it were all in jest.

It's certain Charlie was struck by the change in Brooks, who, only months before, was completely paranoid and hardly able to function. It's equally certain that had Brooks known about the murders, he would not have been so cool.

But it wasn't Brooks or me that Charlie was baiting, it was Crockett, who, after a cordial "howdy" and a hand-shake, had lapsed into silence before his cards. Charlie wasted little time in sending several of the girls with Bruce Davis to check on the Meyers ranch; then he sat beside Crockett and began rapping about Helter-Skelter. Crockett just listened while Charlie laid out his trip, pausing just long enough to ask Crockett for a cigarette. Crockett handed him one. A couple of times Crockett muttered "yeah . . . uh-huh" but little else. It wasn't until Charlie got into his "we-are-all-one" routine that Crockett seemed to perk up and listen more intently. Brooks was standing in the doorway to the kitchen. I was seated at the opposite end of the table beside Brenda.

As Charlie spoke, Crockett nodded, his hair falling in tight ringlets around his eyes. Charlie leaned forward, his elbows on the table, his hands gesturing freely.

"Dig it," he said. "I am you and you are me."

"No," Crockett interrupted. "No . . . that ain't true."

Charlie's hands came to rest on the table; he just stared as the old man went on to explain, while I exchanged glances with Brooks.

"We are both spirits . . . that's true, both capable of postulating and perceiving that which we postulate. In that sense we are the same . . . but we have lived different lives and had different experiences, therefore I am not you and you are not me."

Moments later, Bruce Davis came in to announce that everything seemed copacetic at the Meyers ranch . . . ready to move in.

Charlie glanced at Crockett, who had returned to his game; then he addressed me. "Come on, Paul, let's take a dune-buggy ride."

We hiked down the trail and I climbed into the dune buggy.

"Look," Charlie said, climbing in beside me, "get this straight—I don't release you of your agreements. I don't release you from nothin'!" He fired up the engine and backed the buggy into the road.

"You know, you broke my heart, man . . . just when I needed you."

I didn't say anything. I felt strangely composed as we

passed the Meyers place and headed up behind the ranch.

"I got a scene going here now, Charlie."

"What kind of scene? What are you doing?"

"Just doin' things with Brooks and Crockett."

"What things?"

"You told me never to put my business in the streets."

"*I'm not the streets!*" Charlie bellowed, slamming on the brakes, his eyes flashing. "What about our trip . . . what about the things we were doing?"

"I'm still doing them, I'm still—"

"I ought to kill that old man is what I should do."

When we reached the summit, Charlie stopped and faced me.

"I'm gonna get you back with me . . . you ain't released from nothin'. . . ."

"It's too late."

"Even if I have to torture your little ass." He glanced at me. "Even if I have to tie you to a tree and slit your belly open; I may just tie you up and have the girls take turns givin' you head till you're about ready to come, then I'll cut your prick."

I remembered Charlie's fear games and was determined not to let him get to me. "You're a riot," I said.

"You know, man, we had to *kill* Shorty." He fired up the engine, his eyes still on mine.

"That right? How come?"

"Got to talking too damn much . . . a real pain in the ass . . . we cut him up real good."

I didn't believe him. I didn't *want* to believe him. Had I gone for it, I would have been overwhelmed with fear, and that fear might have done me in. Yet, when he said it, I felt it might be true, that Charlie *was* capable of such an act. Only minutes before, I'd seen him put his knife to Brooks's throat. Yet it was all for show, all done to get to Crockett. Crockett was the one Charlie wanted —not to kill, but to discredit and invalidate in front of the Family. Winning me back would be one way to do it.

Charlie recognized and respected Crockett's power (the fact that he asked permission to come up to the ranch was proof of that); there was also a part of him that sought to learn what Crockett had to teach. By that time Charlie had created a void around himself; he had fallen "into the hole" of his own madness. He could only grow if he were challenged, and by then there was no one to do so—just a band of followers programmed to heed his every whim. Just how far they were programmed to go (and had gone), I had no idea.

As we approached the Meyers ranch, Charlie described his plans to move in immediately. He spoke to me as though I had agreed to rejoin the Family, which I hadn't. He said he was bringing in enough supplies and weapons to outfit an army. He said Helter-Skelter would go down in recorded history as the grand finale.

We had just pulled in and parked in front of the Barker ranch when Charlie asked if I'd heard about Bobby Beausoleil and Mary Brunner.

"What about them?"

"They're in jail, man . . . for murdering Gary Hinman."

"Did they do it?"

Charlie hopped out of the dune buggy. "Sure they did it . . . you did it, I did it . . . we all did it."

By the time it was dark, Charlie and the Family had moved, lock, stock, and barrel, into the Meyers ranch, leaving Brooks, Crockett, and me alone at the Barker ranch, just a quarter of a mile away.

20

The following morning, the three of us were up early, Crockett was scrambling eggs and frying bacon while Brooks and I packed the mining gear and filled the canteens. We'd stayed up much of the night discussing what had happened. I'd told them what Charlie had said to me. Brooks suggested we split. Crockett said no.

"I ain't goin' anyplace . . . we got our work here, and I'll be damned if I'm gonna be run off."

Our "success" with Charlie during that initial encounter was due to several factors: for one thing, Crockett anticipated Charlie would use fear tactics to influence us; though I knew nothing about the Tate–La Bianca murders (which was also in our favor), I had experienced

Charlie's fear games before. Too, Crockett had been prepared for Charlie by Brooks and me. We'd been spouting his rap for months, so that nothing he said was new to Crockett. Crockett's validity, meanwhile, had been established in Charlie's mind by the mere fact that Brooks, Juanita, Bo, Stephanie, and I had defected. Equally disturbing, perhaps, in light of my claim of a "psychic barrier" on the canyon, was Charlie's inability to get his trucks and supplies up to the ranch. Charlie knew enough about psychic power to realize that such phenomena were possible, and after meeting Crockett, however briefly, it became clear to him that the old miner was for real. In a single afternoon the stage was set for what was to become a battle of nerves. The month that followed was both bizarre and frightening.

While we ate that morning, Crockett reiterated what he'd said the night before. "The idea is not to take anything from Charlie—not even Snake, Paul. We don't need to make any agreements with him . . . we have all we need right here—a mine to dig, a good garden, plenty to keep us busy. We put our attention on what we have."

Brooks and I both sensed that Crockett was intrigued by Charlie and that part of his motivation to stay was prompted by his own curiosity. Crockett loved games. When Brooks asked him what he thought about Charles Manson, Crockett replied succinctly, "He has a lot of power."

We'd no more than stepped out the door when Snake appeared at the gate and motioned to me. Dressed in skin-tight Levi's and a transparent silk halter top, she stood leaning against the fencepost. Charlie wasn't wasting any time. While I spoke with Snake, Crockett and Brooks started down the wash. She asked what I was doing and I told her we had work to do.

"Charlie wants you to come up and make some music. He brought tapes of the stuff we recorded at Spahn's."

"Maybe later."

Charlie knew my greatest tie to the Family was the music. A lot of the work was mine. He also knew how tight I was with Snake. She asked if I was coming back with the Family.

I said no, and started down the wash after Brooks and Crockett.

"I'll come back later, Paul," she called after me.

It was around nine o'clock and already hot; the sides of the wash loomed up on either side of me as I scrambled over the boulders, then descended to the creek bed. I spotted Brooks and Paul far down the wash, Crockett in front wearing a red bandanna tied around his neck, and Brooks just behind him. I could see the tire tracks from Charlie's dune buggies in the sand, and yellow paint on an outcropping of rock where the vehicles had scraped the canyon walls. I thought about Snake and decided then that I would make love with her. What I had going with her (in my mind) had nothing to do with Charlie. Submitting to any of the other girls would be different, like taking of Charlie's hospitality. But with Snake I had established a separate relationship. That night, when we got back to Barker's, she was there . . . and I was horny. I knew Charlie had sent her, but it didn't matter. I took her up to the bunkhouse and we made love.

Later, when Crockett asked me what happened, I told him.

He shook his head. "You're a fool," he muttered.

"Maybe so, but I feel a lot better."

Around eleven the next morning Stanley Berry pulled into the yard and parked his pickup. Brooks was on the porch; I heard him call out to Stanley.

"Stanley's here," I shouted to Crockett.

Crockett came out of the bathroom as Stanley entered the house, handing me a letter as he did so.

"Letter sent to Bob's post-office box in Vegas." Stanley poured himself a cup of coffee and sat down at the table. He was second oldest of the Berry brothers and by far the mose irascible. He had crew-cut black hair, a chubby face, and walked like a portly, disoriented penguin. He wore a rancid sweat-stained felt hat, which he took off and set on the table.

"Hundred and thirty in Ballarat at eight this mornin'," he said, more to himself than to any of us.

"Got to go to L.A.," I announced. "Induction physical . . . . Shit!"

"Finally gonna do somethin' fer yer country, are ya?" Stanley jibed. " 'Stead o' hangin' around with this no-good rock hound."

Crockett sat down with a cup of coffee and took out his cards.

"How're Bob and Juanita gettin' along?" he asked.

"Got married Sunday . . . no, Saturday . . . and left the state." Stanley slurped at his coffee. "No great loss . . . as a miner, Bob wasn't worth two tits on a boar." He set his cup down. "What's all the to-do up at Meyers'? I seen two spanking-new dune buggies sittin' out front . . . seen a couple of guys down in the wash too, drivin' motor-cycles; said they was headed up here."

"More supplies for Charlie," I said, looking at Brooks. "Probably Bill Vance."

"Well," Stanley said, getting to his feet, "I got to stop at Meyers' and pick up some of my tools, then I'm headin' back to Vegas; anyone want a ride?"

"Yeah, I'll ride with you . . . then hitchhike to L.A. and make that physical by Monday."

Crockett glanced up from his cards. "Good idea."

"Yeah, ya might get lucky," Stanley joked, "get drafted . . . go to Veet-Nam."

"Would you draft him?" Crockett asked dryly. "Either one of 'em?"

Stanley looked at me, then at Brooks. "Yeah, I see what ya mean."

I smiled and flipped Crockett off.

Stanley grinned. "Hey, little Paul, that reminds me, ya know what a taint is, don't ya? Think he's old enough to hear this, Big Paul? . . . Ya know, Brooks?"

"Nope, what's a taint?"

"Ya know that little space in there between the pussy and the asshole?" He paused, his eyes dancing from me to Brooks. "Well, *taint* pussy and *taint* asshole!"

Stanley's laugh sounded like a flock of startled poul-try.

I ripped off a booming fart. "Let's go," I said.

On our way out, we stopped at the Meyers ranch so Stanley could pick up his tools; Clem and Bruce were sitting outside with Brenda and Sandy. The dune buggies were pulled right up to the house; boxes of supplies lay strewn along the narrow porch. Charlie appeared on the porch with Squeaky as Stanley and I got out of the truck. He was all smiles. He told Stanley that he was welcome to any tools or equipment he saw lying around. Stanley thought that right neighborly and immediately loaded his truck with backpacks, picks, and shovels that Charlie had brought up from Spahn's. It was obvious to me that Stan-

ley's eagerness to actually take the stuff pissed Charlie off.
That was Charlie's way with people: offer them everything
so as to immediately put them in his debt. Usually the *offer*
was enough. The first day I met Charlie he offered me food,
shelter, a harem of women—his entire life-style—asking
only that in exchange I "cease to exist," a fate that could
well have become Stanley's had he ever returned to the
Meyers ranch while Charlie was there, which he didn't.
Several days later, Charlie would tell Crockett, "When
Stanley comes back up here, I'm gonna bury him." We
considered it part of Charlie's ongoing fear games, not
knowing that by then he'd been responsible for at least
eight murders.

I attended my physical in L.A. on a Monday morning
and before noon was classified as unfit for military service. A well-thought-out spiel on the virtues of drugs in
expanding consciousness (plus my police record) was
enough apparently to make me "undesirable." That afternoon I hitchhiked up to Spahn's to find Juan, only to learn
that he had left for Golar Canyon. In the meantime,
Brenda had returned to Spahn's to deliver a message to
Clem and Gypsy: Charlie wanted them to come to the
Meyers ranch at once and to bring a load of motor parts.
Brenda hailed me as I approached the boardwalk, and I
walked down to the corral, where she and Clem were
sitting on the chassis of a dune buggy smoking a joint.

Brenda informed me they were driving back to the
desert later that afternoon and that I was welcome to
ride with them. I thanked her and told her I would. She
asked why I hadn't come back to the Family, saying that
Charlie was hurt by me and that I was needed. By then,
Brenda had become one of Charlie's heaviest and most
dependable girls. She could talk his rap and get things
done. And in contrast to some of the others, she never appeared spaced-out or lethargic. Yet, Charlie had a firm
hold on her. Like everyone else, she had been ordered
to work on me.

Clem, on the other hand, was totally blitzed, and sat
slouched over the steering wheel of the dune buggy, his
eyes glassy, his hair matted and snarled; he wore buckskins and a hunting knife on his belt. He appeared stiff,
almost cadaverous, as though the essence of what was
once Steve Grogan had been drained out of his body and

replaced by a recording that mumbled bits and snatches about Helter-Skelter and the piggies and how beautiful it would all be when the young love came to the desert.

Later, on the ride back to the desert, he became animated. He was driving, while Brenda sat between us. "Hey," he said, "heard about Shorty . . . huh?"

I didn't reply. I just looked straight ahead over the tops of boulders fronting on the horizon, and beyond them to the mountains, which were cast in crimson, as if a fire were burning somewhere beneath my vision. I did not want to believe what Clem was saying, but I knew it was true, and he didn't stop talking.

". . . Yeah, it was a trip, you know. I never seen so much blood . . . it was all over everything. But he wouldn't die . . . he jest wouldn't die . . . he kept sayin', 'Why, Charlie, why? Why, Steve, why?' And we just kept stabbin' him . . . me and Bruce and Tex and Charlie. 'You know why, motherfucker?' Charlie says . . . but he wouldn't shut up. . . . So when Charlie told me, I took the machete and chopped his head off so he'd stop talkin' . . . and it just rolled off the trail, bloop . . . bloop . . . bloop . . . into the weeds."

I didn't tell Brooks and Crockett what Clem had said. I justified it by trying to convince myself it wasn't true, that it would be a weakness. I wanted to be strong and not tell them. Yet, deep down, in the truest part of myself, which was only then becoming partially accessible, I knew it was true, that everything I had been committed to in the Manson Family had turned foul, irrevocably malignant.

Juan spent two days at the Meyers place with Charlie and the Family, then moved into the Barker ranch with us; he said very little, but I sensed he knew a lot. Meanwhile, more supplies arrived for Charlie—stolen dune buggies, Harleys, weapons, food supplies. Helter-Skelter was in full swing, happening just as Charlie had described. There was still a part of me, even then, that thought maybe he was right; Brooks and Juan expressed similar feelings, yet we all recoiled at "the reality" of what the Family had become. It is not easy to see people you love become subverted, twisted, rendered into robots.

Crockett became our island of sanity, something solid like the mountains we could turn to and feel assured. Crockett had agreed to this position, consciously pitted himself against Charlie. Juan's defection became Crockett's victory. But the battle was only beginning.

Juan's decision to join us wasn't made until he had taken off for a week (with a canteen and some dried figs) and hiked into Butte Valley to be alone. Juan Flynn was a deeply sensitive man, by nature happy and thoroughly outgoing. During the course of our friendship, I saw evidence of his compassion and generosity. His experience in the United States (after coming from Panama) had been no picnic. Immediately upon arrival, he was drafted into the army and sent into combat in Vietnam. He later confessed to all of us that his battlefield experiences were terrifying and that only by smoking hashish could he keep from being totally paranoid.

"I was scared," he admitted. "Sometime I theenk I will die and that eet would be better to die than to be so frightened . . . that I just have to fight and fight and kill anyone who might kill me. In war every man become a child who want his mother . . . because there is so much he will never understand alone."

It was not hard to comprehend how Charlie's rap on making love and facing your fears had appealed to Juan, particularly in light of his infatuation with Brenda. Charlie continued to use her, as he did Snake, as a means of luring us back to the fold.

With each new day the scene became more nerve-racking—like two armed camps in the throes of some bizarre and arcane psychological warfare. At odd hours during the day Charlie would send down contingents of women—Snake, Ouisch, Brenda, Sandy, and Squeaky—to work on us all. When that failed, he'd come into the yard with Clem and Tex, brandishing shotguns, and start shooting them off around the property. We learned to size up a situation and turn it around without panic. On one occasion Crockett borrowed Clem's shotgun and began taking target practice in the front yard.

Often Charlie would engage Crockett in verbal exchanges, which sometimes lasted hours. But Crockett played it perfect; he did not fight with Charlie or openly disagree in a way that might provoke anger. He merely expressed opinions which left Charlie utterly flabbergasted. He later confessed that he and Charlie shared many of the same opinions about the world but that Charlie "had a hole in his humanity." One evening they were out in the yard near the porch—squatting on their haunches like two Indians taking a shit. Brooks and I were inside listening through the window. Charlie was discussing karma, how every man and every spirit has a destiny that is inevitable. He insisted that part of his destiny was to bring about the revolution through Helter-Skelter. As usual, he did most of the talking. Finally, after a long silence, Charlie asked Crockett, "Look, do you always keep your head like that?"

Crockett seemed to ponder several moments, then said, "If you were beating me with a stick, Charlie, don't you suppose I'd know it?"

"Dig it . . . why don't you teach me? . . . How 'bout that . . . you teach me?"

"Teach ya what?"

"What you know."

"I can't teach ya . . . ya already know everything." We watched through the window as Charlie got to his feet and stretched, then knelt down again beside Crockett.

"Naw," he said. "I don't know nothin' . . . really, I don't."

"Well, that's about the same as knowin' everything. Can't teach a man who knows nothin' . . . ain't nothin' to build on."

Charlie just couldn't get a handle on Crockett; he couldn't get any agreements with him, nor could he get any disagreements. Their exchanges served only to exasperate him; yet he would not give up. The dynamics of the situation were curious. Charlie wanted me back in the Family; he, perhaps, knew better than I how deeply I had been affected and that only Crockett stood in his way. Crockett was the first guy Charlie had encountered who (Charlie believed) had more knowledge than he did. The rules of warfare were different because of it; he couldn't just kill Crockett; it would prove only that Charlie had been defeated. Rather, he had to psych him out, discredit him, con him. Getting us back into the Family would accomplish all three objectives. But up until that point it had all gone against Charlie. Not only had Juan Flynn joined forces with the Crockett-Posten-Watkins contingent, but there were others who were contemplating similar maneuvers.

If the murders were weighing on Charlie's mind at that time (certainly he was aware of the hysteria they must have created and that the Man would seek a just revenge), it didn't manifest itself physically in his outward behavior. Such was not the case with many of the others. Within a matter of weeks nearly everyone broke out in hideous open sores on their arms and legs—sores that would not heal.

21

In late August, while Charlie's dune buggies roared across the Panamint Valley, police in L.A. sought leads in the Tate–La Bianca killings. Roman Polanski offered $25,000 reward for information leading to the arrest and conviction of those responsible for the Cielo Drive slaughter. Meanwhile, motives for the Tate and the La Bianca murders were being postulated by police, detectives, newscasters, and Hollywood celebrities. Famed psychic Peter Hurkos, after a visit to the Tate residence, claimed that three people, all of them homicidal maniacs under the influence of massive LSD doses, had committed the crime during a black-magic ritual. Truman Capote, author of *In Cold Blood*, appeared on the Johnny Carson show to state that in all likelihood the Tate murders had been committed by one man who had been "triggered" into a state of acute paranoia. By the end of September, authorities confessed they had "little to go on." No connection between the Tate, La Bianca, and Hinman murders had been established; odd, since the word "pig" or "piggie" had been written in blood at all three murder locations.

"Pig" was the word Charlie had used to describe Stanley Berry when he told Crockett (the afternoon I left with Stanley for Las Vegas), "I think I'll chop up that piggie and find a good hole to dump him in." Crockett ignored the remark and went about his business, not realizing that slowly we were helping to push Charlie Manson to his karmic turning point.

Near the end of September, Manson was making numerous forays into Death Valley, looking for caves, exploring the terrain, choosing strategic hideouts in which to store his burgeoning supplies—still searching for the mystical "hole" in the desert where the Family could go to wait out the ravages of Helter-Skelter and make "a new beginning." Traveling in caravans of three to five dune buggies, he led these expeditions for days at a time, leaving Clem and Bruce and a few girls behind to watch the Meyers ranch in his absence. At one point Charlie asked me to search for "the hole" by diving with scuba gear into Devil's Hole, a vast, murky water-filled cavern just across the Nevada border. Only months before, two professional divers had gone into Devil's Hole and had never come up. I said no thanks.

Still, I was playing both ends against the middle. I had accepted favors from the Family—played music with them, made love to Snake, and at times had listened to Charlie's Helter-Skelter rap, still half-believing it was true. I didn't *want* to do this; more, it was like an unconscious reflex born of habit. It was also, as Crockett had said, "foolish"—a game I was playing that was rooted in conditioning and based in part on my fear of completely severing ties with the Family, even after I sensed there was nothing left to salvage. Accepting *this* was to admit I had been a fool, a dupe, just another of Charlie's pawns; which I had. Describing my feelings is not easy, since they changed often and there were many levels and much confusion. Inside, I told myself, "They did not kill Shorty." I'd seen him less than a month before. I'd waved and he'd waved back. Charlie was merely trying to manipulate my fears. It was easy to say, "Yeah, we had to kill Shorty." But where was the proof? Charlie was always boasting of his macho exploits, but I had never actually seen him so much as step on a bug. Yet, deeper down, I sensed it *was* true. I'd felt it. At that point I still had no idea how deeply programmed I was, how much work it would take to free myself.

Early one morning sometime around the first of October, Charlie spotted me on the hillside and hiked up to where I stood surveying the valley while sipping a cup of hot coffee. He reminded me that a year had passed since we had first come to the Barker ranch as a Family. He told me he was taking an expedition over to the Saline Valley and asked if I'd take the younger girls—Snake, Kitty, Ouisch, Sherry, Barbara, and Patty—up to the Lotus Mine to "hide out" for a few days while he was gone. Charlie frequently moved his "young loves" to different locations, calling it "survival training." Yet part of it, I knew, was his paranoia that if left alone at the Meyers ranch they would be vulnerable to outside influences.

"You don't have to go all the way with them or nothin', just show them how to get up there—that's a pretty tricky trail, you know, and they've never been up there."

"I don't mind, Charlie," I said.

An hour later I met the girls at the head of Golar Wash and we started for the Lotus, a defunct gold mine located about midway up Golar Canyon at the top of the mountain, a strategic spot from which to survey the entire valley. The climb from the base of the wash to the mine and the small stone dwelling beside it followed a steep, twisting trail, replete with switchbacks and spots where the footing was treacherous. Halfway up, Sherry and Barbara announced they had left their packs and canteens at the bottom of the trail and went back to get them, and I continued on to the mine with the girls. After helping them make camp, I hiked down the *quebrada* and back four miles to the Barker ranch.

Later that afternoon when Crockett, Brooks, and I went down to retrieve supplies from the foot of the wash, Sherry and Barbara Hoyt suddenly appeared from behind a rock, claiming they wanted to hike out of the valley and go back to L.A. "We're afraid of Charlie," Barbara declared.

Crockett listened while they confessed their fears, his face expressionless, his eyes scanning the alluvial fan that stretched twenty-three miles toward Ballarat; he reached over and felt the canteen Barbara had strapped to her waist.

"Gettin' dark," he said. "Might as well go up with us, think this out."

That night we sat around the table drinking coffee and listening to Barbara and Sherry. Both girls were relative latecomers to the Family, Barbara arriving at Gresham Street at a time when Helter-Skelter was in its incipient stages; they had not been exposed to the in-depth indoctrination of some of the original girls, whose loyalty to Charlie was never in question.

Barbara's voice was high-pitched and agitated. "Charlie says we're free, that there are no rules, but we're not free. He says we can do what we want, but we can't. He said about two weeks ago that if we tried to leave he'd poke our eyes out with sticks. He—"

"All we want is to go to Ballarat," Sherry added. "From there we can get to L.A."

After the girls had gone to sleep, I discussed it with Crockett and decided that I would take them to the base of the canyon, drive down the gorge in the power wagon, and leave them at the edge of the valley.

"Give 'em enough water and tell 'em to keep a steady pace . . . they won't have no trouble . . . we'll feed 'em a good breakfast in the mornin'."

At noon the next day I dropped them off at the edge of the canyon, then headed back in the power wagon. I drove slowly, bouncing and weaving along the valley floor, avoiding eroded gullies and boulders. The sun blazed off the hood of the car, casting a blinding reflection. To cut the glare I put on a pair of dark glasses that were lying on the dashboard; it was well over 120 degrees in the shade, the air bone-dry. Sherry and Barbara would have to go slowly in the heat, but they had enough water and I knew from experience that barring unforeseen circumstances, they would make it with little problem.

I was nearing a point just south of Halfway House Spring, a particularly rocky stretch of ground, almost directly beneath the Lotus Mine, when something distracted me. I looked to my left just as Charlie's head appeared above the rocks in the gully, where he'd been filling his canteen. At the very instant our eyes met, the left-rear tire popped, the echo reverberating against the walls of the canyon. It was as if all the pressure generated by our gaze had caused the blowout. I sat stunned, listening to the hiss of escaping air as Charlie scrambled toward me over the rocks. He was shirtless and had Snake's binoculars around his neck. I knew at once he'd been watching me from the Lotus Mine. He had a shit-eating grin on his face as he approached me, dusting off his buckskins with his hands. He took off the hat he was wearing and held it out as though appraising it, then looked at me.

"Thought you were headed out to Saline?"

"Just wanted to check on the girls," he said evenly. He leaned against the fender of the truck and put his hat back on. "Hey, brother," he drawled, "you wouldn't lie to me, would you?"

"No."

"You didn't take Barbara and Sherry down the canyon, did ya?"

I looked Charlie dead in the eye.

"No."

Charlie grinned. We both knew I lied, yet for some reason he reacted as though I had said yes, as though my lie had been programmed by him. That was Charlie's way. When things went against him, he often acted as though he had programmed it, so that no matter what was said, he was in control.

"Well," he said, "you want to drive me down there so we can pick them up?"

"Got a flat. . . . no jack."

"How 'bout walkin' with me?"

"I gotta get back to the ranch . . . get this truck fixed."

He gave me a long, hard look. "Guess I'll have to get them myself." With that he turned and trotted down the wash.

Frightened and confused, I scrambled up the wash. Sherry and Barbara had a three-mile start on Charlie, but they didn't know he was after them, and we'd told them to conserve energy and go slow. Had the car been running, we'd have caught them in twenty minutes. I figured they had a fifty-fifty chance of making it. If he did catch them, I didn't know what he'd do. But it wouldn't be pleasant. For the first time I was really scared. Up until then, my actions had all been open and aboveboard insofar as Charlie was concerned; there was still the implication in the game we were playing that I might be won back to the fold, that Charlie might still invalidate Crockett. But helping his girls escape—I couldn't have crossed him in a more blatant fashion. I had an impulse to go back and find him. I felt like a condemned man, sensing that unless I confronted him right away, I'd never be able to face him. But I wanted to talk to Crockett.

"I think you're right," Crockett said after listening to what had happened. "Better go on back and meet him

. . . tell him straightaway. That lie puts you on the run, and the longer you got it hangin' over ya, the more it's gonna wear ya down."

I filled a canteen and put on my boots. Crockett went out on the porch with me.

"What you can do," he said, "is process yourself on the way down there so there's minimum tension when you meet him. You just imagine everything that could possibly happen when you see him, everything, as vividly as you can, as many times as you can . . . all while you're walk-in'; that way you run all the excess tension and energy off the actual confrontation, so it's cleaner. See what I'm drivin' at?"

"Yeah, I see."

"It ain't like you imagine they're *gonna* happen . . . it's just takin' the tension off the *possibilities*, like makin' them pictures go away, so you don't bring them up when you get there . . . you just do it."

I knew Charlie had eight or nine miles on me, but I took off anyway. It was dusk by the time I reached the base of the canyon and started out across the valley. I must have gone at least ten miles when I realized the futility of trying to catch Charlie at night. I knew, too, that if I remained in the valley he might not see me when he returned to Golar Canyon. It was bitter cold and pitch dark when I reached the base of the valley, wondering how I could ever stay warm through the night. Just moments later I stumbled through a clump of brush and my foot struck something soft. I reached down, to find a sleeping bag—brand-new and still encased in a cellophane wrapper, probably dropped during one of the supply runs. It was uncanny, but no more freaky than the flat tire earlier in the day. I was dumbfounded as I pondered the workings of fate while hiking back to the mouth of the wash. By then I was totally exhausted. I laid my bag down in the middle of the trail (at a spot where Charlie could not help but see me), and despite my apprehension, fell asleep almost at once.

About midmorning the next day, Tex, Bruce, and Brenda came bounding up the wash in a bright red Toyota. They stopped just five feet from me and honked, jolting me from sleep. They'd been staying at the hot springs. When I asked where Charlie was, they said he was behind them a few miles in another dune buggy.

"Are Sherry and Barbara with him?"

"Naw . . . why?" Brenda asked.

"Just wondered." I got out of the sleeping bag and started rolling it up.

"You need a ride back up?"

"Got to talk to Charlie."

For the next hour I waited, still processing all the confrontation possibilities in my mind. I was apprehensive but in control. It must have been close to noon when Charlie finally rumbled into view about twenty yards from where I sat hunched against the cool wall of the canyon. The moment he spotted me, he stopped the buggy and leaped out with a forty-five pistol in his hand.

"You motherfucker," he shouted, "I should blow your head off!"

My heart was thudding, but I didn't panic. Charlie's eyes were bloodshot, his face windburned and dry. He pushed the barrel into my chest.

"You ready to die?" he bellowed.

I held my breath, but didn't flinch, then said, "Sure, go ahead . . . I fucked up, maybe I deserve it."

"I'd be doin' you a favor!"

"Maybe so."

Then he thrust the gun at me, and I took it. "Maybe you ought to kill me . . . see what it's like!"

"No, Charlie, you know I don't want to do that."

"How 'bout if I just cut you a little!" He pulled out his knife and shoved the point against my throat. I took a step back. "Well, then, you cut me!" He offered me the knife, and I shook my head.

"You know what I ought to do . . . I ought to kill that fucking old man . . . he talked those girls into leaving."

"No, he didn't. All they wanted was food and water. They were leaving anyway."

"Well, he put discontent in their heads. . . . Get in!"

Charlie pointed toward the dune buggy, and we both climbed in. He laid the forty-five in the back and fired up the engine. "I caught up with those girls in Ballarat," he said, without looking at me. "They wouldn't talk. . . . I gave them twenty bucks and sent them back to Spahn's."

Moments later, Charlie was laughing. He put his arm around me. "Nothin's changed, you know, between you and me. What goes round comes round; we're still brothers, and no redneck piggie miner is gonna change that.

'Cause one day he's gonna wake up and find that he just ain't here."

Near the top of the canyon we came up behind Juan and Brooks hiking toward the ranch. Charlie stopped and they climbed in.

"Where you been, Juan? Seems like I hardly ever see you anymore."

Juan didn't reply, but he held Charlie's gaze through a rearview mirror. Charlie pulled up at the gate and stopped. We all piled out.

"Say hello to that old man for me," he said. Then he lurched forward in a swirl of dust, and we headed into the yard as Crockett came down to meet us.

22

Juan Flynn had difficulty sleeping at night. He knew too much. Charlie had told him "things." When we asked him what "things," Juan remained evasive, preferring to keep his knowledge to himself, thinking perhaps as I had, that by disclosing such information he would only spread fear. Juan suspected Charlie of many things, but he wanted to be sure; he was like that—the kind of person who comes to his own conclusions. I always admired Juan for that quality. We all did. Also, having a six-foot-five Vietnam vet on our side was reassuring. Still, Juan's insomnia permitted only intermittent rest, and he spent hours with a shotgun sitting on a hillside outside the ranch house—"on patrol," Crockett used to call it.

We were staying in the bunkhouse then, the four of us on cots in one small room. At night we'd play bridge and games of concentration. Sometimes Juan talked about his Panamanian mother, who "knew voodoo." "She have, my mother, strong powers to keep thee spirits under control. One day I walk out in thee street in front of my home and find a dagger stock in thee ground and my mother she tell me not to touch, that eet keep away thee *locura* . . . how do you say . . . craziness."

Following my episode with Charlie in the canyon,

Juan put his shotgun on nails above his bunk. By that time Crockett had convinced him to try to sleep.

"We got a psychic umbrella around the ranch . . . it's there. Soon as anyone enters that area, we'll wake up . . . ain't no way Charlie's gonna sneak up on us."

One night about two o'clock he tried it. We were all asleep, bundled up in sleeping bags. The nights had turned cold; we had a small wood-burning stove set up in one corner. I was awakened by Juan thrashing around in bed, talking in his sleep. Crockett and Posten were also awakened; we lay there watching and listening to Juan.

"You . . . son of a beech . . ." he muttered. "You motherfocker. . . . Ah . . . ah . . . okay . . . okay. I got you, you! *I got you!* Hah! *No, no,* you ain't getting away. There, I'm in your lung. *Now . . . burn. I'm burning real good . . . Sisss . . .*" Juan's legs flailed inside the sleeping bag, his body dangling over the edge of the bunk at both ends. Finally his foot struck the shotgun, and it fell on top of him.

When he opened his eyes, I was looking straight at him from my bed just adjacent to his. Across the room, Crockett lay there wide-awake on his bunk. Brooks was already sitting up.

"What's going on, Juan?"

"I got him," Juan muttered.

"It's Charlie, ain't it . . . he's sneaking up on us out there."

"Yeah, but I got him good . . . I burned in there . . . in his lung."

"It's Charlie and somebody else," Crockett said.

"I got him," Juan repeated, his voice still groggy.

"Yeah, but he's still coming," I said.

Crockett sat up. "He may be comin', but by the time he gets here, he's gonna be so wiped out he won't be able to do much."

Juan slipped out of the bag and climbed down from the bed. He picked up the shotgun and checked the chamber before setting the weapon on top of the bunk. Then he walked to the door and went out onto the porch.

Seconds later we heard him. "Hi, Charlie . . . what you looking for?"

Charlie's response was unintelligible. Then we heard Juan. "And you too, Clem, you sneaky motherfocker. . . . I know you're out there. And you, Bruce, *cabrón!*"

Charlie followed Juan inside the bunkhouse. Charlie was white. He looked totally disoriented. Crockett grinned, lit a cigarette, and offered one to Charlie. "Kind o' late for a social call, ain't it?"

Charlie wore buckskins and carried a leather thong over his shoulder.

"One of these nights I'm gonna sneak up on you motherfuckers," he said evenly, forcing a grin, still trying to regain his composure. "And when I do . . ."

"Now, that's impossible, Charlie," Crockett said. "Ain't no such thing as sneakin' up on people. You know it and I know it . . . all that sneakin' up is just make-believe, somethin' people do to keep up a little intrigue in their lives."

"Yeah," I added. "You taught us too well."

Charlie grinned, and some of the color returned to his face.

"Yeah, well . . . you folks just sleep tight." He turned and walked out the door, and Juan called after him, "Hey, Charlie . . . thee next time, *cabrón*, there ain't gonna be no next time!"

Two nights later we all woke up simultaneously.

"Charlie," Brooks said. "Creepy-crawly."

"Son of a beech!"

"He don't give up, does he?" Crockett sat up and reached for his shirt.

I put on my pants, then hopped back up on the bunk—Juan's shotgun was under my sleeping bag. I tossed it to Juan.

We were all sitting up and Crockett was smoking a cigarette when Charlie pushed the door open and came crawling in on his hands and knees.

"Hi, Charlie," I said.

"*Buenas noches, cabrón.*"

"Lose somethin', Charlie?"

Charlie was utterly humiliated, but he didn't lose his composure. "One of these nights . . ." he said. Then he got up and walked out of the bunkhouse. We heard him say something to Tex and Bruce, and I went to the window and watched as they walked to the gate.

Crockett got to his feet and stretched. "Let's head down to the main house and make some coffee. 'Bout time we had a little powwow."

It was clear that we'd pushed Charlie to his limit. Up until then, the rules of the game had dictated a certain bizarre etiquette that we'd all adhered to. But Charlie's karma was turning; it had started to turn from the day he met Crockett. Charlie could not get to Crockett. Charlie needed the paranoia of the city to work his fear tactics; in the desert Crockett was on home ground, amid surroundings which were a part of his consciousness.

Before, there had been no doubts; Charlie's belief in his "destiny" had been reinforced by an entire Family of followers. Two months had passed since the Tate–La Bianca murders, and still the law had nothing on him. They'd busted him for stolen vehicles but could not hold him. This made Charlie strong, made Helter-Skelter even more of a reality. It validated Charlie's power. The fact that people had actually gone out and committed murder for him was proof of that power; proof that his revolution, despite all odds, was meant to be, and that he was beyond the law.

Then Crockett appeared and the Family began to disintegrate. Charlie sought to beat Crockett at his own game, but without success. He could not discredit the man. Maybe Charlie was wrong. Maybe Crockett actually had more knowledge than he did; if that were the case, then perhaps Charlie had created a myth; he had killed for nothing. Maybe Helter-Skelter wasn't real. That's when Charlie began to doubt himself, and that's when his karma turned and he grew desperate. Though we didn't know it at the time, Charlie's rampages in the desert had begun to reflect his frustrations; just days before his nocturnal visits to us, he and Clem and Tex set fire to a construction site and several pieces of large earthmoving equipment—a sure way to bring the Man down on him.

Crockett had sensed the dangers but had no intention of letting someone drive him away from the canyon. He had also been curious to play out his hand with Charlie. Until that night.

"Seems to me," he said, once we were seated around the table with our coffee, "that things are gettin' a little out of hand. What's nice about bein' here is the peace of mind . . . but there don't seem to be much of that left . . . more like the city up here now. Old Charlie

brought his Helter-Skelter with him. But I hate like hell
to pull out . . . just when we're having success with our
prospectin' and findin' that yeller stuff."

Juan picked up his shotgun and walked to the door.
"I don't stay," he said. "I'm going back." He walked out
onto the porch.

We took our coffee and joined him, sitting on the
steps. The night was cold, studded with stars, but there
was enough light to see the craggy spine of the Panamints cutting sharply across the sky.

"We'll give it one more week," Crockett said. "Make
one more supply run. We can't stay too much longer,
'cause the cops are gonna swarm this place. I can feel it."

The following morning Juan and I set out for Las
Vegas. The trip took six hours; most of it was made in
silence. Several times I tried to engage Juan in conversation, but he wasn't in the mood to talk; he said only that
he planned to return to Spahn's and to pick up his back
pay from George. After that, he confessed, he didn't
know what he was going to do. "Maybe when you and
Brooks and Crockett find a good mine, I come and work
with you . . . but I don't come back to Barker ranch . . .
no more."

I let Juan out on the outskirts of Las Vegas. While he
hitchhiked south toward Baker, I drove on into town. It
took three days to get supplies, round up parts for my
BSA, and deliver a couple of messages for Crockett. By
noon on the fourth day I was on my way back.

Like Juan, I too thought of leaving. Charlie's terror
tactics, even though they had backfired, had transformed
our quiet, productive scene into a perverse kind of torture. I had gained a certain satisfaction in seeing Charlie's
interaction with Crockett, since it reinforced my with-
drawal from the Family and served to convince me I had
made a wise decision. But I knew Charlie couldn't and
wouldn't be pushed much farther; his own credibility was
on the line. There was too much at stake. Had I known
just how much, I would never have returned that afternoon.

By the time I parked the truck at Barker's, it was too
late to carry in the supplies, so I left everything and
hiked back up to the ranch. When I got there, all the
lights in the ranch house were on. I saw Snake and
Squeaky walking up the path to the house. Two dirt bikes

were parked at the gate, and three or four dune buggies beyond the bunkhouse. Clem and Bruce Davis were sitting beside Brenda when I entered the gate. I saw Sadie coming down the road from the Meyers place with Ouisch and Kitty Lutesinger, one of Bobby's old girlfriends. As I reached the porch, I spotted two of the girls getting out of the bus, followed by Tex and Bill Vance, who had driven a new dune buggy up the back route by way of Furnace Creek.

My heart was pounding as I walked into the house. Charlie sat at the table across from Snake. Katie was cutting Snake's hair. Snake smiled, but she looked ghostly. She laughed nervously when I sat down.

"Glad you're back, brother," Charlie said, getting to his feet and stretching his arms over his head.

"Where's Brooks and Crockett?"

"Don't know." Charlie walked past me to the door. "But I got to dig a couple of graves before it gets dark."

He let the door slam as he walked out.

Fear, rage, utter desperation commingled inside me. Tex came in with a shotgun and sat down at the table. Then Squeaky, Sandy, and Brenda entered the house. All had short, uneven, recently cut hair. The sound of the scissors slicing through Snake's hair sent chills down my back.

Bruce came in and sat down across from me. His face was red and puffy; some of the sores on his arms had healed, but new ones had erupted on his neck, just under his chin. "Where's that Panamanian piggie?" he rasped.

Before I could respond, Charlie called to him from the porch and he walked out. I got up, went into the bathroom, and closed the door. I had to compose myself. I had to face Charlie without blowing it. I heard him and Bruce walk past the house. I heard Bruce's coarse pneumatic laugh as I started to take a piss. Then I heard Charlie speaking to Phil Simms, an ex-con and friend of Charlie's who had apparently just arrived.

"How's your wife, Jean?" Charlie wanted to know.

"Real pain in the ass at the moment . . . you know how women are."

"Well," Charlie blurted, his voice hard and without a trace of humor, "why don't you bring her up here and we'll throw her down a mine shaft. Then you can move in with us."

I didn't wait for Phil's reply, but went back into the living room. Katie, Stephanie, and Cappy were in the kitchen preparing a meal. Cappy said, "Hi, Paul," as I passed the kitchen doorway and took a seat by the table, just as Charlie and Bruce walked in from the porch and sat down.

In addition to Charlie and Bruce, there were two other males seated at the table—a kid they called Zero, and a part-time wrangler from Spahn's named Larry Jones; there were also two new girls, introduced to me as Beth and Shelly. With his Family slowly disintegrating around him, Charlie felt the need of recruiting additional followers. But I paid little attention to any of them. All my focus was on Charlie.

He grinned at me. "Let's make a little music." His eyes were dancing. I knew it was test time, and sensed, as I held his gaze, that what lay in the balance was everything.

While he tuned the guitar, he told me that the tapes we'd made at Spahn's were set to be recorded and that an LP record would soon be released; he said it was long overdue but that our hard work would pay off. I put all my attention on Charlie, on the music. I listened to the sounds he made on the guitar. Then he sang, and I sang with him, and it was like one sound. Afterward he came over and put his arm around me. "You're finally back, huh . . . where you belong. . . . It's about time."

We ate a huge meal together that night; then the girls moved the table and chairs and brought in mattresses and laid them on the floor; Tex built a fire and we all gathered around Charlie to make music. I sensed that it was all a means of showing me that the Family was still unified, that the love was there, that we were still one. But going through the motions was not enough. The people sitting around me, Snake on my left, Brenda on my right, then Katie, Sadie, Stephanie, Ouisch, Cappy, Tex, Kitty, Bill Vance, Crazy Patty, Sandy, Clem, and Squeaky —seemed lifeless. With their close-cropped hair, the girls looked like a gaggle of militant dikes. There was no feeling, there was only a strange, depraved momentum set in motion by Charlie. When I looked at Snake, I felt sick inside; her eyes were glassy, lusterless; she looked insane. When Charlie made a joke, everyone laughed, yet the laughter was soulless and without joy. At times I found the girls looking at me as though I were a stranger, or perhaps someone they had seen before but could not quite remember. Still, there was a connection, however vague and nostalgic, and I felt it. I also felt Charlie's attention on me, particularly after he began to play the guitar. Like the others, I went through the motions.

We were getting ready to drop acid when Bruce Davis came stumbling into the room to announce that the truck was stuck in the wash. Charlie flew into a rage.

"*Motherfucker!*" he shouted. "Can't you do anything without someone holding your hand! I might as well send a girl to drive the truck! We got to drop off that gasoline and get supplies!"

"I can get the truck out, Charlie," I said.

Charlie's eyes found mine. He got to his feet and walked across the room muttering to himself.

"Yeah," he said finally. "Why don't ya do that. Deliver them gas drums and pick up supplies, then come back here. You go too," he said to Bruce. "Make sure everything gets back safe and sound—everything!"

Bruce nodded.

Charlie was taking a chance, yet he probably saw it as an opportunity to teach Bruce a lesson while testing me at the same time. In a way, it was a continuation of the power games he had been playing with Crockett. With Crockett gone, he may have considered his position stronger. He knew that Bruce, having assumed my position within the Family, would keep a close eye on me.

Charlie went into the bedroom and came out with a wad of folded bills, which he laid in my hand. "Here's three hundred bucks. Buy some camping gear and a couple of parachutes, then play the slot machines for me . . . okay?"

I interpreted this gesture as a vote of confidence, and as a means of castigating Bruce. Less than a week before, I had been on Charlie's shit list. Now he was entrusting me with money and responsibility for supplies. He was also, he believed, securing an implied agreement from me—to return.

My plan at that point was simple: to get the truck unstuck, get to Vegas, and start looking for Brooks and Crockett. I had a growing sense that they were safe. I wasn't that worried about Bruce Davis.

Charlie walked with us down to the gate, Bruce on

one side, me on the other. For a long moment we stood in silence looking down the road that leads to Golar Wash. Charlie lit a cigarette and exhaled into the chill night air. I was aware of a low rumbling sound that seemed to seep up out of the canyon, the same psychic vibration that preceded Charlie's arrival at Barker's just weeks before. I had an impulse to ask Charlie and Bruce if they heard the sound, but thought better of it. Even then I knew what the sound was. It was a sound Brooks and Crockett and I had heard a week earlier. The sound of the Man closing in.

As I stood beside Charlie listening to his final instructions to Bruce, I recalled the words he had spoken to me at Gresham Street over six months before. "You know, once Helter-Skelter comes down, I'll be going back to the joint. After that, it'll be up to you."

It was after three A.M. by the time we got the truck out and drove it to the base of the wash. I told Bruce to stop while I lifted my BSA out of the pickup. Without a word he helped me load it onto the flatbed. Then we headed out across the valley toward Ballarat, to deliver Charlie's gas drums and continue on to Las Vegas.

Bruce did a lot of talking on that trip. He told me about going to London and studying Scientology; he told me Helter-Skelter would stun the world. He also told me something I'd heard before; how hard it had been to kill Shorty Shea.

Once we got to Vegas, I ditched Bruce long enough to make a phone call to Shoshone. I spoke to Don Ward. When I asked if he knew where Crockett and Posten were, he said, "Maybe, but we got to talk to make sure who *you* are. . . ."

The next day I unloaded my bike and drove it to Shoshone. Brooks Posten and Paul Crockett were in Don Ward's office when I got there.

The following morning, the Barker ranch was busted.

Part Four

The Truth Will Set You Free

23

Leaving the Family that night with Bruce for what I thought to be the last time did not break my ties with Charlie. Even after he was sent to L.A. county jail as a murder suspect. On the contrary, and for a variety of reasons, not the least of which, perhaps, was Charlie's physical absence, I was drawn back to the Family.

Charlie's powers, though he was behind bars, did not diminish. For months he would manipulate not only a large segment of the public and mass media but also law-enforcement officials, lawyers, even judges. He also managed to hold the Family together. Unwittingly, I helped him. He had attempted to program me for this long before: "When Helter-Skelter comes down, I'll be back in the joint, it'll be up to you." While my motives were never completely clear, being at times as much subconscious as conscious, my actions did serve, as Crockett put it, "to hold the Family together when you should just let it die." I continued to work with Crockett and Brooks, but I was divided within myself. I can honestly say that no time in my life was more agonizing than the months between Charlie's capture and his conviction. I walked a mighty thin line. The view from the middle often gives a panorama of all sides. But my balance was precarious at best, and what I paid for that vantage point in suffering was more than I could afford. That I survived at all appears, in retrospect, something of a miracle.

The hillsides around Shoshone are riddled with man-made caves, dug originally by itinerant miners, prospectors, and other vagabonds, who, over the years, found the town a convenient oasis in the scorching lowlands of the Amargosa Valley. Shoshone was also a water stop on the railroad line and for a time the site of a thriving hobo jungle which centered in and around the tufa caves. Crockett and Posten were broke and living in one of those caves when I arrived on October 9. Don Ward had told them (as he did me) not to leave Shoshone, that the Barker ranch was about to be busted.

The following day, just before dawn, while the three of us slept off a reunion celebration on the floor of the cave, officers from the highway patrol, the Inyo county sheriff's office, and the National Park rangers assembled near Golar Wash for a raid on the Barker ranch—a raid that lasted three days and resulted in the capture of Charlie and most of the Family. All were taken to the Inyo county seat in Independence (just four hours north of Shoshone) and booked for auto theft.

I didn't know then, nor did Brooks or Crockett, that during the raid Stephanie (Schram) and Kitty Lutesinger (Bobby Beausoleil's girlfriend, who was then five months pregnant with his child) had been trying to escape from the Family. They asked the police for protection and were taken to Independence to be interviewed by detectives. When it was learned that Kitty was Bobby's girlfriend, she was asked what she knew about the Hinman murder. She said she had heard that Manson had sent Bobby and a girl named Susan Atkins to Hinman's house to collect some money and that when he refused to pay, they had killed him.

On October 13, Brooks, Crockett, and I were escorted to Independence by Don Ward and officers of the highway patrol. Brooks and Paul had already made statements to law-enforcement officials (including Ward) as to the nature of "goings-on" at the Barker ranch. They had talked about Charlie's philosophy and Helter-Skelter. The law, however, at that point appeared little interested in such bizarre and unlikely tales. Their primary concern, it seemed (at least on the surface), was that Manson and the others be identified and linked to the stolen vehicles found at the ranch. We were shown photographs of dune buggies and Harleys and asked to identify them. We did; both privately to Dave Steuber of the highway patrol and later that week during Charlie's preliminary hearing in the Inyo county courthouse.

But during that hearing, things changed drastically.

One morning flocks of reporters appeared in the courtroom; not only L.A. and local press, but foreign correspondents as well; what had started out as a quiet, routine procedure became suddenly a circus of spectators, reporters, cops, and lawyers. Word was out that this was not a simple case of auto theft. Charles Manson had become a murder suspect.

Independence, though it's the seat of Inyo County, is a small, immaculate town located in the heart of the Owens Valley at the foot of the eastern Sierras. From the center of the main drag, snowcapped peaks are visible year round. The county itself is the second largest in the state but has fewer than 17,000 inhabitants. During the court proceedings it seemed as though all of them had flocked to Independence. I remember Crockett saying one morning, "Jesus, there just ain't no place to hide." Everywhere we went, we were hounded by reporters. Crockett told us to keep quiet and let things blow over a little. But that didn't happen. It just got more intense.

Finally, one morning while we were drinking coffee in a waiting room outside the courthouse, Crockett said it was time we told some of the story to the press.

"Look at it this way," he said. "Old Charlie always wanted his story told . . . we might as well tell it. It ain't all pretty, but it needs to be told; people should know what the hell went on . . . what can happen to the mind. Most people ain't gonna believe it anyway, but eventually there's gonna be a lot said about it . . . hell, there's gonna be books written about it."

Another of Crockett's motives, though he didn't express it at the time, was money. We were stone broke. We couldn't go back to the mine; police had made Golar Wash a restricted area. Meanwhile, foreign correspondents were clamoring for information. The more we refused to talk, the more they wanted "to make a deal" for our story. Two days before leaving Independence, we agreed to meet in L.A. and give it to them.

Around the middle of November, at approximately the same time Sadie was at Sybil Brand Penitentiary for Women telling her story to Ronnie Howard, Juan, Brooks, Crockett, and I met with reporters (Don Dornan, Iver Davis, and Jerry Le Blanc) in Sherman Oaks and told them what we knew about the Manson Family—includ-

ing the murder of Gary Hinman and what we'd heard re
garding Shorty's death. The interviews lasted five day
and resulted in the publication of articles in both Spai
and Germany as well as a book (which we did not agre
to) that was later released, called *Five to Die*. We wer
paid eleven hundred dollars each for our informatio
Afterward Crockett, Brooks, and I went back to Shoshone
while Juan remained in L.A.

It was a scary time for us. Word had it that Charli
had issued more threats; most of the Family, includin
Clem and Bruce, had been released from Inyo Count
and were back in L.A. living at Spahn's. Our own livin
conditions in the cave were by no means pleasant. With
out electricity or water we were forced to use candle
and to transport water a mile up the mountain fron
Shoshone in five-gallon containers. Since Golar Canyo
was off limits, we could not go to the mine and we had t
find work in Shoshone. I managed to get hired washin
dishes in the Shoshone Café and also worked with Brook
and Crockett doing town maintenance for the Charle
Brown Company; we worked our asses off; did every
thing—trimmed trees, painted buildings, laid concrete
dug ditches, pumped cesspools.

In late November we moved out of the cave an
rented a house on the main highway across the stree
from the high-school football field. It was a small place:
two bedrooms, a tiny narrow kitchen, and a fair-sized
living room. There was also a small fireplace, which be
came essential as weather turned colder in winter. In
front of it, Crockett set up his table, and at night after
work, while we practiced our music, he spent hours play
ing solitaire. Around Christmastime, Juan Flynn moved in
with us. By then Charlie, Sadie, and Leslie had been
charged with murder and indicted. Katie and Tex were
still out of the state. Juan brought us further news; others
associated with the Manson Family had reportedly been
killed. One of them was Joel Dean Pugh, Sandra Good's
ex-husband; the other, a young man I'd met only two
months before, John Philip Haught, better known as Zero.

Shoshone was far from mellow for any of us. People
didn't take to ex-Manson Family members living in their
midst, particularly after the story in the L.A. Times:
SUSAN ATKINS' STORY OF TWO NIGHTS OF MURDER. Notices

were posted advising that people keep their children, particularly their young daughters, under lock and key while we were in town. Petitions were circulated to have us removed; letters were sent to the district attorney. Being glared at, ignored, and verbally berated became a part of our daily experience, and while, in time, it lessened somewhat, it never stopped completely. The only saving grace was that Don Ward, one of the few people who sought to understand the dynamics of the Manson Family, became our friend and to some extent served as a buffer between us and the public at large.

Sometime around Christmas, shortly after Charlie had been granted the right to defend himself, I felt the urge to go to L.A. and see the Family. I don't know if it was a programmed response, an implant Charlie had made months before—curiosity, guilt, or a perverse sense of my own confusion. I don't know what it was. But I did miss the Family and still considered many of its members my friends. When I told Crockett, he said it didn't surprise him. He said it would take a long time to get free of Charlie's programs and my ties to the Family, and that I wouldn't ever do it by avoiding the issue. I'd read the newspaper accounts. I'd listened to Juan. I could well imagine the paranoia at Spahn's. But I wanted to see for myself. I wanted to see Charlie. I wanted to see the others. At a deeper level perhaps, I wanted to extricate some meaning from all the horror and carnage, to step back into the nightmare and find something worth salvaging.

When I asked Juan if he'd heard anything about Snake, he said he had. "They send her to mental hospital."

The first thing I did when I got to L.A. was call Patton State Hospital. They said Diane Lake was there but that I couldn't see her. Afterward I went directly to the Los Angeles county jail to see Charlie. The meeting was arranged by Charlie's lawyer, Daye Shinn, who escorted me to the small glass-enclosed room where we both waited. Moments later Charlie came in—all smiles —clean-shaven and wearing his blue-jumpsuit prison garb.

"Hey, brother . . . hey . . . where the hell you been?" He gave me a hug and grinned at Daye Shinn. "This is the man I been waiting for," he said.

"How's things, Charlie?"

He shrugged. "I'm just here for Christmas." He winked at Daye Shinn. "I always come home for Christmas."

Charlie lit a cigarette and pulled the ashtray in front of him. "Lot to do," he said. "The girls need your help, you know . . . all this legal shit to attend to. They got a place on Chandler Street in Van Nuys. Got the scene going at Spahn's too. We're getting the album out. You got to help them out, keep things together."

Listening to Charlie rap, you'd have thought he was free. He spoke as though nothing had changed and that being in prison for murder was merely a temporary inconvenience. He was, in fact, in excellent spirits. Overnight, he'd become an internationally known figure; he'd made the cover of *Life* magazine. There was also a small yet vocal segment of radicals who were calling him a hero. My impulse was to ask him about the Tate-La Bianca murders, but with Daye Shinn sitting beside me I remained silent.

"What you been doing?" he finally asked me.

Before I could reply, he went on. "You still with Crockett?"

I nodded.

"Hey, tell me something . . . does he try? I mean, psychic energy. . . . You know, does he *try*, or does it just happen? I mean, I sit in my cell and put all my attention on the bars to make them dissolve . . . but they won't do it, you know. They won't do it because I try."

I told Charlie that Crockett didn't try.

I realized even then how dangerous a game I was playing. You can't be on all sides at once. Yet that's what I was doing. I *was* with Crockett. I was also with those who sought to prosecute Charles Manson. Along with Brooks and Juan I had told the D.A. and other cops all I knew about the Family. Yet when Charlie asked what I'd said to the law, I didn't lie. "We're just telling your story, Charlie . . . you know . . . just tellin' it like it is, 'cause your story has to be told . . . the true story."

"Dig it," Charlie quipped, glancing at Shinn. "The truth will set you free . . . even Crockett will tell you that."

What struck me then, and continued to amaze me during subsequent visits with Charlie, was his preoccupation with Crockett. Invariably he would ask about my relationship to him, and if he had taught me anything I might pass along. I told Charlie that if I could think of anything I'd let him know.

After leaving the jail, I drove directly to Spahn's Ranch in a battered Chevy pickup I'd borrowed from a friend of Juan's. As I wound my way up Santa Susana Pass in second gear, I flashed on all the journeys I'd made on that road with Charlie and the Family; of the day Brenda and Snake had first taken me there. All that had transpired since then seemed beyond comprehension. I felt apprehensive as I turned into the driveway. On the surface, things hadn't changed. George and Pearl were still there; so was Randy. Gypsy and Squeaky continued to minister to George's needs. The wranglers worked; the tourists came and went. So did the law. The paranoia Juan spoke about was all too apparent. Driving up to the boardwalk was almost eerie.

Squeaky, Brenda, Sandy, and Clem were standing by the saloon when I pulled in. While Clem, as usual, was pretty spaced-out, the girls seemed alert and animated. They greeted me with open arms.

"Charlie said you'd be back," Brenda said, beaming.

I spent the afternoon at Spahn's. I saw George and Pearl, then took a walk up to the outlaw shacks. I watched the wranglers herding horses toward the corral. I thought of the first summer at Spahn's, when things had been good. I thought of Shorty Shea. That night I went with the Family, or what remained of it—Squeaky, Brenda, Gypsy, Sandy, Clem, and a kid named Kevin—to the Chandler Street house in Van Nuys. On the way, Squeaky told me about the trial; about Leslie, Katie, and Sadie. She said things were working out well; that Charlie would handle his own defense and that he would get off. She also said that the album was being cut in wax and would soon be released.

The Chandler Street house was a two-bedroom, two-bath structure in the center of an upper-middle-class residential area in Van Nuys. The property was surrounded by a thick hedge on one side and a chain-link fence on the other; there was an outdoor patio in the back, where we convened to discuss legal matters, entertain reporters, and play music. The living room was cluttered with amplifiers, and musical instruments, but was otherwise orderly. At that time the Family had three vehicles, two of which were parked out in front of the house—a late-model Volkswagen van (belonging to another new guy named Mark Ross) and an old Studebaker sedan. There was also a pickup truck, which was kept at Spahn's.

My return to the Family changed the nature of things immediately. If the girls harbored any suspicions as to my loyalty, they didn't show it. I was needed. The Manson Family was based on male leadership; Charlie's absence had created a real void, a void Clem (and later Bruce Davis) would never be able to fill, nor the young recruits like Kevin and Mark, who began hanging around after the arrests. Unconsciously I fell into the role at once.

While Squeaky continued to brief me on all the legal issues—who needed what, which lawyers had to be fired or hired—I began instituting my own programs, a return to the original philosophy of being unified in love and music. It was completely insane. Charlie was on trial for mass murder. Deep down, I was coming to believe he was guilty of those murders. Yet, there I was, working with the girls on Charlie's behalf in court, while trying to regain some semblance of what the Family had once been. All of which seemed fine with Charlie, since the image he was then trying to project to the public was that of the enlightened hippie guru who had become the victim of a degenerate society. When I called Crockett and told him I was moving in with the Family, there was a long and pregnant silence on his end. Crockett never gave advice. He didn't then. He merely quoted something from the Bible: *"Fools go where angels fear to tread."*

To this day I don't know just what forces were impelling me. I was later accused of being a spy for the police, but this was never the case. In part, it was the fulfillment of my role in the Family. Charlie had said, "I am you and you are me." That statement was always more applicable to me than to anyone else. He had also said, "Someday you'll be taking over." Too, I may have been motivated by a sense of guilt for having deserted the Family, not just Charlie, but everyone. I wanted to get back to what we once had. Perhaps with Charlie gone there was a chance. But I knew that this was a false hope. Charlie was never gone from the minds of his followers. Though there were times when I realized how much danger I was in, I could not let go. *That is the power of programming, and what this book is about.*

When I saw Juan in L.A. several days later and told him what was happening, he said I was crazy. "Seem to me like you try and commit suicide."

By that time, Crockett, Brooks, and I had all made statements to the D.A.'s investigators. This information, *I knew,* would be turned over to Charlie once a *motion for discovery* was made by the defense, which means that all evidence of the prosecution—documents, reports, interviews, everything—has to be submitted to the defense for examination. Charlie would see at once that my testimony against him was some of the most damaging, particularly what he had told me about killing Shorty Shea. Even so, there was a part of me which believed that Charlie would realize the wisdom of his own words: "The truth will set you free," that by telling the truth I was doing him a favor. Admitting this now is not easy; admitting to being a fool never is. But it was not merely a question of judgment; it was, in large part, the result of a process in which I had been locked up for more than a year and which left me completely fragmented; the power of programming, hypnosis, call it what you will. I *was* telling the truth. But I was telling it differently to different people; to Crockett; to the police; to the Family. In the face of all the horror—the real truth—I turned my head. It was not a question of personality, character or reason; it was like being a victim of a destiny I had to trust. I did know one thing; it couldn't go on indefinitely.

For the next few weeks I met with Charlie, discussed strategy, helped the girls secure new lawyers; I spoke to Sadie and Leslie and conveyed Charlie's messages. Meanwhile, at the Chandler Street house I reinstituted therapy sessions and love therapy and began indoctrinating the new guys in the arts of sex. For a time I did become Charlie in a way that I never had before.

Perhaps unconsciously I was proving that I could do in the Family what Charlie had done in the beginning; and by doing it, that it wasn't such a great achievement. In some sense this would invalidate Charlie or at least prove to me that the programs I had accepted were not so important. Perhaps I was trying to free myself by walking a tightrope in front of Charlie's nose, playing his game even better than he had played it. By the end of January 1970 the only thing I hadn't done was to make love to Squeaky (Charlie's number-one girl). I sensed that some of the other girls were generating pressure in that direction.

Only at night did my anxieties really surface. I began suffering from acute insomnia. When I did sleep, I'd invariably have nightmares. I fell into a habit (both at Spahn's and sometimes at the Chandler Street house) of walking all night, alone. Only through total exhaustion could I relieve some of the tension. But I couldn't go on living like that, and I knew it.

One morning (the day after I'd been told that Charlie had warned the girls to "Watch Paul!"), I returned from Spahn's following an all-night hike. Though totally thrashed, I borrowed Mark Ross's camper and drove it out to Topanga Canyon. I felt the need to see the ocean. Near the base of the canyon, just before it enters the coast highway, I stopped to buy a cup of coffee. As I pulled into the parking place, I saw a guy get out of his van and trot across the street toward the gas station. He looked familiar, but I wasn't sure. I rolled down my window and shouted.

"Hey, Charlie . . . Black Beard Charlie!"

24

Black Beard had changed only slightly since I'd seen him more than a year before, just a few miles away from where we now stood facing each other in the middle of Topanga Canyon Boulevard. His fleecy, tousled hair hung to his waist; his smile was infectious. He said he'd rented a place up the canyon and invited me there for breakfast. I followed him in my car. Five miles back up the canyon he turned up a steep side road to a small house built beneath a stand of oak trees, and parked.

Before going inside, we stood on the porch and smoked a joint. I told him about Charlie and the Family and what I'd been doing. To my surprise, he knew a lot

bout the Manson Family—firsthand. In July 1969 (just
fter I had split for the desert), Black Beard had inherited
ome money and had moved into Topanga Canyon
ith a friend named Bob Kasabian. A short time lat-
r, he met Bob's wife, Linda, who had just joined the
amily and who, on orders from Charlie, had ripped off
lack Beard for five thousand dollars. When Black Beard
ried to get the money back, Charlie merely showed
im the sword he'd used to chop off Gary Hinman's ear.
lack Beard got the picture and a week later took off to
outh America. He'd only recently gotten back, and was
gain living with Bob Kasabian.

During the weeks which followed, I visited Black
eard regularly, thereby adding another dimension to my
ragmented state, another tendril of extended energy I
ould ill afford. When I confided to him the many roles
was playing, maintaining at the same time that I had
aith that things were going the way they should, he said
e wasn't surprised. He recalled the night we were
usted at Half Moon Bay, saying, "I never seen anyone
urn a scene around like you did that one. It was karma,
an . . . the real McCoy, you blew those pigs' minds. . . ."

In early February 1970 we were still living in the
handler Street house during the week and repairing to
pahn's on the weekends to do music and unwind. I con-
inued to confer with Charlie, to help arrange for attor-
eys, and to convey his messages to Leslie and Sadie. I
as also in touch with Crockett and Posten by phone.

About that time Bruce Davis was arrested again and
ent to Inyo County on charges of grand theft. I was sub-
oenaed and told that without my testimony they couldn't
old him. I'd hitchhiked to Inyo with a new girl in the
amily named Ginny who was carrying twenty-four tabs
f acid, all but two of which we'd sewn into the lining
f a sleeping bag. Squeaky had suggested we slip a tab of
cid to Bruce during the trial; in part it was a means of
esting me. Charlie had told them to watch me closely.

During the proceedings, while Don Ward sat with
rockett and Posten on one side of the room and Ginny
n the other, I took the Fifth Amendment, refusing to
nswer on the grounds that what I said might incriminate
e. Steuber, and Inyo's D.A., Frank Fowles, were furious.
hey needed the testimony to hold Davis. While they had

interviews from me which more than implicated Bruce Davis, they could not be used in the court. Brooks and Crockett knew the game I was into and they looked pretty dejected. It got even more insane when Ginny got up and, while passing in front of Bruce, slipped him a tab of acid in the courtroom. Bruce dropped it on the floor, but before anyone could react, picked it up and ate it. A cop meanwhile had seized Ginny's purse and found the other tab of acid. She was held for two days, then released.

A few days later they let Bruce go, and my loyalty to the Family was, for the time being, reconfirmed.

In the meantime, the scene had been set for my sexual number with Squeaky. It was never talked about directly, but the promptings were there, a feeling that the Family would benefit by such a consummation of power.

It happened one afternoon at the Chandler Street house. I'd been at court all morning and had just returned to change clothes. While I was changing, Squeaky entered the bedroom and flopped down on the bed. She was talking about how great things were going, that Charlie was going "to walk." The free press was taking up the cause. This was during the time that Bernardine Dohrn told a convention of Students for a Democratic Society "Offing those rich pigs with their own forks and knives and eating a meal in the same room, far-out! The Weathermen dig Charles Manson." It was also at the height of Charlie's flamboyant courtroom theatrics, when he wore embroidered shirts, kept his hair combed, and paraded around the courtroom like a peacock. I walked by Squeaky, telling her to follow me into the other bedroom. I heard her giggle as she waltzed in behind me, removed her blouse, and tossed it on a chair.

I'd all but forgotten the day at Barker's when I'd seen Charlie bring Squeaky out of an epileptic seizure following sex. And I was momentarily stunned when, after making love to her, she began to shake and convulse. Within minutes she had lost all control. It was as if her entire being had been reduced to a quivering mass of jelly. Then her body stiffened and she clenched her fists until her knuckles turned white. Her head thrashed from side to side.

"It's okay, Lynn . . ." I said. "It's okay. It's Paul . . . just relax." I climbed on top of her and grabbed her by the wrists.

"Ohhh . . . Ohhhh," she moaned. "Aghhhh." Her breathing came in short pants and gasps.

"Go ahead . . . go ahead," I said. "Tighten your fingers . . . yeah . . . good . . . tighter, no, tighter. . . . Now, relax them . . . relax. . . . Now tighten . . . relax . . tighten . . ."

Using the method I had seen Charlie employ, I was able to settle her down, but it wasn't easy. By the time I'd calmed her, we were both exhausted. Afterward we drove to Spahn's and Squeaky behaved as if nothing had happened. But the incident stayed with me, a graphic expression of the control mechanism Charlie had implanted in Squeaky and by which he had been able to dominate both her mind and body.

After that episode, things happened fast. Later that same week I was coming out of the court building when a dapper little guy sporting a goatee and dressed in a double-breasted suit approached me, saying he was a lawyer and wanted to ask me a few questions. I walked with him to a chauffeured limousine and we drove up to Hollywood. He introduced himself as Jake Friedberg, saying he just wanted some information about the Family and that he'd make it worth my while to provide it. He asked if I'd mind staying at the Continental Hyatt House for a couple of days, and when I said no, he made a reservation for me in the penthouse. I spent two days there telling him what I knew; on the morning of the third day, as I was leaving the hotel, I was paged to the phone. It was Crockett; I'd called him the day I arrived and left my number.

His voice was hard and clear, like a pick against granite.

"Where the hell you been?"

"Nowhere."

"I been tryin' to get you. D.A.'s office called us up and said that guy Friedberg is a Mafia man . . . somethin' bout La Bianca's connection with the syndicate . . . he say anything about it?"

"Nope."

There was a long pause. Then Crockett spoke. "Where you tryin' to take yourself anyway, oblivion?"

I didn't answer. I didn't know.

"When you comin' out to the desert?"

"It won't be long."

I waited for Friedberg to come back, but he didn't. And I never saw him again.

A couple of days later, we moved out of the Chandler Street house and back to Spahn's. George had mellowed enough to allow us to move in again on a permanent basis. The day after we moved back, Clem was released on bail and joined the rest of us in a small wooden structure built just beyond Randy Starr's trailer, a beautifully symmetrical building we called the Story-Book House. The day we moved in, I was standing on the boardwalk with Sandy when a car with two men in it pulled up beside me and stopped.

"You Watkins?" the driver asked.

I nodded. Both men got out of the car. Both wore baggy sports jackets and gray fedoras. One of them had on sunglasses. They asked if we could talk, and I led them into the saloon, where Squeaky and Brenda were sitting on the floor working on Charlie's vest.

"We'll make it fast," the shorter of the two men said. "We hear Charlie wants to be sprung."

"Huh?" Brenda stood up.

"We don't know nothin' about that," Squeaky said. "Where'd you hear that?"

The man didn't look at Squeaky. His eyes were on mine. "So what's the deal?"

"I don't know anything about it." I didn't.

The two looked at each other. Then the short one grinned. "Well, that's cool . . . just forget it ever happened." They walked out, climbed in their car, and drove away. To this day I have no idea what their visit was all about.

That same week a motion for discovery was made by the defense, and all the prosecution's evidence (including my statements) was turned over to Charlie and his ever-changing team of lawyers. I had known this would happen eventually, but I didn't think it would be that soon. I would later learn that on the very day Charlie was presented with those documents we at Spahn's had set things up for an acid trip to celebrate our return to the ranch.

It was rather chilly the night we gathered inside the saloon to play music and smoke a little grass. I had Mark Ross pass out the acid, and we all dropped at the same

ime. It was good acid and we each took one tab. Sitting
t the head of the circle on a pillow, with Sandy and
Brenda on one side and Squeaky on the other, I felt as
hough I had assumed control. I sensed at once that Kev-
n and Mark were uptight. I signaled for Cappy and
Ginny to move closer to Mark. We all joined hands and I
nitiated some motion into the circle. It was then that I
aw Mark's eyes kind of roll back in his head. I knew we
night lose him if I didn't intervene. I knelt in front of
im and raised his hands, setting his palms against mine.
"Hey, Mark . . . hey, man, don't fade away on us." I began exerting a slight pressure against his palms until he
net the pressure with some resistance. When he did, I
gave in to his motion, then applied pressure again. Pretty
oon our hands began moving in a series of synchronized
movements. I watched his eyes and saw he was coming
round . . . the motion was bringing him around. I'd seen
Charlie do the same thing countless times; pretty soon ev-
ryone was tripping out on me and Mark. Finally he
ooked me dead in the eye. As he spoke, so did I; the
vords we said were the same words:

"Are you doin' that or am I?"

Afterward we all made love, then lay around raping and listening to music. Sometime before dawn we
eard three vehicles pull up in front of the saloon. Brenda
lew out the candles, and Mark and I laid a cross beam
cross the door. We could hear the static from squad-car
adios and the cops as they climbed out of their cars and
egan flashing their lights along the boardwalk.

"Go on down by the corral and take a look," one of
hem said. "We'll take a peek up this way." The board-
valk creaked as they clomped past the saloon toward the
ack room.

"Check the back door," I whispered to Cappy. She
valked quietly to the rear of the saloon, then came back
nd sat beside me.

"It's locked," she said. "Somebody must have told
hem we moved back here."

Had they wanted, the cops could have gotten inside,
ut in listening to them, you got the feeling that they
eally didn't want to. Finally they convened in front of
he saloon, got in their cars, and split.

The next morning (though I was scheduled to appear

in court on a traffic violation), I accompanied Clem t
the Hall of Justice. He too had to appear in court. It wa
a simple procedure; he merely wanted to change atto
neys, substituting Daye Shinn (at Charlie's suggestion) fo
Charles Hollopeter. All that was required of Clem was
one-word answer: "Yes." But by then Steve Grogan wa
pretty far gone.

When he was finally called before the judge, h
stood there dumbly, with a leering grin on his face, hi
hair disheveled across his forehead.

"Mr. Grogan, the court is informed that you no long
er wish Mr. Charles Hollopeter to represent you, that yo
have decided upon Mr. Daye Shinn as your new actin
attorney. Is that true?"

Clem turned and looked at the girls who wer
seated among the spectators.

"Is that true?" the judge repeated.

"Huh?" Clem muttered.

"Young man, I'm talking to you . . . do you under
stand what I'm saying?"

"Huh?" Clem blurted again.

The judge then asked that Clem be taken next doo
and examined for being under the influence of drug
Forty-five minutes later he was escorted into the court
room again, it being determined that he was not unde
the influence of any drug or stimulant. When the judg
repeated the question, however, Clem's response was th
same. We asked for a recess, and I took Clem outside.

"Look, man, all you got to do is say one word, 'Yes
When he asks you if you want Daye Shinn, you say, 'Yes.'"

"Huh?" he repeated.

Finally I just rared back and slapped him full in th
face with the flat of my hand and shouted his name
"*Steve . . . Steve . . .* what the fuck is the matter?"

His eyes fluttered and he looked at me.

"What's the matter?" I repeated. "Where the hel
have you been? You okay?"

"Sure."

"You want to keep Hollopeter or do you want Daye
Shinn?"

"I'd rather have Shinn; he seems to know more
what's happening."

When court reconvened, we went back inside and
he told the judge he wanted Daye Shinn.

Seeing Clem so completely "dodoed out" that morning unnerved me; he'd played the idiot so long that he'd literally become an idiot; all his responses were idiot responses—implants by Charlie. Steve Grogan had for all intents and purposes "ceased to exist." Why this particular episode jolted me so, I don't know. Unless it was the realization that my own idiocy was no less blatant. I didn't go back to Spahn's that afternoon. Instead, I drove out to Topanga Canyon to visit Black Beard and spent the night there.

The following morning I appeared before the judge for my traffic violation. Brenda and Squeaky went with me. Since I'd failed to show on two previous occasions, the old man was in no mood for excuses, and fined me sixty-five dollars or five days in jail. I asked the girls to go out to the car and get some money I'd stashed under the dashboard. They went out but didn't come back, and I spent five days in the cooler, not knowing that Charlie had already given the girls copies of my statements to the D.A.

Charles Manson had spent twenty-three years in prison. To me, five days seemed an eternity, particularly since I knew I'd pushed my own games to their limit. Though I was in a cell with six other guys—half of them murder cases on appeal, the others alcoholics—I felt totally and utterly alone. I thought about the others in jail. I thought about what going to prison actually meant. I thought about Snake, sitting in a mental ward. I would later see a transcript of a statement she'd made to the police. When asked who she was, she replied, "I am a butterfly in a flower palace . . . I live on a sea of sand." Perhaps for the first time I began to see what was happening. Not the sensationalism, the publicity, the theory, the great spectacle that was being created to glut the public's craving for "meaning and justice." What I saw was the truth, that the distance between good and evil is short; that the fine line between sanity and insanity is one we all walk; that I was on the brink of self-destruction. Around me were four walls and barred windows and men, who, in the face of life, preferred to stay drunk.

I was released in the morning (sometime around the end of March) and immediately hitchhiked up to Spahn's. Five nights of insomnia had left me completely oblit-

erated. Sandy, Brenda, and Squeaky were there waiting
with copies of my statements to the police.

"What is this shit?" Squeaky shouted, springing to her
feet.

"What?" I mumbled.

"Your goddamned testimony to the Inyo County pigs!"

"It's the truth . . . it's the—"

"*Truth?*"

"Charlie always said we had nothing to hide . . . the
truth will set you free."

"It didn't set you free, did it?" Brenda lashed out.

"You want to be free?" Sandy asked.

"Judas . . . you're a Judas!"

"Get fucked!"

I walked out of the saloon and up to the Story-Book
House. I grabbed the keys to Mark's van, then trotted up
the trail toward the outlaw shacks where it was parked.
I didn't know where I was going, but I was getting the
hell out of L.A.

I stopped in Chatsworth and put some gas in the car,
then headed for Topanga Canyon, deciding to see Black
Beard before I split. I was completely disoriented, feeling
disgust one moment, anguish the next. My entire being
seemed molten, slippery, and out of control, as though all
levels of consciousness belonged to the sea—to its currents,
its waves, its vastness. I felt like some hapless sailing vessel on the brink of a storm. Part of it was exhaustion; part of it was I had reached the end and the
beginning at the same time.

25

*But Jesus said unto him: Judas, betrayest thou
the Son of Man with a kiss?*

Judas; looking back, I see that my relationship to
Charlie was like that of Judas to Christ. Christ needed a
Judas; together they made the legend. Someone had to
tell the story; someone had to tip off the law. Of all the

disciples, only Judas tried to explain what Christ was preaching. But they wouldn't buy Christ's blasphemous statements: "I and my father are one." Christ was seized, tried, and crucified. But Judas never lived to witness the crucifixion; he hanged himself the night before.

I parked my car in front of Black Beard's place and went inside. Black Beard wasn't there, but Bob was. I didn't feel like telling him what had happened, so I remained quiet while he discussed the trial. He said Linda's testimony would be enough to get Charlie and the others convicted; he said Linda had gotten her head together and was ready to tell everything. He said if I agreed to testify, "Charlie's goose will be cooked." I listened for a while, then went out to the van. It was dark by then. I lit a joint and turned on Mark's stereo and lay down on the bed in the back. I guess that's when I fell asleep.

Sometime around midnight I woke up gagging; the inside of the van was filled with smoke. Flames were licking up around the front seat. I tried to kick open the rear door, but it wouldn't budge. The smell of burning plastic and enamel permeated the air. My lungs sputtered; there was no oxygen, only the toxic, white-hot smoke which funneled into my throat. I tried to scream, but the sounds were muted, choked off in guttural groans. I smashed my fist through one of the side windows, but the cold air only fanned the flames, bringing them closer. For what seemed like minutes I remained in a state of panic, continuing to kick at the rear door while my mind lapsed into a slow, reeling, kaleidoscopic rerun of deaths by fire. It was like the freak-out all over again. I felt the hairs on my body being singed. The smell sent me into convulsions, and I vomited, choking on my sickness, feeling as though I was about to die again. Finally an impulse prompted me to dive headlong through the flames onto the front seat. I kicked open the door and rolled out onto the ground, then got up and raced to the house to wake Bob and Black Beard.

By the time the ambulance arrived, I was in shock. Black Beard had wrapped me in a blanket. I stood in the corner of the living room asking for morphine. But they didn't understand me. They couldn't; my vocal cords had been burned to a crisp. Black Beard rode with me to the hospital. I remember that. I remember him sitting next to me. "You're gonna be okay, Paul . . . you're gonna be okay."

As it turned out, the nightmare of that experience was just beginning. It took over an hour for them to admit me to a bed in the emergency room of the Santa Monica Hospital. Since I couldn't talk, Black Beard had to interpret. I wrote down my parents' phone number. But that wasn't enough. Before the hospital did anything, they wanted to be certain I had medical insurance. By that time, I'd given up on trying to communicate and just lay back, feeling more pain than I could ever remember having felt. The next thing I remember was being given a shot of morphine and being wheeled into a room.

There were two nurses hovering around me when I felt blisters forming on my throat and started choking.

"Pop the bubbles," I gagged. "Poaap do boabbles!" But the sounds were garbled and they didn't understand.

"What?"

"Da baubbles." I pointed to my throat.

"He's going into convulsions," one of them said.

"No . . . no . . . pauup da baubbles!"

Then a doctor appeared and ordered them to prepare for a tracheotomy.

"*No! No!*" I wailed. That's when I started to vomit again, but it was mainly dry heaves. I tried to swallow hard and make the bubbles pop myself. I tried to force my tongue down on the bubbles, but it wouldn't reach. I stuck a finger in my mouth, but the nurses jerked my hand away.

"Pauup the babules! *Paaup the bauubles!*"

A little cart was wheeled in. My eyes were puffy and swollen; all the hair had been singed off my face. I could scarcely see, and it hurt to keep my eyes open. But I saw the scalpel and the hypodermic needle, and I knew they intended to cut my throat.

"*No! No!*" I kicked and thrashed while one of the nurses held a pan under my chin to catch the puke. "Please try and hit the tray," she said primly.

I kicked at her, but someone grabbed my legs. Two dudes had been called in to strap me down.

"He's hysterical . . . hurry!"

They'd pinned one arm down, but before they could grab the other, I seized one of the surgical instruments, shoved the butt end of it down my throat, and popped the bubbles.

I remained unconscious three days. When I woke up, my mother was sitting beside me cutting what remained of my hair. She said everything was going to be okay and for me to rest. She said too that my brothers and sisters were waiting to see me. So were Paul Crockett and Brooks Posten. I remember seeing Crockett and Brooks, but I don't remember what they said to me. The next day, my parents took me home to Thousand Oaks.

During the week I spent at my folks', reporters and police continued to call and come by in droves. My parents kept them away. I couldn't talk anyway. Fate works with the psyche in mysterious ways—at the very time I am asked to testify in court, in front of Charlie, before the world, I am rendered voiceless. Perhaps I had programmed myself, driven myself unconsciously to the outer limits of several realities at once. The questions were obvious ones: did the Family try to kill me? Were my actions and impulses, as Juan had suggested, suicidal? Or was it an accident? Clem later boasted that it was he who tried to kill me. In light of other murders and murder attempts, it would appear a very good possibility. But I don't believe it. Even if it were true, the responsibility was mine. I drove myself into that situation as a means of coming to grips with a game I knew could not go on. Perhaps it was inevitable. I took myself to a place where there was no voice. The voice I burned was not mine; it was Charlie's, the Family's; it was Crockett's, the Man's; it was the voice of society. Those voices had to go up in flames. The voice I needed if I were ever to survive was *my own voice.*

After a week, I left Thousand Oaks and flew to Monterey, then headed down the coast to Big Sur. I wanted to be alone. I wanted to sit on the edge of the cosmos and watch the sea in silence. For several days I hiked through mountains around Esalen, stopping once to visit my sister, who was preparing to go to Chile with a group she helped organize, called Arica. I hiked along the same trails Black Beard and I had once traveled, and I stopped at Garapata Canyon long enough to take a peek at Kevin's house. But I didn't go in. I didn't want to. By the middle of March I'd decided to go back to Shoshone.

The day I got there, Crockett, Juan, and Brooks took me to Las Vegas and bought me a steak dinner with all the trimmings. They didn't talk much about the fire, but I sensed what they were thinking. They talked about the music scene they were putting together, plans to do gigs in towns throughout the desert. We laughed and told stories, and they showed me the depth of their friendship. Crockett found it amusing that I couldn't talk, insisting when I did manage to rasp out a jibberish of inarticulate utterings that my singing had improved immensely. They didn't tell me that night that the D.A.'s office had been calling them regularly, asking them to exert pressures on me to testify in the Tate–La Bianca trials. At that point I didn't want to testify. I had a perfect excuse. I couldn't talk.

By that time the retrial of Bobby Beausoleil for the murder of Hinman was in progress. Mary Brunner, in exchange for complete immunity, became the chief prosecution witness, testifying that she had seen Bobby stab Hinman to death. Bobby, meanwhile, put the finger on Charlie. But the jury believed Mary. While this was happening, Charlie was busy juggling lawyers, not just his but Sadie's and Leslie's as well. In May he acquired the services of Irving Kanarek. Judge William Keene, meanwhile, who had presided over the preliminary trials, was replaced by Judge Charles W. Older. By the middle of June they began the long process of selecting a jury for the Tate–La Bianca trials.

My feelings during that period fluctuated. The trauma of the fire stayed with me. At times I woke up at night in a cold sweat, in a state of utter panic. I was high-strung and subject to fits of convulsive crying, torrential outpourings which carried away the sludge of repression which had locked me away from my feelings and from seeing the stark horror of an evil I had been part of. The fire had burned away the facade. I was left face to face with myself. The pain of that has never left me entirely.

While Juan had talked about testifying, he was undecided. None of us gave advice one way or the other. Meanwhile, we worked on our music. Though I couldn't talk, much less sing, I could play the flute. Brooks had become something of a virtuoso on the guitar; Juan was dynamite on the conga drums. In early June we did a gig in Lone Pine, calling ourselves the Minstrel's Magic. A week later we were hired to play at a dance in Tecopa. For the first time in months I began writing songs—songs for the new voice I didn't yet possess.

One night we were lounging in the living room by the fire. We'd worked all day laying a pipeline for the gas company. Crockett as usual was dealing cards to himself. Juan was writing a letter. Brooks had gone to Tecopa to pick up the amplifiers we'd left there the weekend before. I'd begun groaning about the fact that I still had no voice, that it looked like I'd have to be content to just play music, not sing it.

Crockett glanced up from his cards.

"You ever *decide* to get your voice back?"

"Decide?"

"Well, if ya ain't *decided*, are ya sure ya even want your voice back?" He scooped up the cards and shuffled them. "Maybe ya want to just leave that voice behind ... get ya a new voice. Or did ya like the old one?"

I gawked at Crockett.

"If ya want a different voice—might as well, ya ain't got one now—why not decide on that ... decide on the kind ya want ... one for singing and talking. Figure out what style ya want ... ya know ... low, high ... once ya decide and picture it in your mind, just relax and it'll come."

Juan grinned.

"Way it is now," Crockett intoned, "yer holdin up the show. We got a singin' group here, like to have it complete ... see what I mean?"

That night I *decided* to get a new voice. I pictured and *felt* the voice I wanted in my mind's eye. A few days later, while trying to sing in the shower, my wheezy, disjointed raspings began to give way to sound—the first fledgling tones of my new voice. Moments later I was belting out a song I'd written called "Is It That You Recall." I was exultant as I dried off, wrapped a towel around my waist, and strutted into the living room, where Crockett and Brooks were seated on the floor, rewiring the amplifier.

"Well," Crockett said, glancing up at me, then at Brooks. "It ain't Caruso, but what the hell."

Shortly after that episode, on a windy afternoon when Crockett and I were in Shoshone buying groceries, we ran into Clem, Gypsy, and Mark Ross riding around in a jeep. We had just crossed the street when they pulled up alongside us.

"Got a message for you piggies," Clem barked. "Charlie says when he gets out, you better not be around the desert."

I glanced at Gypsy, and she stared back with all the vehemence she could muster. She looked pathetic. Clem, his hair scrambled and windblown around his ghoulish face, looked even more ridiculous. Suddenly the pent-up rage and resistance I had felt for so long fell away into a kind of clarity. I knew then that I'd testify in front of a jury, in front of Charles Manson, in front of the Devil himself, and that I'd tell the truth.

The same afternoon I wrote a letter to the D.A.'s office, to Stovitz and Bugliosi, telling them I would testify for the prosecution.

Later that night I took a walk downtown with Juan. I told him about the letter, but he didn't say anything. Oddly enough, in all the time we'd known each other, Juan and I had never shared the information we had on the Family. I mentioned that to Juan, saying, "Let's not discuss it now, either . . . let's just go down there and tell the truth. There's just been too much dying . . . Charlie's trip is nothing but death."

Juan agreed to testify, and so did Brooks; it was an agreement that would commit us to an odyssey of trials that lasted more than nine years.

"Best thing for ya," Crockett said when we told him. "Them trials will be like a deprogramming process. Yer gonna have to remember specific incidents and tell them to lawyers who'd like nothin' better than to make you look dumb, crazy, or drugified. And ya can't fake it, 'cause they got it all on them transcripts. Ya can't remember what ya told one guy . . . ya just remember the incident and tell the truth, and that will serve to bring your mind through all those things again and get ya free of them . . . and with Charlie sittin' right there lookin' at ya . . . it will finally cut you loose."

"The truth will set you free," I muttered distractedly.

"Exactly," Crockett said.

We weren't called to testify that summer, but we followed the progress of the trial and all of Charlie's antics and manipulations. We saw photos of Ouisch, Sandy, Cappy, Squeaky, and Gypsy sitting on the sidewalks, their heads shaved, their foreheads carved with Charlie's stamp, just as their souls had been. From time to time we received telephone threats, but it did nothing to alter our decision to testify. Linda Kasabian's testimony alone was devastating for Charlie. But he continued to operate; manipulating lawyers, judges, the jury. Meanwhile, people continued to disappear and to die, people like Ronald Hughes, Leslie's lawyer. But those stories have been told—the story of a murder attempt on Barbara Hoyt, the story of Charlie lunging at Judge Older with a sharpened pencil in his hand. Whether in or out of jail, Charles Manson was dangerous. The prospect of facing him in court was not pleasant. But in a strange ironic way, I was looking forward to it. To me it was a part of the destiny of my relationship with Charlie and the only way to really sever that relationship once and for all.

In September, when Tex was finally extradited to California, I told Crockett and Posten that I wanted to see him. We drove to L.A. the next day and met with him for over an hour. If I had any doubts whatsoever about testifying, seeing Tex removed them.

Sitting before us, he looked emaciated, skin and bone, like a torture victim at Dachau. His eyes were lifeless. The prosecution would later claim that Tex was faking it, that he was trying to cop an insanity plea. But I knew Tex Watson and he wasn't faking anything. He was paying for the crimes he had committed. If I've ever seen a specimen of living death, it was Tex. When we asked him what really happened at the murder scenes, he told us. He didn't explain, he just narrated the events in monotone as they happened. The bodies of the Tate and La Bianca victims had received a total of 159 stab wounds; most of them had been inflicted by him. "I just killed them . . . that was what I had to do. I heard Sadie cry, 'Help me,' and I helped her. It seemed like there was a lot of time between events . . . then Katie needed help and I helped her. It seemed like I had to do everything. . . . And then it was over."

As we were walking out to the jeep, Brooks remarked to Crockett that Tex might just as well die, 'cause he'd never be able to get that horror out of his head.

Crockett just grunted. It was clear that seeing Tex Watson had disturbed him too.

"I don't know," Brooks said, looking at me. "I remember just after Charlie came up to Barker's after the murders. I was sitting in the bunkhouse and he come in, said he'd been looking for me and that the only time he could talk any sense to me was when Big Paul wasn't around. He takes out his knife and says to me, 'You know, it might be a good idea for you to take this knife, go to Shoshone, and kill that motherfuckin' Sheriff Ward.'"

"What'd ya say?"

"Somethin' like, 'Yeah, far-out.' But I was thinking in there, looking at Tex, what if he had stayed at Barker's and met Crockett 'stead of me." Brooks glanced at Crockett, who climbed into the jeep and fired up the engine. I sat in the back while Brooks, seated on the passenger side, faced me, his eyes squinting. "I mean, shit, if I'd never met Crockett or come to the desert, I'd still be like a junkie hooked on Charlie. Who knows, I might have taken that knife . . . I might have wound up where Tex is now."

26

Is it that you recall being in harmony
Is there something in you that yearns to see
Or do you remember a time
When you were free

Did you ever wonder what you're living for
Is there anything of which you are sure
Have you asked yourself
Is there more

A moment's moment can be an eternity
And all the while time has its flow

So how many lifetimes can you live in infinity
It's all there for us to know. . . .

—song by Paul Watkins, summer of 1970

The book *Helter-Skelter* chronicles events that took place during the Tate–La Bianca trials—the saga of a murder case which lasted longer, received more publicity, and cost more than any other in American history. For me to repeat what was written there would be wasted effort. I can only conclude my own story, which is a part of that saga, a single thread in a legal tapestry which will not be forgotten.

I saw Charles Manson for the last time in a courtroom in the L.A. Hall of Justice in the fall of 1972. I saw him face to face, not twenty feet away, across an odyssey of time and circumstances that in retrospect seems totally unbelievable. What happened that day in the midst of my testimony, when Charlie leaped to his feet and screamed, "Liar!" must remain indelible to all those who bore witness to it. For me it was a catharsis, a moment of utter unwavering certainty, as inevitable as the dawning of a new day. Yet, by the time it happened, I was prepared. By then I had testified not only in the Tate–La Bianca trials and the grand jury proceedings but also in Tex Watson's trial, and the Shea-Hinman trials. I had spent weeks on the witness stand and had been asked the same questions time and time again. I had been examined and cross-examined by some of the best defense attorneys in Los Angeles, including Charlie's most tenacious counselor, Irving Kanarek. I had been referred to as a "robot," drug addict, pimp, thief, social misfit. But through the process of concentration and a commitment to remembering the truth in court, I was able, as Crockett had foreseen, one step at a time, to deprogram myself from the subtle yet profound effects of Charles Manson's philosophy, so that when my final showdown with Charlie came, I welcomed it.

From the beginning the courtroom had served as a theater for some of Manson's best performances. Even those who most wanted his blood could not help but be struck by his spirited charisma. Early in the Tate–La Bianca proceedings, Joseph Ball, the former president of the state bar association and former senior counsel to the Warren Commission, found Charlie to be "an able, intelligent young man, quiet-spoken and mild-mannered." He remarked, further, that Charlie had "a ready understanding of the law" and "a fine brain." Ball said, too, that Charlie was "not resentful against society . . . he feels if he goes to trial and he is able to permit jurors and the court to hear him and see him, they will realize he is not the kind of man who would perpetrate horrible crimes."

Following Ball's remarks, the then presiding judge, William Keene, begged Charlie to reconsider his decision to defend himself. But Charlie wouldn't budge.

"For all my life," he said, "as long as I can remember, I've taken your advice. Your faces have changed, but it's the same court, the same structure. All my life I've been put in little slots, your Honor, and I went along with it. I have no alternative but to fight you back any way I know how, because you and the district attorney and all the attorneys I have met are on the same side and the newspapers are on the same side and it's all pointed against me, personally. No, I haven't changed my mind."

But Charlie didn't defend himself long. His courtroom antics and violation of procedure, much of which was done to play up to the press, forced the judge to appoint an attorney, Charles Hollopeter, with the stipulation that Charlie could enlist another attorney if he so desired. Along the way, Charlie would make many substitutions, selecting, at last, Irving Kanarek.

From December 1969 until July 1970, when the Tate–La Bianca trials finally got under way, Charlie called most of the shots, both in and out of the courtroom. And in the beginning, when he had the support of the free press and radicals like Jerry Rubin, he put on a real show. Together with the girls who came to court daily and kept vigil on the sidewalks of L.A. (Broadway and Temple), Manson was able to hold his own on the battleground of what he called "injustice." But the evidence and testimony against Charlie, Sadie, Katie, Leslie, and Tex mounted.

But neither Charlie nor the girls gave up, and we were continually threatened. I was entering the courtroom one morning when Squeaky approached me just outside the doorway of the Hall of Justice. It was in September, around the time I was to begin my testimony.

"What are you doing?" she asked.

"I'm just telling the truth . . . it's time to tell the truth."

"Are you still my brother?"

"Yeah . . . I'm your brother."

"Listen to your love."

"That's what I'm doing, Lynn."

"There's no such thing as death," she muttered. "It's all love."

"Here, Lynn." I took a five-carat emerald ring off my little finger and handed it to her. Then I walked into the courtroom.

Nearly three years later to the day (September 5, 1975), in Sacramento, California's "city of justice," Lynette "Squeaky" Fromme attempted to assassinate the president of the United States.

My testimony, together with that of Brooks and Juan, not only substantiated the murder charges against Charlie —he had admitted killing Shorty to each of us separately —but provided corroboration of Helter-Skelter (the race war) as a motive. We had all experienced Charlie's programming techniques and were thus able to convey at least in part how Charlie's devices operated. On cross-examination the defense continually sought to invalidate my testimony by suggesting that drugs had destroyed my mind.

During the Bruce Davis trial (Shea-Hinman), after I had testified to hearing Bruce describe the murder of Shorty Shea, the defense attorney approached the bench.

"Your Honor, it is my intention to show that this witness has, over a period of time involved in his testimony, been engaged almost continually in the taking of drugs. That he has acknowledged on examination and cross-examination in prior cases that he has taken LSD . . . and that as a result his mind has been bent."

Hours and hours were spent grilling us on drugs, everything from acid to marijuana. The numerous transcripts of trial testimony read very much alike. From the Shea-Hinman trial, February 1972:

Q. "And now, Mr. Watkins, how about marijuana . . what are the effects on you of marijuana?"

A. "On me?"

Q. "On you, sir."

A. "You get high, or what I would call high. Kind of happy, laughing, feel free, feel good."

Q. "Is this after just one, or does it take several?"

A. "It depends on how strong it is, and how strong you are; who you are with, and what you are doing; and it depends on a lot of things."

Q. "All right. How about hashish?"

A. "It just has the same effect, only much stronger."

Q. "Much faster?"

A. "Much faster."

Q. "And when you say much stronger, does it affect your balance?"

A. "Hmmm. It depends on the type of hashish you're smoking. I never had it affect my balance, like I suppose you're likening it to being drunk, where you are stumbling around. It's not like that, no."

Q. "Does it affect your sense of time?"

A. "Inasmuch as though you may be having a good time, and time would seem to fly."

Q. "Does it affect your sense of vision?"

A. "Not really."

Q. "It doesn't enhance or detract from your ability to see; is that right?"

A. "Well, I may have had it enhance my ability to see at times and detract at other times."

Q. "Does it cause you to have any sort of visions or hallucinations at all?"

A. "No."

Q. "Does it cause sounds to be more . . . cause you to be more keenly aware of sounds and sights?"

A. "You're still talking about marijuana and hashish, right?"

Q. "Right."

A. "Yeah. On certain occasions it would . . . you would be more aware of sounds and sights."

Q. "Well, other than that, does it do anything for you?"

A. "Other than what?"

Q. "Those things we've named."

A. "Well, I don't know how deep you want to get into it. We could leave it right there; if it's okay with you, it's okay with me."

When attempts to discredit me failed along those lines, the defense tried other means. At one point during the same trial, the defense lawyer approached the bench to tell the judge he could prove that I was working with the police and that therefore my testimony was prejudi-

cial and biased. Out of earshot of the jury he explained to
the judge what I clearly overheard:

"I will offer proof that between October and December—and specifically in mid-December of 1969—this
particular witness had several conversations with officer
Dave Steuber and other officers of the highway patrol and
the sheriff's department in Inyo County; that thereafter,
and as a part of the plan of the prosecution, he returned
to the Manson Family, to the Spahn Ranch, specifically
sent there to be a spy; that he saw Charles Manson in
January approximately eight times at the jail—which visits are recorded—and that I contend that this was done
specifically to get information, to pass along to the sheriff;
that therefore his testimony is biased and prejudiced, because of his connections with the prosecution, based on
his background."

Though none of these assertions were true, I felt at
times as though I were on trial.

Q. "Well, you did visit Charlie at least seven or
eight times in January of 1970, in jail; is that correct?"

A. "At least."

Q. "All right. And these were just friendly visits, to
pass the time of day, to help poor old Charlie while away
the hours—?"

The state's attorney at the time, Manzella, objected, and the objection was sustained.

Q. "Well, were these just friendly visits to help
your friend, who was there in great trouble?"

A. "Some—"

Manzella objected and the court sustained it.

Q. "All right, sir," Denny went on. "These were
visits in order for you to try and pump Charlie Manson
for the prosecution; isn't that right?"

A. "No, that isn't right."

Often I felt totally exasperated. I wanted to tear
through the mumbo-jumbo of the courtroom decorum; I
wanted to explain to the court, to the judge, the jury, and
everyone present, the real truth—the torment, the depth
of feeling, the reality of my experience, which seemed
inaccessible and paradoxically out of place in what has
been called the halls of justice. But I had learned the
courtroom games well, and focusing energy on the truth
enabled me to outlast the most determined defense attorneys. The mind games played in a courtroom are com-

plex, and it takes a good deal of awareness to stay on top of them. It is not simply a matter of telling the truth, since everything you say is controlled by the questions, and many of the questions are asked obliquely so that the intent of the lawyers is not always clear. Plus, your consciousness must encompass not only the attorneys on both sides but also the jury and the judge.

But it was neither the judge nor the jury that made testifying traumatic; it was facing the defendants. It's hard to describe the multitude of feelings I had when taking the stand as a witness for the prosecution—facing Charlie, Sadie, Leslie, and Katie in the courtroom eye to eye. Facing girls who had once had beauty in their hearts, girls I knew better than any jury would ever know—girls I had lived with, traveled with, made love with, sung with. All of them, on trial for murder. And the man who had taught me a great deal about music and love and had asked me to submit to that love; a man I had once seen as the embodiment of life but who had become its opposite, but who nevertheless continued to project incredible force and presence even late in the Tate–La Bianca proceedings, after Brooks and I had testified.

Clean-shaven, well-groomed, and articulate, he made a great spectacle, prancing confidently around the courtroom. According to Charlie it was not he who was on trial but the system which brought him there. And in part, he was right. Near the end of the Tate–La Bianca trial, when it was clear that the evidence against him was insurmountable, he took the stand to testify in his own behalf. Even Bugliosi, who had fought so hard to secure the death penalty, admitted to the hypnotic effect of Manson's words. And Bugliosi had not met Charles Manson at eighteen *before* the murders, during the Summer of Love, when the youth of America were riding the crest of an awakening consciousness and were high on life and LSD. But I had. And I had come a long way since then, far enough, at least, to see through Charlie's impassioned soliloquy, shot through with truths and half-truths and the subtle nuances of his madness. Yet, even when Charlie spoke, and he spoke for more than an hour, what he said was not only for the benefit of the court but to manipulate the other defendants—his Family, still programmed to loyalty to the bitter end, ready to die for a man who could have just as easily cut their throats.

Charlie's testimony began slowly, but as he spoke, his voice became clear and resonant; if Charles Manson was anything, he was a performer. "Most of the people at the ranch that you call the Family were just people you didn't want, people that were alongside the road, that their parents had kicked out, that did not want to go to Juvenile Hall. So I did the best I could and took them up on my garbage dump and I told them this: that in love there is no wrong. . . .

"I told them that anything they do for their brothers and sisters is good if they do it with a good thought. . . .

"I was working at cleaning up my house, something that Nixon should have been doing. He should have been on the side of the road picking up his children, but he wasn't. He was in the White House sending them off to war. . . .

"I don't understand you, but I don't try. I don't try to judge nobody. I know that the only person I can judge is me. . . . But I know this: that in your hearts and your own souls, you are as much responsible for the Vietnam war as I am for killing these people. . . .

"I can't judge any of you, but I will say this to you, you haven't got long before you are all going to kill yourselves, because you are all crazy. And you can project it back at me . . . but I am only what lives inside each and every one of you.

"My father is the jailhouse. My father is your system. . . . I am only what you made me. I am only a reflection of you.

"I have ate out of your garbage cans to stay out of jail . . . I have wore your second-hand clothes. . . . I have done my best to get along in your world, and now you want to kill me, and I look at you, and then I say to myself, you want to kill me? Ha! I am already dead, have been all my life. I've spent twenty-three years in tombs that you built.

"Sometimes I think about giving it back to you; sometimes I think about just jumping on you and letting you shoot me. . . . If I could, I would jerk this microphone off and beat your brains out with it, because that is what you deserve! That is what you deserve. . . .

"You expect to break me? Impossible! You broke me years ago. You killed me years ago.

"You can do anything you want with me, but you

cannot touch me because I am my love. If you put me in the penitentiary, that means nothing because you kicked me out of the last one. I didn't ask to be released. I liked it in there because I like myself."

On April 19, 1971, Judge William Older sentenced Charles Manson, Susan Atkins, Patricia Krenwinkle, and Leslie Van Houten to die. Ten months later (February 1972) the death penalty in California was abolished and their sentences were reduced to life imprisonment. But the drama wasn't over. Not yet. I saw Charlie one more time, on an afternoon during the final stages of the Shea-Hinman trials. But by then the flamboyance was gone. He no longer looked like the high priest of flower power but an embittered convict.

He was seated in front of me, twenty feet away, just to my left beside his attorney. His head was shaved, the scar of the swastika stamped on his forehead; his jaw was dotted with a fine stubble. He looked old, worn-out, beaten. Since the early days of the trials, much had happened: a major earthquake had rocked Los Angeles, killing sixty-five people. Spahn's Movie Ranch had burned to the ground. In less than one month of each other Jimi Hendrix (September 18, 1970) and Janis Joplin (October 4, 1970) had o.d.'d on drugs, perhaps symbolizing the end of an era. Someone once said "all universes die"; looking at Charlie that afternoon, you got that feeling. Yet when I took the stand, he looked up suddenly and just stared at me, a strange half-leering smirk on his face.

As I spoke, he just watched me, tilting his head from side to side as if he were an artist attempting to get the right perspective for a painting. Maybe he was remembering, seeing as I had so many times the arc of the circle we had made in time, the journey from one end of the human condition to the other, from a perfect dream into the bowels of a nightmare from which I had awakened just in time.

I was in the midst of my testimony when Charlie suddenly lurched to his feet and shouted, "Liar! You're a liar!"

"Order!" The gavel came down.

But Charlie didn't stop. "*No, no . . . little boy . . . you lie!*"

Charlie was pulled to his seat, but his eyes were blazing, and I looked at him and held his gaze, and after a warning by the court, went on with my testimony.

As I spoke, Charlie raised his finger, grinning, and slowly drew it across his throat.

"You're pathetic, Charlie," I said.

"Order."

Then Charlie was standing again.

"*You're a liar!*" he roared.

"No, Charlie. . . . I'm telling the truth!"

"Order!"

"*Liar!*" Charlie was pulled to his seat.

Then I was standing, filled suddenly with emotion—a surging of rage, remorse, and utter revulsion. "*You . . . you . . . made it all a lie! You calling me a liar proves it! Your whole trip has been a lie.*"

Charlie struggled to his feet and began grappling with the bailiff, but I didn't stop yelling. "It's like you said . . . the truth will set you free. I *know* that!"

"Sit down, Mr. Watkins!"

"I speak the truth, Charlie!"

"Remove Mr. Manson from the courtroom!"

Charlie was seized by both arms, but he continued to kick and struggle. "*You're just an insecure little boy!*" he shouted.

"The truth, Charlie. The truth will set you free!"

They dragged Charlie out of the room.

"Order. . . . there will be order in this courtroom!"

The door closed, and I slumped into my seat.

Epilogue

Ironically, the story of Charles Manson and his Family does us all a favor. It reveals in no uncertain terms the disease of our own society. It chronicles the transformation of communal love into its opposite. There was nothing simplistic in what happened. And it isn't something to turn away from. People seem to feign a horror of blood and carnage, yet invariably rush to accident scenes and fistfights, to anything that will put them in touch with their own blood and something that is primal—to something that will wake them up to the fact that they are not robots but living, breathing organisms. The Manson Family did more than this. It tore the lid off suburban complacency with a vengeance, and left us with a lot of questions to answer.

I thought once the headlines and the novelty had worn off that the questions would cease. But as the days went by after the trials, and the months turned into years, the questions continued. Even after the publication of *Helter-Skelter*, it was clear that people did not understand what had actually transpired in the Manson Family. During the trials, I was approached by producers Robert Hendrickson and Lawrence Merrick, who wanted to make a documentary film on the Manson Family. They had already shot footage around Spahn's while Charlie was on trial, inducing the remaining Family members to make music and rap about Charlie on film. The group obliged, believing not only that Charlie would be set free but that they were helping to program Helter-Skelter. Later, we shot some footage in Merrick's studio and in the desert. I hoped the film, *Manson*, would help explain what actually happened. It fell far short of the mark, but even so, won an award for the best documentary at the

Venice Film Festival in 1974. Merrick signed the distribution rights over to American International Pictures, and he and I toured the country premiering the film in Albuquerque, Chicago, and elsewhere. To me, the film seemed to be popular, but the company reported box-office flops and legal problems and it was virtually scrapped.

After *Helter-Skelter* hit the stands I began touring with Vince Bugliosi to promote the book on TV talk shows. I realized then that there was a genuine need to know what caused the phenomenon of the Manson Family. I remember people asking me, "What can we do to protect our kids?" Often, I became the scapegoat for people's collective outrage. When I appeared on the Tom Snyder *Tomorrow* show, his first question nearly floored me. "How is it that you are allowed to walk the streets and do this show?" Along with Bugliosi, I wasted no time in setting him straight. But I was astonished and angry, and I asked myself: why go through this? I questioned my own motives, realizing that deep down I did feel a sense of guilt. I had played a part and did have a responsibility to explain what had happened. After the Snyder show I got serious about public speaking and learned to handle myself under fire. I began giving lectures on the effects of drugs. I spoke at district attorneys' conventions and on college campuses. I pondered the idea of writing a book. In my own mind, I knew the Manson story had not really been told.

With the exception of the Vietnam war, the Kennedy assassinations, the slaying of Martin Luther King, Watergate, and perhaps the kidnapping of Patricia Hearst, few events in the last twenty years have had more impact on the public at large than the story of Charlie Manson and his Family. People's fascination with death, violence, abduction, and money, it seems, can never be fully satiated—which says something about the public consciousness. Oddly enough, the Manson Family originated as a rebellion against that very state of consciousness and was a direct outgrowth of the psychedelic revolution of the early sixties, grounded theoretically in principles of love and the freedom "to be." What happened to those ideals, to me, and to the minds of Charlie's followers was the story I wanted to tell—the story of mind control and mental programming.

The questions to be answered were crucial—the echoing refrain of a lady from Atlanta who asked me on the Phil Donahue show: "What experiences in your own background would make you susceptible to a man like Manson?" The woman appeared shocked when I told her we had shared many of her own experiences. Like her, we had shuddered through the Cuban missile crisis. We too cried for our country and the Kennedys. We watched in disgust while our natural inheritance turned into plastic and concrete, and bit our lips in rage as our brothers died in Southeast Asia. We saw movies on drugs made by people who knew nothing about drugs. We felt the need to live and to believe that we had inherited a world worth living in. So we hit the road in the mid-sixties, searching for truth, hoping we might recognize it once we saw it. We needed to love and to be loved. One by one we met Charlie and saw in him and his followers the love we were looking for.

It has been too easy to classify the Manson Family as a pack of sick, drug-bludgeoned kids duped by an ex-con. The transformation from a "flower-child" Family whose only revolutionary activity was an alternate life-style into a militant, Helter-Skelter-ready band of death-wielding robots was slow, methodical, insidious. Yet, many still cling to the notion that all Charlie had to do to get people to kill was to stuff them full of dope and say "sic 'em." Had that been the case, the interest in the Manson story would have waned long ago.

No, Charlie Manson was intelligent, and so were most of his followers. Hippies who wanted only to get laid or stoned were neither susceptible nor acceptable to Charlie. In conversation, he would lose the average "lodie" as soon as he opened his mouth. People are still surprised when reminded that Sandy and Mary both had college degrees; that Leslie Van Houten was a homecoming queen and one of the most popular girls at Monrovia High School; that Katie was a Sunday-school teacher . . . and so the list goes. And how could it be that Tex Watson, who took part in so much killing, was not only an A student and a top athlete but was voted the most likely to succeed by his classmates in high school. No, Tex was programmed to kill, just as young soldiers are programmed to kill in the name of democracy or the flag or whatever. But in that case, it's just an all-American boy performing a heroic act. It's possible that had Tex gotten into that kind of program, he'd have been one hell of a marine—a hero with decorations instead of a murderer in jail for life. It may be stretching a point, but it's one that should be made nevertheless.

What drew us to Charlie initially was a real love we helped put there. So we submitted to his trip; we burned our bridges and left our past far behind, to become lost in Charlie's nightmare with nowhere to go. But Charlie always had the "joint" to go back to. The Family didn't realize that he had a home and that the bridge to it could not be burned.

Still, there are questions that remained unanswered. Just how and why did Charlie change? Did he have Helter-Skelter planned from the start, or was it only a bud in his subconscious awaiting its time to flower? Only Charlie knows the answers to all the questions. But ultimately he must be seen for what he was: the worst kind of criminal, a man who subverted the power of love, turning it into the most despicable evil imaginable—the domination of souls.

Charlie did more than give hitchhikers and hippies a bad name. He manifested and expressed not only the mechanism of his own twisted psyche, but the latent evils existing within our own society. You cannot divorce Manson from the culture that spawned him. That too is an easy way out and would be a grave error. I know that his incarceration has not put an end to my own struggles. It has taken years for me to untangle and come to grips with all that I experienced in the Family. But more than anything, in the wake of all the destruction, the killing, the inner crippling of those who survived, I wanted to salvage something, if only the knowledge that what happened to the Family could well have happened to others; *that mind control and programming are a part of our daily lives and that the results, unless people develop an awareness, can be, in the long run, no less insidious and destructive.* Clearly, in a world where the majority of the populace speeds around in varied states of hypnosis, bombarded into stupor by the media, it is necessary to understand the fundamentals of programming.

Perhaps, if there is one lesson I have learned, it is to listen to myself. To be what I am. This is the bottom line of awareness, and paradoxically the greatest link to humanity after all. Had I been so grounded in March 1968, on the day I met Charles Manson, I would probably find it hard now to remember who he was.

But the Manson saga is not over. In June 1977 and again in May 1978 I testified in Leslie Van Houten's retrials, each of which resulted in her reconviction. Whether or not she will appeal that conviction is not certain. I don't know what happened to all the others. I do know that Susan Atkins and Charles Watson, both born-again Christians, have written books about their experiences and are serving life sentences for their crimes, as are convicted murderers Bruce Davis, Mary Brunner, and Bobby Beausoleil. Lynette Fromme is also in prison following her attempted assassination of former President Gerald Ford. Diane Lake (Snake) has been completely rehabilitated and the last I heard was working as a teller in a bank in northern California. As for Brooks, Juanita, Juan Flynn, and Crockett, all are doing well: Brooks is a full-time musician, while Juan lives in Panama, where he works on a ranch.

Charles Manson, meanwhile, now forty-four, is serving a life sentence in California, awaiting his eligibility for parole.

ABOUT THE AUTHORS

PAUL WATKINS was the class president of all his high school classes in a suburb of Los Angeles and student body president in his senior year when he dropped out and took to the road. A series of circumstances led to his being picked up by two girls of the Manson Family and he soon became one of Manson's most devoted followers. Later, however, he became concerned about Manson's predilection for violence and left the family before the Tate murders. He now lives in the desert town of Tecopa, California, and earns his living in construction and by lecturing on the subject of drug prevention and rehabilitation.

GUILLERMO SOLEDAD is the pen name of a member of the faculty of the University of California at Santa Barbara. He has written a number of magazine articles for publications such as *Ms.*, *Playboy* and *Playgirl*.

WE DELIVER
And So Do These Bestsellers